SHIFTING BORDERS

In the series

Mapping Racisms

edited by Jo Carrillo, Darrell Y. Hamamoto,
Rodolfo D. Torres, and E. Frances White

SHIFTING
BORDERS

RHETORIC,

IMMIGRATION, AND

CALIFORNIA'S

PROPOSITION 187

Kent A. Ono and John M. Sloop

 Temple University Press
PHILADELPHIA

Temple University Press, Philadelphia 19122
Copyright © 2002 by Temple University
All rights reserved
Published 2002
Printed in the United States of America

⊗ The paper used in this publication meets the requirements of the
American National Standard for Information Sciences—Permanence
of Paper for Printed Library Materials, ANSI Z39.48-1984.

Library of Congress Cataloging-in-Publication Data

Ono, Kent A., 1964–
    Shifting borders : rhetoric, immigration, and California's Proposi-
tion 187 / Kent A. Ono and John M. Sloop.
        p. cm. — (Mapping racisms)
    Includes bibliographical references and index.
    ISBN 1-56639-916-5 (alk. paper) — ISBN 1-56639-917-3 (pbk. :
alk. paper)
    1. Illegal aliens—Government policy—California—Public opinion.
2. California—Emigration and immigration—Government policy—
Public opinion. 3. United States—Emigration and immigration—
Government policy—History—20th century. 4. Immigration opponents—California. 5. Immigration advocates—California. 6. Public
opinion—California. I. Sloop, John M., 1963– II. Title.
III. Series.

√ JV6920 .O56   2002
    325.794–dc21   2001034070

Contents

Acknowledgments

We would thank the folks at Temple University Press, especially Peter Wissoker, who saw this project twice: initially while he was at Guilford Press and now that he is at Temple. He has been a constant source of support and encouragement. Janet Francendese wrote letters at key moments and helped bring the project along, despite bumps along the way. Thanks also to Doris Braendel at Temple University Press, our original editor on the project. We are also indebted to Debby Stuart, an extraordinary copy editor.

We would also like to thank Sarah Projansky, who read several drafts of this book at various stages and provided much intellectual feedback and research assistance. She has been a constant source of inspiration, even as she was completing her own book. Kevin Johnson read through the entire book and provided much-needed intellectual assistance. Bill Ong Hing answered our questions and guided us through the contract process. Thanks also to the many research assistants who helped us, especially Lena Carla Gutekunst, who did much research and provided excellent feedback on the chapters. Thanks to Suzanne Jackson, Veronica Davison, Hoa Giang, and Danielle Greenwood, all of whom helped us significantly. Finally, we wish to thank Sarah Lincoln and William Knight for making the index and for checking the quotations in the book.

Thanks to the staff at the Vanderbilt News Archives and to the Fellows at the 1998–1999 Robert Penn Warren Center for the Humanities (and Mona Frederick).

Thanks go out to Bruce Gronbeck, who helped us think about the book during its initial stages. Wendy and he were kind to let us talk about the book in their home when we visited them in Iowa City. Angie Chabram-Dernersesian was a constant source of support throughout the project. Thanks to Georges Van Den Abbeele and Liz Constable, who invited us to present an early version of this work at the (Im)migrant Identities Conference at UC Davis (10 October 1996).

Malaquias Montoya provided us artwork for advertising purposes and for the paper cover of the book, which we greatly appreciate.

This research was partially supported by a 1997 University of California, Davis, finishing grant; a Faculty Development Program Award; and the Vanderbilt University Research Council.

SHIFTING BORDERS

Introduction

oday, several years after the passage of Proposition 187, a 1994 California voting initiative, we have the opportunity to reflect seriously on the issue of migration and its importance to human survival. Studying contemporary migration reminds us, for example, that movement and mobility are fundamental elements of living that help us develop and maintain ties with friends and family. Migrants sometimes find their way onto airplanes or boats, seeking economic opportunity or temporary refuge from the threat of death. They may live in makeshift camps awaiting return to their homes or transportation to new ones. Some who sojourn hope to go back home after accumulating wealth. Some die while making the trip. Those who flee their home countries searching for new homes, long-term sustenance, and survivable living conditions become part of an international diaspora. Eventually, those who move build communities in the image of their own culture and produce new, syncretic cultural formations. Whether or not specific people or groups ever actually return home, their migration will have forever altered the web of relationships between men and women, racial and ethnic groups, and, ultimately, among communities worldwide. It will change the histories and saturate the stories they eventually tell about themselves.

This book examines the rhetoric of migration by focusing on contemporary media representations of migration in the United States and, more specifically, on the rhetoric surrounding Proposition 187. The images and information about these and other issues that we receive through newspapers, television shows, and other media come to us through a complex network of information sources. Very little, if any, of it comes from our direct, personal observation, let alone from any substantive understanding of what it means to be migrant people. Stories told by western media often have a generic quality; the images and language used to depict people "elsewhere" have an uncanny resemblance to things we have already seen or heard "at home." All this is to say that in our study, what we are witnessing within the popular press, television broadcasts, in the office, on the streets, and in our homes are contemporary rhetorics of immigration.[1]

Contemporary mainstream media produce information, but they also provide a specific locale, a space, where social issues collide, where political issues are struggled over and subject positions (in this study, immigrants) are constituted. What is at stake is the power to control what is represented publicly as dominant truths. Words and images populate the mediascape, and audiences' understanding of the politics of their communities (e.g., who is in power and who is not) may be based on, among other things, how these representations appear. Thus, "struggles over representation . . . are not just substitutes for some 'real' politics that they inevitably replace or at best delay"; they provide "a different, but no less important, site in the contemporary technological and postindustrial society where political struggles take place" (Gray 1995, 6, summarizing Lipsitz 1990).

After centuries of migrations across U.S. borders, the criss-crossing paths of peoples with many different backgrounds, traditions, and histories, European colonizations of the Americas and its peoples, public policies aimed at drawing and redrawing borders, and military and economic colonial battles waged internationally, historical processes that extend several centuries into the past continue to linger in the minds and imaginations of people living today. But the story of migration extends beyond that history and the trace of so many lives that came before us to the issues that face those living in the United States today: civil and human rights, legal and social memory, race and gender relations, citizenship and membership in communities.

We could study any period of U.S. history to gain a fuller understanding of immigration and the discourses that frame it. We chose to study the discourse surrounding Proposition 187 because this measure invited widespread public discussion about immigration and U.S. citizenship and, as such, allows us to address questions of race, politics, and marginality directly. Proposition 187 is a contemporary example of a popular public policy issue that produced a sustained rhetoric of nativism and xenophobia. The discourse surrounding Proposition 187 shatters the cultural assumption that the United States is a "post-racist" society, that mass, public racism cannot happen today, and that the United States is an open land of opportunity for all those who want to improve their own and their family's lot.

Proposition 187 was profoundly important to those who live in California; rumblings about the issue continue even now to reverberate throughout the state, as well as in the United States generally. During California election coverage in Sacramento during fall 2000, Proposition 187 came up over and over again, this time as a negative issue sure to upend any candidate linked to its having passed in California six years earlier.[2] By 2000, Proposition 187 conjured in many minds a trace of some of the most virulent racist discourse in the history of the United States.

Proposition 187 allows us to study the role rhetoric plays in shaping social borders and constructing immigrant identities and international relationships. It also allows us to reflect on race relations in contemporary U.S. society. Because of events during the past decade in California, the United States, and indeed throughout the world, we can be certain that Proposition 187 will resonate far into the new century. Thus, we examine local, regional, and national mass media rhetoric about Proposition 187.

In November 1994, just over a century after Congress passed the 1882 Chinese Exclusion Act barring Chinese people from migrating to the United States for ten years,[3] voters in the state of California argued over, and eventually passed, the anti-immigration Proposition 187.[4] Developed by a coalition of nativist Californians, together with a then anti-immigration governor, Pete Wilson, Proposition 187 sought to eliminate public health, welfare, and education provisions for undocumented migrants. It recreated demeaning depictions of undocumented workers, primarily from Mexico, and attempted to rally the general public against them. For many, the policy conjured up memories of the racialized "alien" land law restrictions against Japanese Americans; legislation severely limiting Asian immigration[5]; the incarceration of Japanese Americans during World War II (see, e.g., Takaki 1989); the 1930s repatriation campaigns to force Mexicans in the United States and their children to move back to Mexico (see Balderrama and Rodríguez 1995);

and the 1954 "Operation Wetback," in which more than a million Mexican migrant workers were forcibly deported from the United States to Mexico (see Juan García 1980). Proposition 187 was punitive, because the law already denied health and welfare benefits to undocumented workers.[6] Proponents of Proposition 187 falsely suggested that workers were getting "benefits" they were already ineligible to receive; then, using a tortured logic, proponents called for a "new" policy to end such benefits. In addition to further polarizing racialized communities in California and beyond, the campaign helped to construct a crisis surrounding California's economy and its ethnic diversity, which continues to grow apace (e.g., Chicanas and Chicanos will soon be California's largest ethnic group). It also reminded, and continues to remind, migrants and "natives" alike of the privileges of U.S. citizenship and the lack of such privileges for noncitizens.

District Court Judge Marianne Pfaelzer overturned the major provisions of Proposition 187 in March 1998 (McDonnell 1998). The effects of the proposition continue, however, with feelings running high on both sides of the issue.[7] For example, the State Government of California issued an official notice in English and Spanish that one of us found posted in a California doctor's office in spring 1999 directing patients to a telephone number to call if they felt they were unfairly discriminated against because of perceptions produced by Proposition 187. The Academy Award–winning director Laura Simon (1999) admitted around that same time that the lingering resentment about Proposition 187 by people she worked with in Los Angeles was part of her decision to quit her job as an inner-city school teacher and to go into filmmaking full-time. A powerful public protest followed an attempt by Immigration and Naturalization Service commissioner Doris M. Meissner to punish undocumented workers from Mexico in the Yakima Valley by forcing their employers to fire them. Meissner, who had been enforcing border controls and approving workplace raids, was also responsible for racial profiling along the border. One protest sign accompanying a story about the effects of Meissner's decision on the community reads "RACISM HURTS US ALL," and another reads "STOP RACE-BASED I.N.S. RAIDS!" (Verhovek 1999).

Following passage of California's Proposition 187, many states, including Florida, Arizona, and Texas, considered introducing similar legislation. But passage of the federal Personal Responsibility and Work Opportunity Reconciliation Act of 1996 in many ways ended the need for states to establish individual policies. President Bill Clinton signed the bipartisan welfare reform legislation into law 22 August 1996. The federal restrictions on immigration benefits in the bill duplicated many of the provisions of Proposition 187.[8] Responding to much public pressure from nativist voters, newly appointed California Governor Gray Davis, who had originally voted against Proposition 187, decided not to end his predecessor's appeal of Judge Pfaelzer's decision, choosing instead the politically expedient route of letting a court-appointed reviewer make an "objective" decision (Purdum 1999).[9]

The rhetoric of Proposition 187, as we argue throughout this book, will have long-standing effects not only on what kinds of things get said in the media but also on perceptions of immigrants and immigration in the United States, as well as on race relations. The rhetoric of Proposition 187 fundamentally affects the way many will understand the meaning of the "nation" and its "borders." Indeed, we argue that such rhetoric *shifts* borders, changing what they mean publicly, influencing public policy, altering the ways borders affect people, and circumscribing political responses to such legislation. We are suggesting that rhetoric shapes understandings of how the border functions; taken further, because of its increasingly powerful role, rhetoric at times even determines where, and what, the border is. We use the word "shifting" to call attention to the way rhetoric about Proposition 187 continues to alter what the border means and how it functions and to suggest that productive future work needs to be done in order to alter purposefully the meaning of borders, of nations, and of peoples.

Our project is not alone in attempting to change the way people conceive of nations, borders, and migration. Recent research in the humanities and social sciences has addressed many different aspects of immigration in the United States. Such studies range from feminist to critical race theory projects and from literary to anthropological.[10] They range from being case studies to theoretical analyses and from examinations of xenophobia to examinations of transnationalism. Although there have been no books devoted solely to Proposition 187 published in academic circles, many articles look specifically at the subject, particularly from the perspective of critical race theory. Nevertheless, while many of these articles briefly discuss rhetoric (some even state outright the significance media rhetoric played in the campaign), no studies engage in the kind of detailed, sustained analysis of the media rhetoric of Proposition 187 we undertake in this book.[11]

Poems, short stories, and novels on the study of borders and immigration do influence people's thinking, but literary works do not reach as wide an audience, ranging from migrant farm workers to policy makers, as do the newspaper articles, e-mail messages, and television spots that are mediated daily, in some instances transnationally, for public audiences. They are part of the very fabric of day-to-day living—unlike literature, which can more easily be removed from everyday reality—and as such constitute a reservoir of shared images, ideas, and knowledge about matters of public importance. They are the textual residue of daily life. National, regional, and local media have produced myriad news programs, articles, and e-mail messages about Proposition 187. These texts far outnumber the discourses of professionals talking to other professionals and make legal documents accessible by translating them into everyday language. The words and images in the notes, letters, articles, and news spots and stories that are the artifacts of this book fundamentally shape what issues become salient, the way issues come to have meaning, and the audiences who participate in learning about issues, as well as what responses ultimately become possible. Throughout the book, we examine rhetoric publicly spoken and written, question the meanings of texts, and draw conclusions about how people are affected by messages and what kinds of influences such representations have beyond predictable ones. Furthermore, by taking a discursive approach to the study of rhetoric, we assume each text, whether it is meant to be neutral, in favor of, or opposed to Proposition 187, works from existing cultural assumptions about immigrants and immigration and may work in contradistinction to a text's stated purpose. Thus, we assume certain "regimes of truth" may be in operation that do not mirror familiar patterns such as ideologies and class hierarchies.[12] Finally, whether or not people react to these messages, such messages may have long-term political effects across generations of people. By calling attention to the *constructedness* of media communication—that is, to how an utterance, comment, or image depends on previous representations in order to make sense—we attempt to elucidate the cultural fabrics that circumscribe future political acts, discourses, and resistances.

In the remainder of this introduction we first discuss some theoretical issues pertaining to the task of investigating the rhetoric of contemporary culture. The discipline of rhetorical studies has developed a perspective that has much to offer the study of culture and the circulation of meanings and representations. Next, we present an overview of a theory of rhetoric in order to explain our choices of discourse investigated in this study. Finally, we provide a brief preview of each chapter of the book.

Negotiating the Posts in Rhetorical Criticism

Given the attention paid to poststructural theories of discourse over the past two decades or so and given the changes in the overall "postmodern" cultural condition within the United States and outside of it, it was inevitable that there would also be important changes in the reasons people give for studying public rhetoric as well as the approaches taken to study it. "Rhetorical criticism," as it has emerged in the field of communication studies in the United States, provides a unique model with which to address the role of the academy in facilitating social change. Unlike literary criticism and theory, which has roots in aesthetics and textual objects, rhetorical theory, emerging historically from the ephemeral quality of orality, takes as its practice daily participation in civic and political life. Hence, when rhetoric broke from English departments, it did so by arguing that English was too far removed from everyday social life and that the critical study of public speech provided a unique opportunity to help maintain a relationship between the political and social lives of people and ideas circulating in the academy.[13] Philip Wander and Steven Jenkins's call (1972) for a more socially effective rhetorical practice, a call grounded in the work of rhetoric's early twentieth-century proponent Herbert Wichelns (1925), rightly understands the opportunities that rhetorical studies provides in mediating relationships and meanings in the social world. The very basis for Wichelns's rhetoric was social. Wichelns, as well as Wander and Jenkins, recognized that there had to be a way to bridge the incommensurable fields of academic disciplines, academic processes, political institutions, and ordinary subjects and the influence they have within everyday life. Hence, rhetorical studies from very early on had built into it a political edge, even if it takes generational reminders throughout its history to encourage practitioners to pay attention to that political edge and to linking thought with practice.

While rhetorical studies is by definition always concerned with the relationship between politics and civic life, rhetorical criticism has not always "been performed" as an activity directly engaged in politics.

Rather, there has been a general historical tension between using rhetorical criticism as a way to improve the abilities of public speakers who engage in civic life (an "indirect politics") and employing criticism itself as a direct performance of a political act. As in other fields in the humanities and social sciences, in the field of rhetoric the push to see rhetorical criticism as a political performance grew in the early 1980s when numerous calls for a politically engaged rhetorical criticism emerged.[14] As progressive as some of the calls for an engaged rhetoric were (and still are), such arguments posited a politics with modernist assumptions. In this vein of research, the autonomous critic attempted to uncover the "truth" of a given political situation and to improve social conditions in a world or paradigm in which what constituted "improvements" or "right action" was seen as being more universal than contingent (e.g., prescribed by a kind of base Marxist utopia rather than by provisional ideas of social goods). Moreover, outside of the history of feminist public address conducted by such scholars as Karlyn Kohrs Campbell,[15] and outside of Philip Wander's appeal (1984) to study power relationships between reader and writer (a "third persona"), there seemed to be little concern with those individuals who did not have access (either materially or educationally) to public forums.[16] Hence, part of our task in this introduction is to provide an understanding of the function of criticism in general within the changing landscape of our broad cultural condition (postmodernity) and in a theoretical landscape in which various forms of poststructuralisms (e.g., Marxist, feminist) have taken a strong foothold.[17]

Our cultural condition has changed considerably since the early part of the twentieth century when Wichelns wrote.[18] Theorists and critics alike commonly characterize "postmodernism" as a general cultural condition marked by sound bites, a loss of history, nonrational logics, fragmented arguments, a decay of metanarratives (overarching explanations), historical and narrative nonlinearity, an ironic attitude toward social truths, and political disaffection, all of which leads to an overall decline of the modern nation-state. We have come to understand postmodernism as a cultural condition in which metanarratives of all sorts appear less stable or foundational and in which the division between simulation and experience has diminished.[19] Briefly said, the world that is virtual has fundamentally altered what we have come to understand as reality. Postmodernism, then, is part of a changing condition rather than a theory about culture and, as Michele Barrett (1988, xxxiv) notes, it is not something that one can be "for or against"; it consists of the daily assumptions and habits with which one lives everyday life. Moreover, as rhetorical critic Michael McGee (1990) has argued, this condition, and changing media technologies from television to the Internet, have generally altered the way persuasive arguments are made, the way public business gets handled, and the way public arguments "make sense" to consumers.[20] Hence, McGee argues that communication within mass culture (rather than changes in theory) is the primary impetus for changing the task of criticism. For McGee, the task of criticism in postmodernity is performative. Rather than assuming we simply can look at cultural texts and analyze them, part of the major function of criticism is rhetorical—not only to examine, assess, and understand texts but also to build a text out of various fragments of communication that are taking place in a variety of locales throughout mass culture and, with that text, to shape the overall discursive terrain. That is, critical analysis of culture and cultural texts can play a material role in shaping culture. In such a view, rhetorical criticism must see itself as also taking on the function of text construction as well as text analysis. All the while, of course, critics are to realize that their choices of fragments, and the ways they put together those fragments, as well as the outlets they access for the texts that are the outcome of this pastiche of fragments, are political decisions that have influence on the meanings of mass culture.

If McGee offers a program of research based on the changes resulting from mass communication as the impetus for a politically engaged and performative style of rhetorical criticism, then Raymie McKerrow (1989) can be seen as offering a critical paradigm to accompany a shift in one set of theoretical assumptions about discourse.[21] Drawing on poststructural research, McKerrow develops an approach to the study of rhetoric he calls "critical rhetoric." Since the story of the various transformations in rhetorical theory we describe has been amply recounted elsewhere (Gaonkar 1990; Lucaites and Condit 1999; Thomas 1997), we here just touch on some of the assumptions implied by these changes and some of the terminology we use in this work. Whereas postmodernism is a cultural condition, poststructuralism is a theory of discourse (something one logically *could* be "for or against," or, at least, think is largely correct or incorrect); it is a set of assumptions one makes about how humans come to understand the world and the relationship between "words and things." While structuralism, in its broadest strokes, suggests that meanings inhere stably in a number of different structural relations (depending on the particular theory), and that by studying the structure of things one can come to some fundamental Truth or driving force (e.g., economic materialism as a driving force of history in some forms of Marxism), or the objectivity of knowledge and morals, poststructuralism begins with the assumption that all knowledge is interpretive, subjective, and local—knowledge is understood in and through cultural discourses and can be understood *only* through discourse. A poststructural view sees the subjectiveness in claims to rationality and objectivity, and hence to truth. A poststructuralist does not look for general laws or material causes for social phenomena but rather searches for contingent truths and pragmatic means of improving social conditions, with "improvement" itself being a relative term. However, this does not mean that "post" theorists are "ludic," to use Teresa Ebert's (1996) phrase. Poststructuralism, for example does not assume people in ordinary life have no foundational reasons for being, thinking, and acting. Rather, poststructural theories understand that all materials are known by humans only through cultural discourses. While "material" does exist and does "act" within the world, the meaning of materials and the meaning of the actions of materials, whether human actions or otherwise, only have significance in the world as humans make sense of them. As Stuart Hall suggests, while things do exist outside of discourse, "Nothing *meaningful* exists outside of discourse" (1997, emphasis added).

Hence, poststructuralism problemizes the move to understand criticism as a way of using, in Philip Wander's (1983, 18) words, "good reasons" to promote "right action." Poststructuralism renders unavailable if not impossible a universal notion of the social good; it also denies the ability to gain access to some Truth located outside of human experience. As John Lucaites and Celeste Condit (1999, 11) note in their narrative of contemporary rhetorical theory, "On this [poststructural] view, struggle, not consensus, is the defining characteristic of social life; accordingly, social discord is not a pathology to be cured but a condition to be productively managed." Regardless of any single critic's specific assumptions, poststructuralism certainly changes the direction of criticism in terms of both purpose and method(s). When notions of "total emancipation" are removed, when Archimedean points are suddenly obscured, a critic must rethink the meaning and shape of cultural performances, including critical performances.

McKerrow (1989) takes the basic assumptions of poststructuralism and argues that rhetorical criticism needs to reverse its emphasis, seeing itself as "critical rhetoric"—a self-reflective gathering together of fragments from cultural discussions in order to "perform" new meanings. Drawing on McGee's attention to the performative dimension of rhetoric, McKerrow argues that, by performing critical rhetoric rather than rhetorical criticism, our primary task is to be "rhetoricians"—to participate in the process of social transformation, not simply to record the effects of it. The critical rhetorician is a political actor, picking up fragments from the ongoing political struggle over meanings and rearticulating them, becoming another voice in that struggle, thereby bringing different sets of issues and identities to bear in the study of discourses.

As McKerrow's notion of critical rhetoric was refined, it has become evident that one of the major concerns with the influx of poststructural theories and criticism into rhetorical studies is that the practice should not be so self-reflexive, so suspicious of any and all grounded observations or claims (i.e., taking poststructuralism to its logical extreme, if solid foundations and utopias are taken away, why is any given direction better or worse than any other?), that critical observations and political actions cannot be pragmatically useful in bringing about change.[22] That is, as we and others have argued, critical rhetoricians need to be careful not to place a permanent question mark next to the very notions of "good reasons" and "right action." The questions become, and these are questions we have been pondering over the past several years, "How do critics simultaneously take seriously the notions of radical contingency and of political action? And if it is possible to take both seriously simultaneously, then what shape does criticism take?"[23]

This book is intended to provide a model of a critical rhetoric that could be useful in consensus formation and policy making in the social sphere. Rather than bemoan the loss of rational culture and complain about the increasing apathy of new generations, we are working through a critical rhetoric to incite social change with the future in mind, while simultaneously recognizing contingency and not assuming a simplistic Utopian agenda with a capital *U*. Our work up to this point, and the work on which this project is based, illustrates the chronological and theoretical path of what we see as a *purposeful poststructural critical rhetoric*, a critical rhetoric that engages cultural studies while taking a uniquely rhetorical studies vision to the study and politics of cultural discourses.[24] Before discussing the specifics of our vision of this particular rhetorical project, we first outline several concepts that are key in carrying it out.

The Assumed Audiences and Logics of Discourse

Our interest in this book is to illustrate a poststructural critical orientation that engages and utilizes meanings, logics, and arguments from multiple areas of discussion, and so we need to lay out some general contours of just what types of discourse we are studying. After providing more detail about each of these discourse types, we then explain how they intersect conceptually. This is fairly tricky ground, however, because while we recognize the need to have a loose set of terms describing our "object of study" (and how we are in fact studying it), we also want to be careful not to reify these terms as being somehow objective or unchangeable. That is, we are fully aware that our choices of categories and the definitions we give them here are pragmatic ones, useful in conducting our specific project. The categories we describe can be seen as tools of criticism rather than as objective categories into which given discourses fit snugly. We want to note that while the "grid-like" nature of the types of discourse we describe has been comfortable for some anthropologists and sociologists who have reviewed this work, literary and cultural critics may find them somewhat formulaic. The "logics of discourse" should be seen simply as conceptual guides rather than as indicators of actual, existing material divisions. We are not building these distinctions for the sake of typology; rather, we suggest that these intersections provide the critic with a "grid of intelligibility" through which to make decisions concerning which discourses to investigate, to make meanings of discourses, and to establish ends for these investigations (Hall 1997).

Civic versus Vernacular Discourse

The first distinction we make is between the target and the potential audience of a given media text. We use "civic discourse," to signify those discourses that are either meant to provide information (entertainment, persuasion, etc.) for a large population of people (regardless of the demographics of actual consumption patterns) or that a broad-based consumer group purchases or consumes. Although we realize that the word "civic" may connote a nostalgic and romantic view of social life, we do not mean to align ourselves with this view. We define civic pragmatically: simply as a descriptor of discourse meant to be viewed universally, not necessarily as a "civil," "civilizing," or "proper" discourse, and certainly not as a discourse in which all members of society have equal power to participate. We distinguish civic discourses from "vernacular discourses," which emerge from discussions between members of self-identified smaller communities within the larger civic community.[25] The origins of identity as a community are not important for this project (i.e., Is this a label applied from mass communication outlets? from within self-identified members of the community? from both?); instead we focus on discourses that grow from smaller communities, are spoken with in-group purposes in mind, and are directed to audiences composed of members of the smaller community. The first distinction, then, is between communication available to people in general, *civic discourses*, and communication that is assumed to be for the direct purposes of supplying information to more limited demographic groups within that larger community, *vernacular discourses*.

Civic discourses include newspaper articles in the *New York Times* and *USA Today* and television shows on any of the "major" networks (e.g., ABC, CBS, NBC, UPN, WB, or Fox). These and other such media are represented (and at times represent themselves) as providing information or entertainment serving all consumers. For example, the *New York Times* line "*All* the news that's fit to print" (emphasis added) illustrates a self-presentation as civic discourse, no matter how limited or specific the actual reading audience of the newspaper is. To a certain degree then, "civic discourses" appear to be invisible (much like the invisibility of, say, "whiteness"). While *Jet* magazine is clear that it attempts to serve the interests of at least some element of the African American community (granting that its publishers might not mind if everyone chose to read it), the *New York Times* does not declare itself as the publisher of news for any specific race or class. Rather, it appears as the daily record of what has occurred, claiming as much "objectivity" or "non-biasedness" as possible.

Especially in this era of narrowcasting in contrast to the historical era of broadcasting, it is doubtful, of course, that one could point to a media outlet that claims to cover all people's interests (it is much easier to point to publications that claim to cover the interests of limited audiences, such as specific ethnic groups and gendered audiences). Hence, here we are conceptualizing a continuum: At one pole is communication presented in generic terms in order to reach the largest possible audience; at the other pole is communication presented for particular in-group members, which includes conversations that take place routinely in the informal contexts of everyday life.[26] Where the line is drawn on the continuum is determined by the critic's purposes.

Vernacular discourses refer both to everyday conversations and to mediated communication directed toward specific communities. We are not suggesting, however, that all such communication is politically resistant or that by virtue of its marginal status this communication should necessarily be valorized. Indeed, the next distinction we make involves the difference between vernacular discourse complicitous with, and vernacular discourse resistant to, dominant discourse. Hence, while vernacular discourse includes chats on street corners as well as popular mass media directed to specific audiences (e.g., Black Entertainment Television), the discourses in any of these venues will at times be more resistant than complicitous and at times more complicitous than resistant to "dominant" ideas and dominant logics—ideas and logics we refer to in the next section as "governmental."

Dominant versus Outlaw Discourse

We make a second distinction based on the "logics of judgment" used within a discussion. The polarities of this distinction are "dominant discourses" and "outlaw discourses."[27] Dominant discourses are those understandings, meanings, logics, and judgments that work within the most commonly accepted (and institutionally supported) understandings of what is just or unjust, good or bad. Outlaw discourses are those that are incommensurate with the logic of dominant discourses.

Dominant discourses operate through a logic of judgment or decision-making dependent upon the general cultural ideology found in public discussions, educational textbooks, legal decisions, legislation, and so forth. They work along the lines of judgment that would appear to emerge naturally, for example, within general popular cultural discussions of an extortion trial or in discussions about the importance of a good secondary education. These are the types of logics and judgments with a materiality in the sense referred to by Ronald Greene (1998, 22) that is focused on "how rhetorical practices create the conditions of possibility for a governing apparatus to judge and program reality." Dominant discourses are implicitly endorsed by governing bodies, and, because ideology so thoroughly saturates most educational and entertainment institutions, the logic of these dominant discourses tends to take on the form of common sense—or in the classical sense *doxa*—both at a civic level and at the level of the individual.

Outlaw discourses, in contrast, are those that represent a position incommensurable with dominant positions.[28] The outlaw position is not simply a disagreement, a conflict, or a controversy regarding a differing of opinions (Ono and Sloop 1999; Sloop and Ono 1997). Outlaw discourses are not, for example, those that enter a plea of "innocent" in a court case to which a judge or jury can weigh the evidence using legal criteria to determine the defendant's guilt or innocence. Outlaw discourses are not simple inversions of dominant discourses; they do not refute or counter dominant positions; rather, they are discourses outside the logics of dominant ones. While dominant logics allow for litigation and arguments within governing structures providing logics of "governmentality," or the logics by which governing bodies rule (Greene 1998),[29] outlaw discourses by definition operate by a different logic, that of the *differend*, what Jean-François Lyotard (1988, xi) defines as a "conflict, between (at least) two parties, that cannot be equitably resolved for lack of a rule of judgment applicable to both arguments. One side's legitimacy does not imply the other's lack of legitimacy."

We can borrow a fictional narrative example from Maurice Charland (1998) to illustrate the line between outlaw and dominant discourses, revealing how differences in logics might play themselves out in practice and how the intervention of litigation may sidestep outlaw logics and discourses. In "Property and Propriety," which draws on Lyotard's discussion of the *differend*, Charland provides an example in which a judge is asked to decide whether to zone a particular section of land for a golf course or for commercial use. Key to the question before the judge is that a community of Mohawk Indians says the land is an ancient burial ground and cannot be "owned" by anyone. In this traditional court case, the court requires representatives from each position to be present for a legal hearing. In Charland's story, however, when the Mohawk people go into the courtroom they "testify" by reciting poetry, telling stories, and singing songs. Their testifying in the fashion the court prescribes or waging an official legal battle, they believe, would signify recognition of the court's legitimacy and submission to the logic by which it operates. Thus, while appearing and communicating within the physical space of the courtroom, the litigants from the Mohawk nation do so in a language that is incommensurable with the language of the court, that is, in a language that does not imply the legitimacy of the court, the law, or the judge to adjudicate on the matter. Even if the court were to decide on behalf of those trying to stop the golf course from being built on sacred Mohawk land, the a priori legitimacy of the court to render such a decision is put into question here. The basic claim made is that the land cannot be used, and no one, not even the judge who is the principal legal representative of the state in this case, has the right to consider the issue, regardless of the outcome of the decision. In Charland's example, when the court eventually does grant the land to the developer, the Mohawk people residing on the land refuse to leave. When they behave in "outlaw" ways (e.g., remaining physically on the land and placing their bodies in front of tractors), their actions are described by reporters and by the developer as the actions of "terrorists." In this example, then, there is a clearly marked *differend:* to settle the case in any single language (e.g., of "ownership," of "sacred grounds") would necessarily enact symbolic violence to any other language or logic being used to make sense of the issue. That violence would not be the same if there were a simple disagreement, conflict, or controversy over who held ownership of the land.[30] Simply recognizing the court's legitimacy would be an act of discursive violence against Mohawk people.

What does this discussion help us say about the logics of judgment? As a critic of this case, one could probably find much civic discourse to study, including court documents, local news reports, and discussions at local businesses and in classrooms. No doubt a large percentage of the published discourse on the case would operate through dominant logics. First, the decision itself, made within a court of law, reinforces dominant ways of making decisions. Second, most of the reporting on the case would make the unquestioned assumption that legal means of settling disputes are the correct methods, and hence the reporting be aligned with dominant logics. Furthermore, most of the local vernacular conversation on the topic would also support dominant logics, even if disputing the outcome of the case. That is, while those outside of the Native American community might take the part of the Mohawk people, many would very likely base their support on dominant grounds (e.g., that private ownership of land is guaranteed under the Constitution). Those supporters outside of the Native American community might argue that "the land was originally their land" and would expect the law to reflect the basic principle of land ownership, recognizing this fact. In a similar fashion, the supporters of the developers might suggest that they have "proper" ownership of the land and that they went through "proper channels" to have the land appropriately rezoned. People on both sides of the dispute might all agree that the Native Americans should have been willing to make "legitimate arguments" in court if they expected to keep the land. Such expectations would of course simply reify the dominant logic of the courts and, arguably, that of the larger dominant U.S. society.

As soon as the differences between the Mohawk people and the developers are phrased within the terms of litigation, the voice of the outlaw is muted within the public. So, if the Mohawk Indian litigants had been willing to argue to the court that they owned the land, and as a result of making that argument had actually won the case, then the dominant logic by which the court operates generally would have been reaffirmed. The land would then be owned by the Mohawk people but the reasoning process they generally used, which we can say for the sake of example did not include the concept of private ownership, would be silenced, the *differend* erased, outlaw logic lost. They would materially win the land but would lose the fight for respect, honor, and legitimacy of the cultural logics of Mohawk people and the "war of position" over what is regarded as public knowledge. Hence, as Lyotard notes, what generally occurs (and this is by no mere accident, since the legal system, as well as all other contexts in which dominant logics are in play as a matter of course, make it occur) is that, when a case is litigated, a judge phrases the *differend* in such a way that it becomes no longer a *differend*; rather, it is filtered by terms, meanings, and logics of dominant discourse: Any resolution reached erases the logic of the outlaw and reaffirms existing law and the process by which decisions are reached. Hence, choosing to engage a system in which dominant logics predominate is treacherous for those practicing outlaw logics.

For our purposes, then, discourse can be distinguished along two key axes, one representing the difference between the producers, content, and audience of a text (i.e., civic and vernacular) and one representing the logic in which an argument or position "makes sense" (dominant and outlaw). To repeat, while each category is necessarily fluid, their intersections as concepts (and hence as critical tools) are useful in carrying out the critical rhetoric project as we envision it. In simple visual terms, if one envisions dominant and outlaw discourse on an x, y axis, with one on top and one on bottom, and civic and vernacular discourse, one on the right and one on the left, one can envision the four points of intersection we discuss below (see Figure 1). While there is a potential for

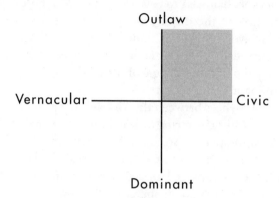

Figure 1. Outlaw/Dominant and Vernacular/
Civic Discourses and areas of intersection.
Shaded area (Outlaw/Civic) is ephemeral and
eventually disappears.

four areas of overlap or intersection—Outlaw Vernacular, Dominant
Vernacular, Outlaw Civic, and Dominant Civic—in real terms no discourse or logic ever remains Outlaw Civic for long (see shaded area in
the figure), for as it moves out of localized contexts into areas of the general culture, three possibilities emerge: (1) it becomes popularized and
hence productively leads to social change, (2) it is disciplined to become
part of the dominant discourse and thus loses what is resistant and challenging about it, thus rendering it unable to alter the status quo power
relations, or (3) it remains Outlaw, which means it never becomes part
of the larger civic discourse and is, in a sense, remarginalized. An independent feminist film titled *Born in Flames* offers one example of the
ephemeral nature of outlaw civic discourse. In the film, while members
of the Women's Army manage to take over a major television station and
broadcast their social message, their outlaw logic has no permanence and
is thus remarginalized. In the end, they give up on even accessing a civic
space and instead choose to blow up the building that houses the television station. Thus, were one to take over a national television station
and air a film with an outlaw logic, the film would either be accepted
and blend in seamlessly with the prevailing modes of thought or (as in
this example) it would remain outside of the realm of mainstream thinking and logics and thus retain its outlaw status.

Critical Rhetoric with an Attitude

In the most general terms, the critical rhetoric project we envision and use in this book is based on the four areas of discourse described in the previous section. According to theoretical arguments that have arisen concerning critical rhetoric, we suggest that criticism should be oriented with an eye toward (1) deconstructing the assumptions of dominant civic discourses, (2) illustrating the complicities of dominant vernacular discourses, and (3) highlighting and promoting what we see as progressive outlaw vernacular discourses. By drawing attention to outlaw vernacular discourses and logics, we are developing a "critical rhetoric with an attitude," one that attempts in part to change the assumptions (i.e., the logic of judgment) of dominant civic discourse while recognizing the contingencies of this change.[31]

We begin the book with a study of dominant civic discourse. While perhaps always a presence in the study of "knowledge," the study of dominant civic discourse can be seen in work emerging from cultural studies, the study of popular culture in rhetorical studies, and in American studies. What we are calling the study of dominant civic discourse would include Michel Foucault's *Discipline and Punish* (1977) or, in rhetorical studies, McGee's essay on ideographs (1980a), or Hall and colleagues' *Policing the Crisis: Mugging, the State, and Law and Order* (1978).[32] Such works attempt to understand discourse at the level of mass popular culture by seeking out the most common meanings for terms in public discussions. They get closest to Paul Bové's discussion (1990, 54–55) of the study of discourse as being made up of the study of "the organized and regulated, as well as the regulating and constituting, functions of language; . . . its aim is to describe the surface linkages between power, knowledge, institutions, intellectuals, the control of populations and the modern state as these intersect in the functions of systems of thought." What is at stake in such studies is how meanings and ideas become "naturalized," how they come to be the "common sense" at the broadest levels of popular culture. Such discourses are always already commensurate with the dominantly shared procedures and values constitutive of a culture at any given moment. For example, when one is watching television and notes peculiar symmetries between, say, episodes of the television series *Buffy, the Vampire Slayer* and the 1999 killing of students at Columbine High School in Colorado, one recognizes that what is common about life and television is the cultural context that produces the material for both references.

Because the study of any and all vernacular discourses is uncommon, at best, the study of dominant civic discourses, and to some extent the unquestioned acceptance of the logics of dominant civic discourses, has made up a large part of rhetorical studies as well as studies in other fields (Ono and Sloop 1995). The deconstruction of dominant civic logics—or "ideology critique"—became popular in the social sciences and humanities in the 1970s. Challenges to ideological criticism focused primarily on the relatively uniform set of assumptions about economic materialism critics used; however, not until the development of post-structural theories in general throughout the academy, and more recently in rhetorical studies, did a thoroughgoing deconstruction of ideological criticism emerge, critical rhetoric. Both shifts, to ideological criticism and to poststructuralism, were meant to provide an outlet for political acts that sought to understand the predominant meanings and pleasures on a mass cultural level.

What was already at least implied in a political challenge to the study of dominant civic discourses was a related move to study discourses as used by a particular subset of communities or the discourse of conversations on the level of everyday life (i.e., vernacular discourses). That is, once critics began to turn away from the history of ideas and toward the study of cultural practices on a political level, it was an easy step to move to everyday conversations and communication within some of those communities that constitute the very fabric of culture generally. As Robin Cohen (1991, 108) notes in a discussion of types of protests against, and challenges to, existing immigration rules, these "hidden forms" of protest are more important than discourse on the mass cultural level, at least in terms of political change, because vernacular discourses are a "bedrock" of incremental changes in consciousness that are necessary for moving immigrants to a more politicized consciousness. Hence, in our own work (Ono and Sloop 1995), we made a turn to vernacular discourse.[33] Spurred on by a general optimism in cultural studies at the time concerning uses and consumption of mass mediated messages as resistant acts, our initial assumption was that the discourses of everyday life, especially those of marginalized communities, would necessarily and automatically be in large part resistant to dominant discourses. It was in fact our study of the discourse of Japanese American newspapers during the World War II incarceration period that led us to reconfigure our argument by noting the more general existence of, to use the terms of this section, both dominant and outlaw forms of vernacular discourses (both complicitous and resistant pleasures, consumption, and meanings). In our research, we often encountered vernacular discourses that were more in line with dominant logics of judgment and dominant ideologies of gender roles (behavior, etc.) than resistant to these logics. While the Japanese American newspaper we studied was certainly resistant at various levels to the prevailing ideology of race and war during the World War II incarceration period, many articles in the newspaper carried in them dominant logics that were problematic, specifically regarding gender roles and sexual exploitation. Hence, while a focus on vernacular dominant discourses serves a number of useful purposes (e.g., exposing complicity, delineating the ways that seemingly alternative or resistant voices ultimately reproduce systemic logics), in and of itself the study of vernacular dominant discourses does not represent the fulfillment of a critical project to actively change dominant discourses.[34]

Therefore, in our essay on outlaw discourse (Sloop and Ono 1997), we suggest (albeit not in the terms we develop here) that in addition to studies of dominant civic and dominant vernacular discourses, one role of criticism might be to study and provide criticism of outlaw vernacular discourses. Outlaw vernacular discourses are produced by marginalized communities and are logically incommensurate with dominant ideologies and logics. As Iain Chambers (1994, 97) notes, rather than the abstractions of dominant ideology critique, here one looks for how "people go about using and inhabiting this culture, invariably domesticating and directing it in ways"—sometimes subtle and often contradictory— "unforeseen by the producers."[35] We suggest an approach examining specific outlaw logics made on the level of everyday life; thus, critics should be interested in logics at odds with dominant ones. The goal of the study of outlaw logics is to understand and highlight logics and ideologies at odds with with dominant logics and that, in the judgment of the critic, could make society a "better" place if they were to be widely circulated. Critics, as Chambers (1994, 120) points out, can bring change by understanding the ways in which their "dialogues" with mass culture do not merely reflect culture, history, and differences but also produce them. Hence, in highlighting particular logics, critics aid in the process of transforming what is constructed and what is accepted in making yesterday's outlaw logics today's current assumption.[36]

Outlaw discourses are heterogeneous with regard to one another and with regard to dominant logics; that is, outlaw judgments challenge one another as well as dominant judgments (i.e., outlaw judgments are not homogeneous simply by virtue of differing from dominant logics). For example, in this book we highlight several outlaw understandings surrounding California's Proposition 187. While we also highlight dominant civic discourses and dominant vernacular discourses, one of our tasks is to illustrate those arguments against Proposition 187 (and other anti-immigration measures) that do not rely on broadly accepted, traditional understandings of citizenship, borders, and legal procedures. However, the simple fact that an argument can be considered an "outlaw" argument does not make it one that should be endorsed by the critic. A critic must carefully reflect upon which positions to denounce, to reject, to accept, and to champion. Indeed, our own values force us to turn away from the logic of some outlaw arguments made against Proposition 187.

To the degree that critics highlight particular outlaw vernacular judgments, they are implicitly attempting to move these logics from the position of vernacular outlaw judgments to the arena of outlaw civic judgments. That is, by public-izing outlaw discourses, one exposes them to larger arenas of public presentation, in part legitimizing them. The category of "outlaw civic" discourses should be seen as one that is always already in a state of disappearance: outlaw discourses become "civic" discourses through a process in which they either are rejected and hence remain an outlaw logic or become ideologically disciplined so that they no longer challenge dominant logics and hence become dominant;[37] or, because their logic is found to be appealing, they become widely accepted and thus change the larger dominant civic discourse that adapts to it and hence redefine what is dominant.

Raymond Williams's observation (1961) that revolutions are always, in terms of the generational pace of discursive and ideological change, "long revolutions" is similar to what we are suggesting here. Revolutions are necessarily long discursive struggles. Certainly, it is possible to imagine transforming government by replacing every key government leader with someone else; however, the memory of the way things were would continually haunt the new leadership, because discourse of the immediate past has great bearing over the meanings of the present. Change does occur, admittedly; it is simply generational rather than immediate. Fredric Jameson (1981) suggests in *The Political Unconscious* that large-scale political change, which is necessarily incremental, entails shifts of entire frames of discourses and institutions. And, as Celeste Condit (1987, 83–93) notes in her discussion of changes in the relationships between African Americans and whites in U.S. history, as discourse changes and as meanings change, what people are able to say and not say publicly while still remaining within the realm of "proper" etiquette changes.[38]

Similarly, discursive change also has a slow pace because outlaw discourses, to be spoken aloud in "dominant" forums and to be understood, must be spoken in large degree in "civic" language necessarily biased toward dominant logics (because dominant logic is by definition the most common logic used within a larger community). That is, when a radically disjunctive way of thinking (outlaw) moves from a zone of vernacular discourse to a zone of civic discourse, not only are its re-presentations phrased relative to words of civic discourse but so are its logics. In some ways, this issue refers us once again to Audre Lorde's (1984) question, "Can the master's tools dismantle the master's house?" True social transformation, we suggest, necessitates multiple strategies as well as acknowledgment of the many positions available inside and outside of the master's house from which to contest and challenge oppressive institutions and logics.

To the degree that outlaw discourses are used and legitimated by speakers in civic spaces, the more likely it is that elements of that discourse will have some influence on other vernacular discourses as well as more broadly accepted knowledges, traditions, and logics. It is our task in this book, in moving toward a renewed "critical rhetoric" perspective that works toward forwarding particular outlaw discourses, to do the following in turn: In the next five chapters, we illustrate the role of critical rhetoric in an investigation of dominant civic discourses (Chapters 1–3) and dominant vernacular discourses (Chapter 4), and then, by examining a number of outlaw vernacular discourses (Chapter 5), we attempt to draw together some of the logics and judgments played on by some opponents of Proposition 187 that could shift overall cultural understandings and logics if they were taken up in civic spaces. We see each of these tasks as valuable—the criticism of dominant and assumed understandings of the world; the criticism and illustration of the problematics of a vernacular discourse that remains within the logic of the dominant while resisting dominant judgments; and the attempt to bring forth and encourage judgments by outlaw logics. In the following chapters, we illustrate the value of a project that combines these elements.

Overview

Robin Cohen (1997, 196) in his overview of "global diasporas" poses the following question, which is relevant to the issue of immigration laws and discourses in the United States: "Will the rash of new diasporas provide an enduring, additional or alternative focus of loyalty and identification to the fealty demanded by the nation state or traditional religions? Or will they melt away in the face of even more powerful forces like the juggernauts of internationalization and globalization?" We believe that the ultimate influence of such diasporas on contemporary culture is contingent in part on how they are "talked" about generally. For this reason we provide critical readings of dominant discourses surrounding immigrants and immigration policies and bring "incommensurate" discourses about immigrants and immigration to the fore.

Driven by a critical project that has grown out of contemporary changes in rhetorical criticism and in contemporary culture, we take each of the following chapters as part of an overall political project. Chapters 2–6 provide step-by-step critical analyses and articulations based on the domains of discourse set out in this introduction. Chapters 2–4 analyze dominant civic discourses, beginning with television news broadcasts and news articles indexed nationally and moving to two chapters about discourse in the state of California, specifically articles in the *Los Angeles Times*. Chapters 5 and 6 analyze vernacular discourse based on an examination of e-mail posts on a listserv dedicated to anti-Proposition 187 activism. Chapter 5 examines dominant vernacular discourse that, while not mainstream, nevertheless functions by way of dominant logics to make appeals. Chapter 6 analyzes the few outlaw vernacular discourses we found on the listserv. Finally, Chapter 7 reflects on immigration and Proposition 187 and the absence of popular discourse about Asian Americans and undocumented Asians in relation to Proposition 187.

Given our commitment to rhetorical criticism, or critical rhetoric, as a political performance, the ultimate success or failure of this project will be determined by how well we have drawn together fragments concerning immigration policies and how well we provide a narrative that alerts the reader to the problematic ways in which "nation," "race," and "immigration" are being articulated in contemporary culture. As Pierre Bourdieu (1994, 164) notes, "It is when the social world loses its character as a natural phenomenon that the question of the natural or conventional character . . . of social facts can be raised." The story we tell is not meant to be entertaining; rather, it is meant to be an impetus for readers to continually deconstruct the discourses of immigration and nationality that appear in daily life, as they are read in newspapers, articulated in political campaigns, and chatted about in hallways and on buses. The project is a success if it forces readers to reflect on the ways immigration and immigrants are called into being by the discourses of dominance and governmentality and if it forces them to consider the possibilities of outlaw discourse. It is a success if it encourages some readers to sometimes use outlaw logics in daily life (e.g., in conversations and arguments about immigration), to make outlaw discourses part of the overall arguments taking place on the wider cultural level. It is a success if immigration and immigrants become denaturalized concepts to readers, ones that are more readily struggled over in a larger variety of ways, ones that are constantly disarticulated and rearticulated. And, for people who have recently migrated, the project is a success if it helps map out the racial dimension of contemporary nationalist/assimilationist discourses and generates interest in constructing alternative subject positions and altering their situation for the better in order to challenge U.S. society.

2

The Proliferation of Enemies to the National Body

That this struggle over citizenship is so often about the lives and experiences of racial, gendered, and sexual minorities and the working class means that its story will frequently seem to be solely about subaltern bodies and identities, which bear the burden of representing *desire for the nation* generally. But, as we will see, once the national body is exhumed from the crypt of abstraction and put on display, everyone's story of citizenship is vulnerable to dramatic revision.

—Lauren Berlant, *The Queen of America Goes to Washington City*

The mid-twentieth-century narrative of "America" may have been one of an open, inviting "land of opportunity" for those able and willing to migrate, but the story told in the mid-1990s focused on the current membership of the nation—who should be, or should not be, a U.S. citizen. Lauren Berlant (1997, 20) defines citizenship as a "status whose definitions are always in process. It is continually being produced out of a political, rhetorical, and economic struggle over who will count as 'the people' and how social membership will be measured and valued." Citizenship also defines who will and who will not receive social privileges. Furthermore, the contemporary citizenship narrative casts immigration in moral terms: Those who abide by U.S. laws and procedures for how to become U.S. citizens are cast as good and moral citizens; those who do anything but systematically follow expectations of U.S. government officials and their supporters are seen as bad and immoral "illegals."

Implicit in this contemporary contrast of good and bad is a related historical narrative about the benefits and virtues of colonialism for the citizen and the vices of the non-European, noncitizen, migrant laborer who ruthlessly attempts to invade and pollute the nation, thus corrupting the nation's helpless, vulnerable citizens.[1]

This chapter is the first of three that look at dominant civic discourse. Here, we focus on the rhetoric of Proposition 187 as it appeared in nationally distributed news media, which in general constructed the most stereotypically caricatured representations of undocumented migrant workers in the Proposition 187 discourse we examined. Specifically, we examined all evening newscasts on Proposition 187 by the three major networks stored at the Vanderbilt University Television News Archives and all discourse found on Proposition 187 in the Newsbank database[2] and the listing of the Academic Index of Popular Media. Because these media outlets are directed at a national and, to some extent, an international audience, this chapter provides the most "civic" perspective on Proposition 187, and the most general metaphors under which the argument takes place and through which immigrants come to be understood.

Civic Rhetoric about Immigration

Mainstream media discourse on Proposition 187 is one example of the proliferation of representations of new enemies replacing the Soviet Union as the old enemy of the U.S. nation-state during the Cold War. The rhetoric of Proposition 187 offers a particularly important instance of the discursive negotiation of ideographs such as nation, citizenship, and immigration.[3] The rhetoric of "immigration," one of the key ideographs of the United States, illustrates well the production of ambivalence surrounding others within narratives about citizens.[4] The reproduction of this ideograph in Proposition 187 discourse once again implies the anxiety-producing question, "Who will be included as a legitimate member of U.S. society?" The two sides of the ambivalence are the desire for productive laborers and a loathing of the laborer who does anything other than work specific jobs associated with facilitating the interests of efficient capital processes.[5] Highlighting the ambivalence of the post–Cold War construction of "all are enemies"/"each is an enemy" within the discourse reifies the opposition of enemies to the self. Since 1965, in particular, the migrant is a person of color and the terms of the discourses about migration display racial ambivalence; thus, all racialized migrant subjects potentially become the enemy. The rhetoric of Proposition 187 not only constructs the immigrant subject but also constructs the immigrant subject as racialized in particular ways.

In this chapter we first discuss the ways news discourse constructs undocumented immigrants as economic commodities for the state of California in the rhetoric of Proposition 187. This construction portrays undocumented immigrants as either underpaid laborers whose work strengthens the economy or welfare recipients who drain the state's social welfare system. Regardless of whether the argument is for or against Proposition 187, public discourses represent immigrants as economic units, significant only insofar as they contribute to the efficient operation of the state's economy. Second, news discourse constructs undocumented immigrants as criminals, either because they fail to gain proper citizenship or because they are prone to take part in illegal activities such as gang violence if they are not allowed into schools or cannot find employment. Finally, public arguments assert that passing Proposition 187 poses a general health threat to the greater population. This discourse relies on "pollution," infection," and "infestation" metaphors,[6] suggesting that undocumented immigrants and their children will spread disease if Proposition 187 passes, because the proposition denies general health care to them. Hence, those arguing against Proposition 187 do so in part by representing the immigrants, whether with or without documents, through a disease metaphor. This metaphor, despite emerging in anti-Proposition 187 discourse, certainly does not help to construct immigrants as gainful members of society, deserving of all of the benefits of membership every community member should receive.

Throughout the public discourse concerning Proposition 187, whether pro or con, public media produce arguments that distinguish "illegal" immigrants from "legal" immigrants as well as citizens, and do so with multiple effects of power, situating immigrants in terms that can act as material constraints to any later attempts at equality. These arguments and metaphors are neither surprising nor new; they are recurrent themes in U.S. nationalist, nativist discourses. As David Gutiérrez (1995) notes of the 1920s, for example, economic hardship stimulated many "Americans" to alter their position regarding Mexicans: "Believing that Mexican immigrants were responsible for the displacement of American citizen workers, by the early 1920s a growing chorus of critics called for the impositions of strict controls on immigration" (69). Moreover, Gutiérrez observes, the nativist litany employed against Mexicans, "charges that they were disease ridden, that they committed crimes, that they displaced American workers, and that they were, in short, singularly un-American—was raised with new vehemence" (72). As we argue in the conclusion of this chapter, contemporary news images also encourage a coupling of "illegal immigrants" with Mexicanas and Mexicanos and Chicanas and Chicanos and hence construct ambivalent attitudes concerning immigrants along racial and gendered lines.[7]

Economic Units

The argument repeated most often in national mainstream news discourse concerning Proposition 187, and the one discussed most often in coordination with the campaign of California governor Pete Wilson (but also by those in opposition to the proposition), involves the cost of undocumented immigrants to California's economy. Specifically, the news constructs undocumented immigrants as a drain on schools, hospitals, and welfare programs in California. For example, *U.S. News and World Report* ran a story explaining the proposition's success and added, "With their state's economy in tatters, Californians are fed up with hosting some 1.6 million illegal aliens who cost California up to $3 billion a year in services" (Impoco and Tharp 1994).[8] Numerous other sources, including the *New York Times* (Noble 1994) and the *Economist* ("The Missing $3 Billion" 1994), report similar if not higher estimates.

Following the reasoning of this argument, undocumented immigrants cost California money in part because they attend public schools. Alan Nelson, a former Immigration and Naturalization Service (INS) commissioner put it this way: "There is no free lunch because if illegal aliens are going to be educated here, they're going to be depriving citizens and lawful immigrants of educational opportunities" (NBC News 1994a). Moreover, an NBC news report suggests California incurs a debt of five thousand dollars a year for each student. That report discusses the case of the "Juarez family," in which the father labors as a construction worker in order to help support his five undocumented immigrant children. While viewing the family at the dinner table, we are told that the father pays no state or federal income tax and hence, with five children in school, costs the state twenty-five thousand dollars a year in education expenses alone (NBC News 1994e). On the same theme, CBS reports that a population explosion at Belmont High

School in California sent the school from the top of the list in terms of spending per pupil to the bottom of the list. The report suggests that the population increase results from the fact that 40 percent of its students are undocumented immigrants. While cameras pan classrooms and hallways filled with what appear to be Latino and Latina students, the voice-over claims to provide "the facts": "forty students per class. Not enough of anything. From test tubes to computers. Not even enough money to buy paint" (CBS News 1994a).

News reports suggest that U.S. citizens pay for undocumented workers in other ways as well, recasting immigrants in solely economic terms—their cost or benefit to the state. Steven Gillette, a thirty-four-year-old equipment maintenance manager says in the *San Jose Mercury News*, "My main motivation in voting for [Proposition 187] was to see the state save money—my money" (McLaughlin and Ostrom 1994). Similarly, a light-skinned woman interviewed on NBC comments, "Foreigners: they go down and they can get all the services they want. You go down there and ask for services, and you can't" (NBC News 1994c). Pete Wilson argued in news media and on campaign ads during the election that he helped design Proposition 187 to "take back California for the working tax-paying families of this state" (NBC News 1994c). None of these arguments discusses the immigrants in terms of their humanity or human rights. And, as Wilson's comments on NBC illustrate, claims made in support of Proposition 187 often, implicitly, direct their messages at "you" (the citizen audience member of the programs) against "them" (the implicitly non-white, noncitizen foreigners).

Like news reports documenting support for Proposition 187, those featuring arguments opposed to Proposition 187 depict undocumented immigrants in economic terms, also privileging the economic over the human and contributing to a rhetoric of inhumanity. But these arguments see economic value in immigrants. For example, Edward Gaffney (1994), dean of the Law School at Valparaiso University, suggests in *America* that the underground economy depends on the labor of undocumented workers and points out that Proposition 187 will not save California money. The proposition, he observes, "overlooks the fact that undocumented aliens form California's hidden economic infrastructure. They mow the lawns in Pasadena. They are the nannies of Beverly Hills. And they pay taxes on virtually everything they buy." Similarly, an essay in the *New Republic* reports that farmers who had originally supported Pete Wilson and Proposition 187 were changing their minds, because they were beginning to see how the legislation if put into effect would damage their profit base. Harry Kubo, a self-described staunch Republican and head of the Nisei Farmers League, is quoted as saying, "Let's face it. Fifty percent of the agricultural work force in this valley is illegal. We'd sink economically without them" (Rosin 1994, 15). And Jaime Gutierrez, an activist attending a rally against the proposition, wanted Wilson to know, "These people are the backbone of the California economy.... Immigrants are the backbone of the agricultural industry, the service industry and manufacturing. And we pay taxes" (Vasquez 1994).

News reports arguing that undocumented immigrant laborers are necessary to California's economy tend to focus on domestic service and child care. Although these articles consistently criticize Michael Huffington, the millionaire entrepreneur whose run against Dianne Feinstein for a U.S. Senate seat failed when evidence surfaced that he had employed an undocumented immigrant worker to care for his children, most opponents of Proposition 187 tended to reinforce the notion of immigrants as economic commodities. In a CBS News report (1994a), for example, Joan Depew, an educator, notes that Proposition 187 would eliminate the domestic laborers that many supporters of Proposition 187 secretly employ. And no one in California, she points out, "shuns hiring immigrants to do their gardening [or] their child care, [or] to paint their houses." Furthermore, the report makes clear, just as Proposition 187 would eliminate the domestic labor economy undocumented immigrants support, it also would dismantle the system that transforms undocumented immigrant students into productive laborers, for despite the admittedly costly education undocumented immigrant students receive, education will provide benefits later. Or, as Howard Chang, of the University of Southern California Law Center and an opponent of Proposition 187, says, "Expenditures on educating children are really an investment in economic terms.... And like money in the bank, it pays off in the future."[9]

In sum, arguments both for and against Proposition 187 use appeals that assume undocumented immigrants are human capital. Arguments for the proposition regard undocumented immigrants as a drain on the California economy while arguments against it regard them as a boon for it. Both see economic enterprise as a social good and undocumented migrant laborers as expendable; they simply differ on which position, for or against, leads to the greatest economic advantage for the state. Either way, immigrants are represented in terms of economic value, connected to their position within the system of capital rather than, for instance, to their right to be seen and treated as members of a social community. Arguments such as these use appeals to *logics of capital* in order to make sense within a capitalist society. Thus, they use the language generally associated with the dominant institutions and dominant power in U.S. society, a language that is therefore understandable to those who naturally think in terms of capital when making policy decisions.

Criminality and Immorality

The second major representation of undocumented immigrants is of immigrants as criminals taking part in immoral behavior.[10] For example, in an opening editorial for *U.S. News and World Report*, Mortimer Zuckerman (1994) argues that "all illegal immigrants have, by definition, broken the law, and they are guilty of an ethical breach as well [by] jump[ing] the line of people patiently waiting for years for their visas." Their actions not only transgress against existing laws but do so at the expense of those willing to follow the law. Similarly, an article in the *San Jose Mercury News* quotes a seventy-six-year-old man named J. Smothers, who suggests that it is immoral to subsidize people who are breaking the law. While his "teamster friends" did not like his pro–Proposition 187 position, Smothers claims, "I stood up and told them, 'It's the law. You believe in law and order'" (McLaughlin and Ostrom 1994, A10). In the *Sacramento Bee*, Barbara Coe, a member of the Orange County–based California Coalition for Immigration Reform and an outspoken supporter of Proposition 187, also connects not having documents with moral corruption in her statement, "These people do not come to assimilate or contribute to our society. We're talking about the undermining of our laws, our language, our culture, our history" (Hayward 1994, D1).

Just as with the economic cost arguments, those who argue against Proposition 187 also articulate criminality with immigrants generally,[11] making the same clear link between "us" and "them." They position immigrants as potential criminals if the proposition passes. This position is constructed along the following lines: "If Proposition 187 passes, illegal immigrants will turn to lives of crime and gang warfare, rather than gaining an education and becoming productive members of society." This argument directly links Proposition 187 to crime in a causal fashion, suggesting criminal behaviors by undocumented immigrants are inevitable if the proposition passes; an underlying assumption is that, save for public education, undocumented immigrants are by nature delinquents. The *San Jose Mercury News* reported in September 1994 that when those opposing Proposition 187 heard the proposition was favored by 64 percent of California voters, they "raised the specter of a post-SOS California with roving gangs of juveniles, no longer allowed in schools, spraying graffiti and bullets" (McLaughlin 1994, F7). Additionally, groups working against passage of the proposition ran a series of advertisements, with the visual image of multitudes of Latino and Chicano youth running in the streets, and a voice-over that said, "One Eighty-Seven kicks three hundred thousand kids out of school and onto the street. That means more crime" (ABC News 1994a).[12]

In each instance in which texts link passage of the proposition causally to increased crime, a narrative is recounted in which the system impoverishes youths who in turn rebel violently against the system that impoverished them. An ABC News report (1994b) by Peter Jennings and accompanying film footage imply that violence resulting from the passage of Proposition 187 should be expected. While the camera pans over a McDonald's restaurant in Mexico City that appears to have been ransacked, Jennings provides the following voice-over: "Given that most of the illegal immigrants in California are coming up from Mexico, perhaps this is not a particularly surprising development. Today, several men in masks ransacked a McDonald's in Mexico City to protest Proposition 187. Mexican McDonald's are owned and operated by Mexicans, but they are still one of the classic symbols of the USA." The report situates Mexican people, whether migrants or not, as behaving destructively and calls their behavior "not particularly surprising."

Thus, arguments both for and against Proposition 187 use appeals that assume undocumented immigrants are prone to criminality. Arguments for Proposition 187 see undocumented immigrants as "illegal" because they have broken laws by entering the United States and immoral because they cut in front of others to do so. Arguments against Proposition 187 view undocumented immigrants without public education as naturally prone to delinquency and very often to violence. Both view law as the proper mechanism to stem the tide of criminality intrinsic to undocumented immigrants and both argue for protection of the citizen populace against "other" people who are either potentially or already criminal. The biologistic racialization of Mexicanas and Mexicanos and Chicanas and Chicanos in this discourse focuses on them as more prone to criminality and to violence and more in need of "proper" public education than other groups.

Disease

The third theme of public argument common to the civic rhetoric surrounding Proposition 187 concerns the health of the social body. The logic of the argument, raised solely by opponents of the proposition, goes as follows: "If health care clinics deny medical care and preventive maintenance (such as immunizations against viruses) to undocumented immigrants, as carriers of illnesses undocumented immigrants will become a health hazard to all U.S. citizens." In these arguments, the risk posed by denying health care to undocumented migrants is only to citizens who might come into contact with them. Indeed, the discourse constructs the undocumented immigrant within the social body as a carrier of disease that will ultimately fester if left untreated. For example, in *Christian Century*, Edward Gaffney (1995, 229) writes, "If an undocumented alien is carrying an infectious or contagious disease, to leave it untreated foolishly risks spreading it to other citizens." Furthermore, an ABC news program airing just after Proposition 187 passed (but before it could be implemented because of lawsuits challenging its constitutionality) shows scenes of an empty health care clinic in Los Angeles where, according to the report, one-third of the normal clientele consists of undocumented immigrants. The report notes that patient visits are down by 60 percent and immunizations by 80 percent. The clinic director, Rudolfo Diaz, argues that it is U.S. citizens who pay when these people do not get immunized, for citizens then risk exposure to disease (ABC News 1994c; see also CBS News 1994b). Finally, in a *New York Times* article focusing on the impending health care crisis that would result were Proposition 187 to pass, John M. Leedom, chief of the Division of Infectious Diseases at the University of Southern California School of Medicine, asks, "Who's your maid? Who's busing the dishes at the table where you eat? Who's around your children in day care?" ("Fearful Aliens in California" 1994). In each example, the report positions the immigrant as a foil, a threat posed to "us" and "our children," the constructed audience for the report.

The discourse concerning Proposition 187 objectifies bodies of undocumented immigrants, asserting a difference between "their" bodies and the threat "their" diseased bodies would be to "our" bodies.[13] The discourse attaches little importance to the bodies of undocumented immigrants, except insofar as they might serve as "carriers" of diseases to "our," or citizens', bodies. Furthermore, as Leedom's comments suggest, scrutiny of bodies near the bodies of citizens will illuminate precisely how intimate and close their bodies really are to "us." As "maids" who ostensibly make "our" beds, who carry "our" dishes away, and who take care of "our" children, undocumented workers occupy a space ever so close to our bodies. Any disease they get could easily be transmitted to "us"; thus, as a result of the threat posed to our bodies, Proposition 187 should be opposed.

The Proliferation of Enemies

In this section, we discuss the proliferation of enemies to the nation-state that has emerged in contemporary popular discourse largely since the dissolution of the Soviet Union, and we discuss the specific way undocumented migrants from Mexico are figured within that discourse as the basis for the mechanical proliferation of enemy others.

Throughout the Cold War, the U.S. nation-state was constructed as a "nation of opportunity," a refuge for those, such as Martina Navratilova and Mikael Barishnakov, "escaping" from lands "without freedom." In this story, the nation is made up of loyal "citizens" who, as "individuals," enjoy the "opportunity," "freedom," and "equality" that "democracy" affords them, citizens who will succeed if they are honest and hardworking. The projection of fears onto "alien invaders" was a natural aftereffect of the Cold War and the concomitant dissolution of a clear and coherent enemy, the Soviet Union. Ronald Reagan's Cold War rhetoric that dominated the late 1980s and early 1990s focused much of its attention on the "Evil Empire." Although the so-called Evil Empire has dissolved, news media continue to uphold the concepts of the nation as in need of protection and of an overall "us versus them" worldview. Thus, we could say the enemy, which was the Soviet Union, has been dispersed and now appears in numerous and diverse forms. As a result, news media represent many different versions of enemies who threaten the moral, cultural, and political fabric of the nation-state and therefore must be evicted, eliminated, or otherwise controlled.[14]

The production and proliferation of new enemies to blame, to oppose, and to conquer is part of a distinct contemporary culture.[15] Mainstream media discourses, whether fictional or documentary, portray terrorists, welfare mothers, people with AIDS, homeless people, young black men, swarthy international "thugs," "drug kingpins," lesbians in the military, militia group members, feminists, and Generation Xers (to name just a few) as threats to the national body. As Lisa Lowe (1996, 56) notes, "Dramatizing the construction of others—as enemies—is a fundamental logic of national identity."[16] We would argue that such dramatic constructions proliferate and take on new meaning in the post–Cold War context, in which it is more likely that both internal and external enemies are needed to explain existing political, economic, or social problems.[17] We are not suggesting that such enemies are "new" but that they play a new role, since an anti–Soviet Union stance is no longer possible, and since new media technology has made it easier to fragment the old enemies and to proliferate new ones. Furthermore, the proliferation of multiple enemies was facilitated by the fact that during the rise of Proposition 187 the United States was in an overall economic crisis and did not need numerous "extra" workers "lowering the employment rate."

In the contemporary post–Cold War context, the other and stereotypes of the other are always shifting. According to Ron Burnett (1995, 283), the contemporary dispersion of possible aliens is an outgrowth of a particular collision between postmodern culture and contemporary media. Burnett argues that as we move to more diverse forms of electronic communication, "communities" necessarily shift and fragment, bringing about a kind of circularity between self and other in which alterity and insularity are unstable.[18] The loss of an identifiable other, which might be the self,

> is so unsettling that the only result may be violence and despair. The image of the Other seems lost, out of control. The fulcrum upon which identity can be sustained has been removed. The shared enemy dissolves, and the result is insularity, fragmentary, almost tribal, configurations, defined by their private mythologies and with no immediate desire to share experiences.

Indeed, the diffusion of media technologies contributes to this post–Cold War phenomenon of the dispersal of enemy others and is arguably a product of it[19]; the same can be said for shifting community boundaries.[20] The greater the number of transnational relocations and the greater the overall diaspora, one would assume (at least according to a particular logic) that borders would shift, and possibly disappear, as well. However, systems of identifying, classifying, and surveying the other adapt to the changing contexts, and the border that seems so porous and crossable may become reified through these contemporary discourses.

Hence, the transformation from Cold War enemy to post–Cold War enemies means a transformation from an integrated, coherent enemy to a disintegrated, incoherent enemy. The enemy is mobile. It lacks fixity. Indeed, like the migrant itself, the new enemy perpetually moves to new locations, producing anxiety, uncertainty, and fear. The lack of an identifiable other, produced by the fragmentation of the other's body, creates an anxiety of not knowing whom to fight, against whom "we" are to be.

In this atmosphere, all enemies are the enemy, and each enemy is the enemy; while contradictory, in this postmodern context both statements can hold true simultaneously. Within the post–Cold War environment, which we would argue has accelerated certain features of contemporary postmodern culture in the United States, the Cold War enemy is present in a multiplied form and therefore is part of every post–Cold War enemy but also still exists in the very same (old) form.[21] The multiplication of enemies in the post–Cold War era means that, despite their difference, every enemy has many similarities to every other enemy, since the many enemies themselves are effects of a consciousness that has for so long had only one "Evil Empire" against which to fight.

Ron Burnett (1995, 283) notes that the difficulty of differentiating between self and other "is so unsettling that the only result may be violence and despair." This unsettling schism between self and other characterizes anti-immigration rhetoric, as does the rhetoric of the stereotype generally. In public arguments concerning Proposition 187, the "we" consists of citizens and documented immigrants (insiders), while the "other" consists of undocumented immigrants (outsiders). Furthermore, because one cannot see the difference between a "legal" Chicana or Chicano and an "illegal" Mexicana or Mexicano, the media environment in effect helps create a situation in which all Mexican-descent peoples are under suspicion as "other." That is, despite some infrequent, but nevertheless existing, representations of invading outside Mexicanos and Mexicanas threatening patriotic Chicanos and Chicanas, news media representations of "apparent" Mexicans conflate nonresidents and nonpermanent residents of the United States with permanent residents and citizens. Thus, the right for Chicanos and Chicanas to be in the United States, let alone be members of the U.S. citizenry, is challenged.

George Lewis begins his NBC News report on California's views on Proposition 187, for example, with a short clip of numerous men, presumably Mexicanos, standing on a street corner, attempting to flag down cars. Lewis's voice can be heard over the images, saying, "They have become part of the landscape in California. The groups of undocumented workers, hanging out; looking for jobs." Lewis goes on to report that while the proposition was written by two former INS officials, "it gets wide support from whites, blacks, and Asians." As he reads this line, images of numerous men crawling under fences or of being arrested by INS agents appear. As Mireille Rosello (1998) argues, there is no way to distinguish between a citizen and a noncitizen visually, yet this discourse seems to assume those viewing are able to make racialized distinctions visually, thus conflating citizen with noncitizen and doing so through the unidimensional, generalized, and uncomplex vehicle of race, which is a narrowing, limiting, and representationally fixing device.

Indeed, newscasts about Proposition 187 air abundant images of dark-skinned people running in streets and across highways and climbing over and under fences. While news reports do not specify where the footage is filmed, they characterize the phenomenon of people crossing the border as so common that cameras easily capture images of them running across highways and up the California coastline, implying that it would not matter when the camera was turned on—the image would be the same. Similarly, an advertisement for Pete Wilson ran during his gubernatorial campaign that shows numerous dark-skinned people running, apparently across the Mexico–U.S. border.[22] This visual message would not make sense alone. As Celeste Condit (1990, 81) points out, "It is in the translation of visual images into verbal meanings that the rhetoric of images operates most powerfully." Along with these images, we see on screen and hear by voice-over narration the following claim: "Three hundred thousand illegal immigrant children in public schools ... and they keep coming. It's unfair when people like you are working hard" (Rosin 1994, 16). The ad implies a "you" of viewers who can vote on the issue (presumably middle-class property owners, perhaps white since race is unspecified)[23]; implicitly then, the ad bifurcates the viewing audience, speaking only to those who are citizens and who therefore can vote.

As one further set of illustrations of news reports constructing distinctions between self and other, on NBC (NBC News 1994d) Tom

Brokaw says, "They have become issue number one in California, the one hundred twenty-nine thousand undocumented illegal immigrants who enter this state every year." Simultaneously, the screen shows a very large number of dark-skinned people with their hands up in the air, followed by officers in uniform. In the shot, what appear to be INS officials surround hundreds of people on both sides marching in a straight line. Those who watch television and read newspapers might, at this point, think of other information they have heard, such as a report by Patrick Buchanan telling audiences to "expel the invaders" (Gaffney 1994, 3). Eleven days later, after federal judge Marianne Pfaelzer initially struck down most parts of Proposition 187, Tom Brokaw reported (NBC News 1994g) that Republican presidential candidate Bob Dole had developed a plan to train armed forces to stand on the border to keep undocumented immigrants from finding a way across it. On a radio talk show with Brokaw, a caller shouts, "If the coward in chief Bill Clinton wants to send troops somewhere, he damn well better get 'em on the border between the U.S. and Mexico." Bosnians don't cause problems, he notes; Mexicans do.

In addition to the conflation of "Mexicans" and "Chicanas/os," the "other" is also expanded through the representation of what could be called the Mexicana or Chicana "breeder." This discourse is gendered feminine in many ways. In relation to the argument that migrants are economic units, there is an argument that migrants produce more offspring than society can care for, leading to a population explosion that ultimately will "soak up" social services. In the discourse on criminality, migrants are loose morally; they will ultimately undermine the national culture, language, and history. Society needs to be protected from the offspring of migrants, who create a threat of violence and disease. In the discourse of a health threat, the maid who is close to "our" (white, citizen) children represents the ultimate threat. Migrants are constructed as bodies carrying disease, as potential polluters of the citizen body, and as carriers of infection—agents of infestation. In each of these examples, the threat of migration is feminized; the threat to the national body is in the form of the Mexicana migrant or the Chicana.

This construction parallels the historical racist, sexist construction of Mexicanas and Chicanas as "breeders."[24] Elena Rebeca Gutierrez (1999) examines the rhetorical figure of breeders as it was employed in testimony during the 1978 case *Madrigal v. Quilligan* to justify the sterilization of Mexican-origin women. The common belief she identifies is encapsulated in the assumption that Mexican-origin women "breed like rabbits." Such a view was not limited at the time of the court case to behind-closed-doors conversations; instead:

> As the coercive sterilization of hundreds of Mexican-origin women at Los Angeles County hospital elucidates, many professionals, including medical doctors, believed that the high fertility rates of Mexican-origin women comprised a significant social problem that portended deleterious effects upon society if not deterred. (274)

Gutierrez argues that this discourse of "hyper-fertility" emerged as an area of public concern in various discourses from 1970 to 1980, when "Mexican-origin women as a group were ideologically, institutionally and politically paired with their reproduction in uniquely gendered and racialized ways" (272). Furthermore, the fear of Mexican-origin women's reproduction built through the 1970s and 1980s, and along with it was a fear that the overuse of public service facilities threatened the California economy and contributed to the state's pending financial crisis.

Gutierrez calls attention to the specific way Proposition 187 was gendered as a problem endemic to Mexican-origin women (281). She suggests that the targets of the proposition—citizenship, welfare, and hospitalization (she does not mention education, but it is implied here)—are all fears relating to women and their children (282).

This construction relies heavily on First World/Third World, civilized/backward, and modern/primitive binaries. The concept of breeders, which rests on the racist notion that the alien can and, worse, does reproduce itself infinitely and mechanically, mirrors the logic of the fragmentation of the enemy in the post–Cold War context.[25] Hence, since the breeder is one of the enemies that take the place of the "Evil Empire," the enemy's own reproduction of self is a hyperreal perversion of the multiplication of post–Cold War enemies needing to be conquered.

As the news articles and television news reports in this chapter suggest, both those for and those against Proposition 187 construct the undocumented immigrant as the invading other and this other as Mexicana, Mexicano, Chicana, and Chicano. The discourse rarely distinguishes between Mexicans and permanent residents or citizens of Latin or Mexican descent and, hence, through this conflation, depicts a generalized brown figure encroaching from south of the border as inimical threat.

Further, the discourse in news sources directed at a national audience constructs immigrants in dehumanizing and objectifying terms. In *Strangers from a Different Shore*, Ronald Takaki (1989) discusses the history of those migrating from Asian Pacific regions throughout the world to the Americas, paying particular attention to the labor history of these groups. He notes that "planters viewed laborers as commodities necessary for the operation of the plantation" (24) and describes how planters in need of cheap laborers in the late nineteenth and early twentieth centuries dehumanized Asian Pacific peoples by including, for example, "Japanese laborers" and "Chinamen" on the same grocery list with "bonemeal," "canvas," and "macaroni" (25) and "Filipinos" on a list with "fertilizer" (25). Similarly, in discourse of immigration about Proposition 187, dehumanizing and objectifying penal, medical, and economic language and metaphors are used to describe immigrants, who seem to be important to California only in their capacity to be useful human capital.

What we are suggesting here is that whether opposed to or in favor of Proposition 187, an ambivalent, and therefore racist, collective rhetoric emerges that uses suspicion of the other as a strategy for the preservation of the self. That is, while at times the discourse valorizes labor of the undocumented immigrant, this valorization is ambivalent. Despite the praise of labor, the threat that the undocumented immigrant who does not receive education, and therefore who is uncivilized, poses to the average citizen counters the rhetoric of praise. Both praise and blame of the undocumented immigrant and desire for and fear of the undocumented immigrant function together to construct a racial logic that fears an invasion of the self by foreigners. By examining the lines of connection between pro and con, we can see the relatively stable narrative about "us"/"them" at work, a narrative we suggest runs through other contemporary discourses as well, such as AIDS and family values.

Collectively, the discourse distances those who are citizens and those who are documented immigrants from those who are not, thus producing an environment characterized by a pervasive fear of the other. Within the post–Cold War context, the undocumented immigrant is a convenient scapegoat on which anxieties over the economy, rising health costs, questionable insurance plans, and one of the poorest public K–12 education systems in the United States are projected. Thus, the focus on immigrants as economic units and as carriers of disease is not a coincidence. Furthermore, the focus on criminality and immorality at home replaces a Cold War focus on immoral "anti-democracy" elsewhere but always also within. Finally, as a national example of civic dominant discourse, the overall focus of texts studied in this chapter tends to rely on already existing logics of legal, racial, and ideological thought. As we show in Chapter 3, the rhetoric that scapegoats undocumented immigrants is an indelible part of U.S. history. However, the context of the contemporary postmodern and post–Cold War environment may, through a hyperbolic construction of the invading undocumented immigrant threatening the coherent social order, enhance and magnify the problematic rhetoric.

3

Pro-187 California Nativism in the *Los Angeles Times*

The previous chapter primarily concerns the national citizen; this chapter focuses on an imaginary relationship citizens have as fellow Californians. Whereas, as we argue in the previous chapter, discourse directed at a national audience conveyed a concern over national citizenship, discourse in the *Los Angeles Times*, despite the newspaper's overall opposition to the passage of Proposition 187, conveyed primarily its own ambivalence over the fraught tensions between immigrants and so-called native Californians. The *Times*'s editorials argued against the measure consistently throughout the period we studied. But those editorials also argued for government economic support to offset the economic burden Californians suffered because of unwanted undocumented migration and its assorted costs to the state.

In the *Los Angeles Times* national concerns are viewed from a Californian perspective. California is often conceived of in today's popular press—and, indeed, has been throughout history—as a barometer for national discourses about race, particularly nativism, because of the state's multitude of cultures. Furthermore, there is a general national perception that trends in California's economy often precede those in the national economy. The influence California's own brand of nativism has on U.S. nation-state nativism has not been given sufficient attention in scholarly research. Thus, a careful examination of the *Los Angeles Times* and its representation of immigration, nativism, and nation in a California context requires an understanding of national issues as well.[1] Migrants, primarily from Mexico, South America, Central America, and the Asian Pacific are "them" in a story in which "nativist" Californians are "us." In this chapter and the next, we examine all articles about Proposition 187 that appeared in the *Los Angeles Times* beginning with the first article on the subject and continuing to January 1996.[2] This chapter addresses themes that emerged in discourse supporting the proposition. Chapter 4 addresses themes that emerged in discourse opposing the proposition. The pro and con arguments in the *Los Angeles Times* contribute in different ways to a dominant civic discourse. In both chapters, we make the point that articles may be pro, con, or neutral; nevertheless, no matter what position the articles themselves take, arguments by or about proponents or opponents may be contained within them.

Nativism Redux

The history of nativism in the United States is well documented.[3] So-called new migrants have always been treated with suspicion because of any number of socially defined characteristics associated with their deviance, including race, gender, religion, ethnicity, sexuality, and socioeconomic class. The specificity of the discourses of alterity shift in response to the particular historical, sociocultural, and juridical forces at play. Because of the importance of Anglo-Saxon Protestantism in the early definition of the United States as a nation-state, immigration of non-Anglos and non-Protestants was very often seen as a threat to a coherent nation-state identity, the destabilization of what makes "America" "America." This threat was, in part, articulated in legislation put in place to regulate immigration. A review of this legislation helps us understand contemporary nativism and the immigration "project" operating within the United States today.

On the national level, immigration legislation in the 1990s seems to mimic legislation of the 1920s. The 1920s saw one of the key oppressive anti-immigrant nativist acts as "Congress made provisions for the enforcement of immigration laws that hardened the difference between legal and illegal immigration: it lifted the statute of limitation on deportation in 1924 and formed the Border Patrol in 1925. In 1929 Congress made unlawful entry a felony" (Ngai 1999, 90). The Immigration Act of 1924 virtually ended Japanese migration to the United States and created one of the harshest laws on record for migrants from Mexico. Thus, between 1924 and 1965, Third World migration was virtually ended in favor of "acceptable" European migration.[4] Indeed, the 1924 act exemplifies, as Walter Benn Michaels (1995, 6) suggests, how newly revised categories of national identity began to occupy "a central position in American culture," redefining "the idea of what an American was" and "the idea of what a culture was."[5]

The 1965 Immigration Act, in contrast, fundamentally transformed the composition of U.S. racial diversity in more promising ways. Put into effect in 1968, the act "had the effect of shifting the immigrants' place of national origin from Old World to Third" (Ramírez Berg 1989, 5), specifically from Europe to the Asian Pacific and Mexico, as well as many places in the world, such as Haiti, that had not previously had widespread migration to the United States. The act also meant a drastic change in the ethnic makeup of Asian Pacific America. The historical numerical predominance of Japanese Americans, Chinese Americans, and Korean Americans was superseded by a new predominance of Filipino Americans, Chinese Americans, and Southeast Asian Americans.

More recent legislation, however, has shifted the overall influx of Third World migration in subtle but nevertheless powerful ways. The Immigration Act of 1990 and the Personal Responsibility and Work Opportunity Reconciliation Act of 1996 together eroded the more open immigration legislation of 1965. Like the Immigration Act of 1924, the 1990 act and the 1996 welfare reform legislation limit access to those thought to be undesirable future citizens. The 1990 act promises a cumulative increase in immigration, a flexible cap on immigration, increased employment-based immigration, and the inclusion of "diversity immigrants" from countries with lower numbers of people immigrating to the United States over the previous five years (Vialet and Eig 1991). In addition to these more obvious changes (some of which appear to be based on principles of freedom of movement and the material fact of migrancy),[6] however, the act also effectively transformed the role INS officers would play in the overall control of seasonal migration across borders between the United States and its neighbors.[7]

The 1990 act also shifted class relations by giving those with enough money to invest in the United States greater leverage in gaining citizenship (Vialet and Eig 1991, 33). It includes provisions for ten thousand immigrants annually who will invest one million dollars or more in the United States, or five hundred thousand dollars in areas where there is high unemployment, and, through this investment, create ten new jobs or more. Harold Ezell, a past director of the INS and a proponent of providing more visas for the wealthy, took advantage of this particular change in immigration law. He began "selling carwashes and Wienerschnitzel hot dog franchises to the soon-to-be-arriving 'yacht people' of the world" (Dunn 1991). Ironically, after the 1990 act Ezell went on to co-author Proposition 187.[8]

The 1996 welfare reform legislation, as discussed in Chapter 1, significantly affected migration to the United States. Unlike Proposition 187, which targeted undocumented migrants, this legislation also targeted documented migrants, thus increasing the stigma and affecting a greater number of people. Together, the 1990 act and the 1996 legislation revealed inconsistencies and anxieties about immigration in the United States, making obvious a fundamental contradiction between the desire for and revulsion of immigrants.[9] The 1990 act simultaneously relaxes and tightens immigration restrictions, and simultaneously expands the power of INS agents and markets visas to wealthy non-citizens. Both policies illustrate continued confusion and anxiety over the meanings of the nation, citizenship, and immigration. These ambivalences, inconsistencies, and anxieties are basic to the very concept of an immigration policy that limits or restricts people from the timeless practice and performance of movement, civic participation, and the formation of publics. The emergence of Proposition 187 is simply another moment, in a long series of moments, in U.S. nationalist, neocolonial history when marginalized communities become a convenient scapegoat for mainstream society's social and economic woes and anxieties about cultural identity.[10]

Throughout history, racialized cases that have drawn public attention at the national level often have been a direct result of nativist rhetoric and activism in California. Keith Aoki (1998) has traced the effects of nativist political climates culminating in the abridgments of legal rights for Asian Americans. His study reveals that in each case—the Chinese Exclusion Act of 1882, the incarceration of Japanese Americans during World War II, and the Alien Land Laws (which limited land ownership and agricultural rights for Japanese Americans)—nativist racial furor that developed in California was followed first by anti-Asian legislation in California and then by legislation at the national level.[11]

California, where white colonialists, arriving in great numbers during the nineteenth-century period of western expansion and Manifest

Destiny, encountered racially marked others, has a long history of racial oppression. George Lipsitz (1998) draws a parallel between the racial climate of Mississippi in the 1960s and California in the 1990s. Focusing primarily on Proposition 209, Lipsitz points out that California politicians publicly argued against racism even as the policies they implemented had the effect of promoting racism: "Our leaders are long on noble pronouncements but short on noble deeds. They preach the politics of inclusion, but they pursue the practices of exclusion" (232). Their stance, however, is neither new nor unique. Indeed, he argues, "California's harsh racial history rivals that of any state in the union, including Mississippi" (229).

Lipsitz goes on to detail the historical racism promoted in California, such as the harsh labor, physical assaults, and murder of Native Americans that meant that by 1850 the Native American population was reduced to half of what it had been when the first white colonizers arrived, and the legal efforts to deny Native Americans the right to be witnesses in court, to own firearms, to go to school, and to be free. He mentions also that California was the setting for anti-Chinese lobbies, organized boycotts of Chinese-owned establishments, and assaults and acts of violence against Chinese Americans, as well as legislation to end immigration from China, disallow Chinese witnesses, deny voting rights to Chinese Americans, enforce property restrictions against them, and limit their employment. For Mexicanas and Mexicanos, the state denied legal rights, limited labor options, established unfair taxes, promulgated racial stereotypes, and failed to prevent lawless incursions, racialized violence, and assault. And the state denied African Americans the right to vote, to own land, to gain an education, to hold public office, and to testify against whites and be a juror in court cases (Lipstiz 1998, 229–31). Lipsitz concludes that "California has long been a racialized state, systematically channeling opportunities for asset accumulation and the exercise of citizenship rights toward whites and away from communities of color" (231–32).[12]

To understand the role nativism played in the passage of Proposition 187 on 4 November 1994, one must look at the political and racial climate in California at the time. By the day of the vote, television programs, newspaper articles, and films were already acknowledging various shifts in immigration policy brought about by the Immigration Act of 1990, including the new role INS agents would play in keeping undocumented migrants under surveillance and capturing and deporting them.[13] The news and entertainment media would soon create the role contemporary immigrants would play in the fantasy of "the nation" and the role media would play in representing political issues along the lines of gender, race, ethnicity, culture, political power, and citizenship.

For example, in 1993, the Hollywood film *Falling Down* took the nativist rhetoric in the air to a new level. Set in Los Angeles, the film tells the story of a man, laid off because of cuts in defense industry spending, who wanders through what is portrayed as the "jungle" of Los Angeles, taking out his hostilities on those he sees—almost all of whom are people of color—as part of all that is wrong with "America." Simply put, the message of the film to impressionable viewers might be: With increasing numbers of hostile dark-skinned immigrants who do not speak English, who are parasites on California's economy, and who break U.S. laws, reject Western Christian morality, and take away jobs from hard-working citizens (primarily white men), as U.S. citizens we have to take the law into our own hands, entertaining drastic measures to ensure that places like Los Angeles will not become suburbs of the Third World.[14]

The cinematic thematization of migrants as aliens needing to be destroyed was not new when *Falling Down* came out. Charles Ramírez Berg (1989) points out that the genre of science fiction films introduced the "alien" theme in 1977 with the Hollywood blockbusters *Star Wars* and *Close Encounters of the Third Kind*. Borrowing from Robin Woods's 1985 essay "An Introduction to the American Horror Film," Ramírez Berg suggests that "on a society-wide level, the Other exists as a projection of what the culture represses" (quoted in Ramírez Berg 1989, 4). Ramírez Berg argues that the Other in science fiction films produced after 1977 may represent the contemporary immigrant from the so-called Third World, specifically, in his study, Hispanic immigrants. But the depictions of immigrants in these films goes beyond simple stereotyping. "The new immigrant 'invasion,'" according to Ramírez Berg, "calls into question the very identity of the nation itself, and the rejection of the Alien in SF is *projected, mass-mediated nativism*" (7, emphasis added).

The narrative of nativism that these examples illustrate is not "seamless": It is replete with serious and significant contradictions. For example, the narrative of nativism contradicts what is very often characterized as the narrative of the "American dream," which goes like this: In order to find better jobs, to take part in the experiment in democracy, and to educate their children, people from all over the world bear the suffering of personal sacrifice, including at times dangerous travel, to come to the United States, where they hope to experience freedom, liberty, and the pursuit of happiness that citizenship guarantees through hard work and moral action.[15] Given the allure of this narrative, how did post-1965 migrants come to be depicted as pesky law-breakers? How did migrant people in the traditional story of "America" as home for diverse immigrant peoples come to be depicted as the nation's "internal enemies," rather than as "American heroes," as they were in the original story?[16] And what are the racial and gender implications of these changes?

To answer these questions, we first need to elaborate on what we mean by the word "immigration." We suggest immigration is an arbitrary construction necessary to a particular narrative of the formation of the U.S. nation-state. Part of its construction depends on its being paired with either "legal" or "illegal." But, "an illegal alien," as Mireille Rosello (1998, 139) adroitly points out, "looks exactly like a legal alien or, for that matter, a citizen. Like any abstract concept, illegality is, by definition, unrepresentable through exclusively visual means." For example, the definitions of illegal immigrant and legal immigrant shifted significantly, particularly in terms of race and class, with the 1924 and 1990 immigration acts. Indeed, since the term "illegal immigrant," which we discuss in detail in a later section of this chapter, is a construct, defined by various gendered, racial, and national associations applied to it, so must "immigrant" itself be a construction. In fact, we argue that "immigrant" is a multilayered construct within discourse on Proposition 187 and, as such, connotes both positive and negative associations. Thus, studying the shifting distinction between "legal" (positive) and "illegal" (negative) immigration provides us with an understanding of the contemporary politics of inclusion and exclusion in U.S. citizenship. *Los Angeles Times* articles that focus on those who support Proposition 187, the subject of this chapter, say immigration should be controlled. They construct immigration as a problem, suggesting that "illegal" immigration is wrong and arguing for the preservation of the state and/or the nation. This mainstream mediated discourse can be organized into three larger themes, each having something to do with the structure of the state: immigration and the nation, immigration and U.S. law, and immigration and the individual.[17] The central concern in all this discourse, though, is California itself—not the immigrant, not the citizen, and not even immigration as an issue.[18]

Immigration and the Nation

The *Los Angeles Times* articles on Proposition 187 portray immigration as a fundamental threat to the character of the U.S. nation,[19] but they generally see the nation through a California lens. For example, narratives about the threat to the nation note the costs immigrants pose to it. In a *Los Angeles Times* article on Howard Ezell's attempt to lure wealthy investors to become naturalized U.S. citizens, news writer Ashley Dunn (1991, A22) quotes Dave Simcox, director of the Center for Immigration Studies, as saying, "There is a recognition of the enormous costs of assimilating thousands and thousands of people from the Third World. . . . The national interest has suffered from this massive influx of cheap labor." Like this one example, many articles in the *Los Angeles Times* focus on the effects of immigration on the nation, and within this context distinct themes emerge. First, many articles discuss the (California) "border": what the border is supposed to represent and how it should function to prevent unwanted migration from Mexico. The border is often discussed as a vulnerable place in danger of being violated. Because it is conceived of as being immobile, it is perpetually threatened by those who cross it. Discourse itself emerges as if to demarcate more precisely what and where the border is. Discourse circumscribing the border is precisely what helps police and INS officers physically distinguish a nation of "selves" from a nation of "others"—or in terms of a body metaphor—"my" body from "yours." Without discourse, legislators, government officials, citizens, and those who patrol the border would not know where the border begins and where it ends. Second, like the border itself, the Mexican flag becomes a metaphor for the Mexican nation; hence, when students and other protesters against Proposition 187 wave the Mexican flag, articles define this rhetorical and symbolic strategy as ineffective, because it celebrates the wrong nation. Waving the Mexican flag is not seen as a celebration of culture by members of the U.S. nation or as the protest of nationalist ethos, but rather it is seen as a celebration of an/other nation and more particularly an inappropriate one. As in mainstream discourse generally, these articles construct migrants from outside the United States as "them" and those in the U.S. as "us." Third, and relatedly, articles portray unwanted migrants as "invaders" who will create a national "underclass." They bring with them "disease," thus "infecting" people in the United States and undermining the "health" of citizens, and metaphorically, the nation. Finally, mass migration from "the Third World" effectively means a "conquest," a subtle, but serious "takeover" of the United States. As illustrated by the focus on the U.S.-Mexico border, the perspective taken on protecting "the border" has a unique California flavor to it. In the *Los Angeles Times*, not just any border, only California's border, could create such calls for national concern.

The Border

Literally and metaphorically the "border" was one of the primary grounds on which Proposition 187 was fought, and it is mentioned or discussed in many *Los Angeles Times* articles.[20] The newspaper depicts proponents of the proposition as favoring a border that maintains the economic and ideological unity of the nation, in part through the process of greater and greater measures of enforcement. Here, we briefly examine three key articles, notable for their greater attention to the issue, written by proponents of the measure who focus on the need to control the border to protect the United States as a nation.

George Will (1994), one of the most eloquent spokespersons for the proposition, sees immigration as a problem needing correction: "When [the Fourteenth Amendment to the Constitution] was ratified, and for many decades thereafter, the nation had essentially open borders. What the nation did not have was a welfare state, the operation of which becomes particularly problematic when courts blithely legislate policies that expand entitlements to public resources that are finite." The paternalism suggested here rests in the assertion that open borders were fine until there was a problem; now there is a problem, so we need to act differently.

Jesse Katz (1995, A12) points out the effectiveness of tight regulation of the border in keeping undocumented migrants out of the United States. He writes, "A year before Operation Gatekeeper was unveiled in San Diego—with the goal of shutting down illegal immigration—there was Operation Hold the Line in El Paso, a human blockade of U.S. Border Patrol agents credited with cutting illegal crossings by more than 70%." And, James Coleman (1994), like Will and Katz, defines the border as fixed and ahistorical, strengthening that representation by distinguishing it from a concept of "fairness," which he allows to shift. He says, "The truth is that fairness is a matter of opinion, but border laws are universally considered necessary to maintain sovereignty."

The Mexican Flag

Like the border, the Mexican flag is regularly used as a symbol of nation-hood. But it is a symbol of the "wrong" nation and therefore needs to be expelled. Specifically, proponents of Proposition 187 saw what David G. Gutiérrez (1999, 483) calls "spontaneous, emotional displays of national identification" featuring the Mexican flag as undermining patri-otism and the United States as a nation. Gutiérrez points out that these displays "provide poignant glimpses of the ways changing social con-texts—in this case the ubiquitous presence of thousands of ethnic Mex-icans in the national territory of the United States—are continuing to destabilize fixed and unitary notions of community, culture, national-ity, and, indeed, of the territorial 'nation' itself."

But, while displays of the Mexican flag generated tremendous and significant tensions, there was no evidence throughout the proponents' discourse of literally and physically *shifting* the border. For example, Patrick J. McDonnell and Robert J. Lopez (1994b, B1) report that for proponents of the measure a march that featured Mexican flags was "an outrageous display of Mexican nationalism that bolsters the case for reducing immigration." Thus, protesters waving the Mexican flag were a sign that the border needed to be policed more effectively to keep out waiting migrants who threaten to make the United States more like Mexico. But, even as proponents called for more surveillance and enforcement of the border, no article ventured so far as to suggest that the United States actually move the border farther into U.S. territories, which would have reified, hence making literal, the discourse arguing that the United States was becoming like Mexico.

Blatantly racist, nationalist, and xenophobic discourse emerged in articles associated with the display of the Mexican flag. In the article just cited, one woman is quoted as saying, "I see a lot of Mexican flags, I see a lot of Spanish writing, and I don't like it." The speaker is described as "a 45-year-old African American mother and resident of San Bernardino who said the march helped her make up her mind to vote in favor of Proposition 187" (B8). In the article, the very sight of a non-U.S. national symbol produced discomfort. In another article, Amy Pyle and Beth Shuster (1994, A25) report that a march by about two hundred high school students "drew scorn from some residents who watched the mostly Latino group chant Spanish slogans and carry Mexican flags. Many of the onlookers said they had planned to vote for

Proposition 187 anyway, but the demonstration strengthened their resolve." One onlooker said, "This is ridiculous to let a Mexican flag go down [the street]. . . . It just makes me angry. I don't like protesters in the first place." Sandy Banks (1994) quotes the complaint of a drugstore clerk "as he watched a cadre of Mexican-flag-waving students march through Woodland Hills": "If they want to be part of this country, they should carry this country's flag."

Well-known public proponents of Proposition 187 argued that use of Mexican flags was offensive, if not un-American. Patrick J. Buchanan (1994), for example, describes "a sea of Mexican flags" in a Los Angeles rally against Proposition 187 and warns readers that "Mexican officials are openly urging their kinsmen in California to vote it down." In another article, Paul Feldman (1994f, A31) quotes Alan Nelson, coauthor of Proposition 187 and INS chief during the Bush Administration, calling the use of Mexican flags "un-American." Jesse Laguna, a Mexican American and a member of the Border Solution Task Force in San Diego, was quoted as saying, "These people certainly have a right to protest, but I don't believe in using a foreign flag" (McDonnell and Lopez 1994b, B8).

In the discourse as a whole, the Mexican flag is a symbol of "otherness," a statement of a preference for a different national affiliation, different cultural belongings and ways of organizing and grouping, and a sign for those who see themselves as rightful citizens or permanent residents that others are invading "our" borders. In contrast to the shamrocks and green clothing that appear everywhere on Saint Patrick's Day and the British flag that still sometimes appears draped over cars or, in miniature, pasted onto windows as a symbol of the punk movement, the Mexican flag, especially when flown in a protest against anti-immigrant sentiment and laws, appears as a kind of "annexation" of the United States by Mexico, a bold reminder of the unhappy resolution of the Mexican-American war,[21] rendering the protesters flying the flag all the more "othered," non-"native," and non-citizenlike. Thus, the Mexican flag is a symbol of nationality, national autonomy, and a refusal to abide contemporary and historical colonialist power. Flying a Mexican flag in the United States suggests the inconclusiveness, the transience, and the irresolvability of any notion of a reified nation and national identity. In the discourse, "floods" of people carrying Mexican flags within the United States are portrayed as the impending—if not already accomplished—invasion of the United States.

Invasion

Infestation and water appear often as metaphors in depictions of proponents of Proposition 187 in the *Los Angeles Times*. Infestation is used to portray undocumented immigrants as invaders of the nation, and hence threats to the core identity of the United States. Patrick J. McDonnell (1994d, B4), whose article is located, coincidentally, next to an article about how the Los Angeles Zoo could control its wasp population, writes, "Supporters say the initiative is needed to dry up the pool of public resources that attracts illegal immigrants." Water imagery, such as Buchanan's "sea" of flags, is everywhere throughout discourse supporting the proposition.[22] For example, Ronald Prince (1994a), another co-author of the proposition, writes, "But it cannot be reversed as long as more illegal aliens continue to pour into the system, demanding more and more special programs." Moreover, water imagery is used in general in nativist rhetoric against Mexicanos, Mexicanas, Chicanos, and Chicanas. Elena Rebeca Gutierrez (1999, 280) cites a key water metaphor used by Pete Wilson: "In an open letter to President Clinton published in several national newspapers Wilson detailed his plan to end the 'flood of illegal immigration' and warned readers to 'make no mistake, our quality of life is threatened by this tidal wave.'"

In addition to the metaphors of infestation and water is the metaphor of invasion. Sam Enriquez (1994c) quotes a North Hollywood Chamber of Commerce member who favors the initiative: "People are saying, 'I don't like this Third World takeover.'" Enriquez goes on to say:

> It is literally an invasion and very upsetting. . . . In fact, Valley business owners who support the measure say it has caught fire among longtime residents who are unhappy with growing numbers of lower-income residents, many of them Latinos, now living in the sprawling Los Angeles suburb that was once nearly all-white and predominantly middle class.

Greg Krikorian and Amy Wallace (1994) quote a pro-187 advertisement as saying, "They keep coming." Martin Miller (1994) quotes the oft-cited proponent Representative Dana Rohrabacher (R.-Huntington Beach) as saying, "This initiative isn't about racism. It's about whether foreigners should be coming here depleting the scarce resources of Americans." Furthermore, "If this doesn't pass, the flood of illegal immigrants will turn into a tidal wave, and a huge neon sign will be lit up above the state of California that reads, 'Come and get it.'"[23]

In colonialist discourse, the metaphor of water is used to lump people together, to suggest their unified agenda, and to reduce them to objects that lack any significant variations, feelings, or emotions, save for physically predictable ones. Like the metaphor of mosquitoes who search for water on which to breed quickly, the water metaphor elicits images of petri dishes, incubators, and harvesters. Furthermore, it has a tendency to be gendered feminine, in keeping with the idea that women "breed" and "soak up" valuable resources, even though men rather than women are very often shown on national television climbing over fences.[24] Once migrants are constructed as objects, albeit objects who should be "contained" by the border, the argument that "they" are using valuable resources that otherwise would go to "us" becomes possible. This rhetoric of disaffiliation, disaffection, and disunity enhances a nativist rhetoric.

Not Just a Border Issue

While much of the discourse focuses on issues of border and border control, there is discourse that suggests the problem with immigration is not a border issue. Newt Gingrich, who favored Proposition 187, argues for greater border control than Clinton's proposal planned, suggesting that "the U.S. Border Patrol should be boosted from about 5,000 officers to 10,000" (Shogren 1994). The *Los Angeles Times*, however, cites those in favor of Proposition 187 as arguing that attending to the border is not enough, because the problem goes beyond simply enforcing already-existent borders. Janice Bierly (1994), a school teacher in favor of Proposition 187, writes:

> If you think a reinforced Border Patrol is all we need, I must remind you that under NAFTA trucks now roll over our borders uninspected, unopened and with no change in driver. Guess what is the most profitable cargo with the least criminal penalty for breaking applicable laws? It's foreign nationals entering the United States illegally. Without some provision like Proposition 187, what defense do we have that is any more humane?

Even though Pete Wilson helped write Proposition 187 and waged his campaign for re-election based on it, in one article in the *Los Angeles Times*, he argues for a "guest-worker program" that would provide for workers from Mexico to live and work in the United States temporarily. This proposal by Wilson replicates heavily criticized programs that have been used before. Under these programs workers, primarily from Mexico, would come to the United States for short-term work and then return to Mexico. Using shorthand, we might call this a policy of mass *importation* and the subsequent *deportation* of laborers, or simply the temporary exploitation of laborers who work on behalf of the nation but who are nevertheless denied the benefits and privileges associated with being a citizen.[25] This policy, as it has been historically employed, is hypocritical. Wilson points out that work done by undocumented immigrants is an economic boon for California; nevertheless, his primary goal was to deny basic work-related benefits and services to temporary employees and to argue that they drain the economy's resources (Brownstein 1994, A1, A18). In short, migrant workers are needed to keep the economy strong but must be returned when they become a drain on the economy.

Immigration and U.S. Law

Some of the discourse in the *Los Angeles Times* about Proposition 187 focuses heavily on the relationship between immigration and U.S. law, specifically on issues such as what is legal and lawful, who breaks the law, how law is enforced, who should control the law, and whether or not public laws agree with the U.S. Constitution. Law, therefore, is a site at which a discussion about the control of power, of history, and of culture takes place. In particular, articles in the *Los Angeles Times* differentiate between "legal" and "illegal" immigrants and between the authority of states versus that of the federal government, and they address the constitutionality of Proposition 187.

Legal/Illegal

Emphasizing the difference between a noncriminal and a criminal, proponents of Proposition 187 make a point of distinguishing between those who migrate legally and those who migrate illegally, hence casting the issues within an "us"/"them" framework. Eric Bailey (1994) quotes Dan Lungren, who would run (unsuccessfully) for governor of California in 1998, as saying he is disturbed over the fact that, in discussions about Proposition 187, "there is no essential difference between the status of one who is here legally and one who is here illegally." Thus, for him and others, Proposition 187 would provide a way to weed out the "illegal" migrants and would protect "legal" ones.

Co-authors of the Proposition Alan Nelson and Harold Ezell are both quoted emphasizing the issue of legality. Nelson says, "This is not an anti-immigrant initiative, it's an anti-illegal immigrant initiative" (McDonnell 1994f, A12). Harold Ezell is quoted by Paul Feldman (1994g, B8) reiterating Nelson's refrain: "It isn't a civil rights issue, it's a legal issue. . . . What about the rights of American-born kids?" Ezell later told a story in which he confronted men he supposed were "illegals." In his own words, Ezell says, "And then one guy was saying, 'La Raza! La Raza!' I said 'Hey man, it ain't La Raza, it's America. It's America, man. That's the deal'" (Quintanilla 1995). California Coalition for Immigration Reform member Barbara Coe (Feldman 1995d, A17) also countered suggestions that Proposition 187 represented something more than simply getting rid of "illegals" when she was quoted as saying, "The [federal] Constitution is to protect law-abiding people. . . . It has nothing to do with minority versus majority rights.'" One article argues that not denying illegal immigrants benefits means denying a host of legal people their benefits. Dan Klinge (1994) writes, "Is it also our moral obligation to feed and clothe illegals, to give them free medical and social services while our own senior citizens and multiple thousands of our homeless are without these services? And is it also our moral obligation to spend twice the amount of money on illegal students than we do on our own kids?" Articles suggested that legal immigrants along with citizens would be harmed by not making a *legal* distinction. James Flanigan (1994) writes, "The emphasis at all times should be on enforcing the law, because not to do so is an injustice to America's legal immigrants, now numbering 750,000 a year plus about 120,000 legal refugees."

Illegal immigration is said not only to deny benefits to rightful beneficiaries but to attack the general institutions of society. Janice Bierly (1994) comments, "It is a strange sort of compassion, indeed, that chooses to shower largess on lawbreakers at the very expense of the perpetrators' victims. The natural result is not gratitude, but contempt toward this country and its people and institutions. Since behavior rewarded is behavior encouraged, all benefits to illegal entrants must come to an end, and soon." Michael Huffington also draws the distinction when he is quoted as saying, "We have cut corners, looked the other way and sent the wrong message—that breaking the law pays, that only fools go through the proper immigration channels. . . . Well, no more. I believe Proposition 187 will finally draw a line between illegal immigration—which is harmful and divisive—and legal immigration—which is beneficial to the nation and California" (Krikorian and Lesher 1994, A1).

Patrick J. McDonnell (1994, A12) quotes Ronald Prince, who draws a specific link to "legal" immigration and citizenship by saying, "'Illegal aliens are killing us in California.... Those who support illegal immigration are, in effect, anti-American.'" Prince (1994b) continues to emphasize citizenship when he later says, "There is nothing more fundamentally American than the ability to elect our own government. When any other country attempts to direct or to control the outcome of an American election, it threatens the essence of our nation."[26]

Some writers emphasize the tautology that "Illegal immigration is a crime." In one article, James Coleman (1994) writes, "To many, it is not even considered a crime, even though its name, illegal immigration, makes it clear that it is," implying that the language itself makes it so. He continues, "People who enter or stay in this country illegally are criminals by definition." According to Coleman such illegality harms the state: "Our state is overrun with people whose first experience here teaches them that the most valuable thing they ever did was to break the laws of the United States." Like Nelson, Coleman suggests that illegality should be sufficient reason to deny a person citizenship: "In the '60s, we were trying to get America to treat Americans like Americans. Illegal aliens have no right to be treated like Americans. Unless they are willing to do what immigrants have done for decades—enter and remain legally—they have no right to our bounty."

Jesse Laguna (1994) reiterates Coleman's arguments about illegality, criminality, and citizenship: "But we are also proud that we are a nation of laws, which means respect for laws, including those we may not like. And illegal immigration is just that: illegal. It is a crime." He further distinguishes between what is a reasonable and an unreasonable challenge to government, once again emphasizing criminality: "It is one thing to petition your own government for fair treatment. It is quite another to make demands on a foreign government and its taxpayers when you have illegally rushed across its borders. And it is a horrible thing to start your life as a would-be American as a criminal." There is a paternalistic view constructed here of the state as a caretaker who knows what is best for everyone (e.g., undocumented immigrants should not want their children to be criminals), and whose knowledge is needed to protect the family.

Some argue that without punishment, undocumented immigrants would take advantage of the helpless state or nation. K. Connie Kang (1994) quotes Gary Kim, president of the Korea American Republican

Association of Los Angeles as he describes the approval of undocumented immigration as generosity to law-breakers: "It's like saying, Hey, break the law, come into our country and we'll provide you all the services you need." And Patrick Buchanan (1994) warns, "If no cutoff is imposed on social benefits for those who breach our borders and break our laws, the message will go out to a desperate world: America is wide open. All you need to do is get there and get in."

While focusing attention on the laws of the nation, this discourse nevertheless maintains an implicit, and sometimes explicit, California perspective. When the nation's laws are invoked, not far behind this plea is a desire to protect California. Bill Stall and Cathleen Decker (1994, A23) quote Pete Wilson, who argues explicitly that the state of California would be harmed by not stopping illegal immigration: "This nation-state is a state of legal immigrants, and proud of it." Wilson's words show how California-centered discourse focuses heavily on nativist concerns and not on concerns of those who represent California's many interests. Therefore this discourse addresses who belongs in California as one of its legitimate members. Throughout the period, Wilson makes clear that for him there is a "right way" and a "wrong way" to immigrate.[27] Immigrating legally is the right way, and immigrating "illegally" is the wrong way. The right way makes one a Californian.

Federal Government versus State of California

Other articles focus on the need for federal compensation for the economic shortfalls of the state of California resulting from "illegal immigration." Articles by or about proponents of Proposition 187 tend to argue that Proposition 187 challenges the irresponsible federal government, which failed to seal off the border and failed to enforce other strict legislation against undocumented migrants. The entire argument rests on a constructed distinction between California and its problems and the nation's problems as a whole, and in casting the federal government as somehow either unwilling or unable to take California's "immigration problem" seriously.

The *Los Angeles Times* reflects concerns about California's being the "gateway" into the United States for undocumented migrants from Mexico. Some nativist Californians say that immigration is a national concern and that California should be compensated for having more than its fair share of undocumented workers, which, they argue, are an economic drain on California's economy. In short, they argue that the entire nation should pay for the INS's failure to control the flow of immigration into California, not just California alone.[28]

Articles depicting proponents of Proposition 187 concentrate on how the proposition would challenge the federal government's lack of responsible attention to California's immigration "problem." The basic argument is that the lack of federal oversight of immigration has an unfair and disproportionate, negative effect on California's economy, suggesting that California is special in the way the federal government neglects it. Most articles in this vein report that Proposition 187 will force the hand of the federal government to act responsibly with regard to California's "illegal immigration problem."[29] As Patrick J. McDonnell (1994d, B4) writes in late July, "The initiative has broad support among voters, and has clearly tapped into a sentiment against illegal immigration at a time of statewide economic stagnation." Two weeks later he says, "Three months before Election Day, the ballot measure known as Proposition 187 already seems destined to join the pantheon of California initiatives that periodically reshape national debate." He continues, the proposition may ultimately shape "national immigration policy" (McDonnell 1994f, A1). Moreover, he suggests its passage might force the federal government to address immigration in California: "With limited influence over Washington, however, proponents have turned to the liberal California initiative process in an effort to involve state and local government in immigration matters to an unprecedented degree" (A12).

By this time, the argument that Proposition 187 will force the federal government to act appears regularly in articles. The logic of "Us [California] versus Them [Federal Government]" is clear in a statement made by Ronald Prince (1994a) in which he explains the argument implied by the proposition: "Once illegal aliens arrive in California, the burden falls on the state, not the federal government. . . . Rather than support and harbor illegal aliens, California will report them to the INS. And, more important, a *yes* vote on Proposition 187 will pressure the federal government to enforce its own laws." He continues, "Proposition 187 deals with the problem of illegal immigration at the state level, where most of the costs are incurred. Its passage will then pressure the federal government to do its part." (See also Coleman 1994.) Similarly, Brian O'Leary Bennett (1994) writes:

> Securing our borders is the constitutional responsibility of the national government, period. Until Washington attaches to the protection of our southern border the same diplomatic urgency it rightly gave to NAFTA, our border

will not be secure. And if Washington won't, pray that at least Gov. Wilson's suit succeeds in getting California reimbursed for a problem that Washington allowed to mushroom into unmanageability.

Indeed, "sending Washington a message" becomes the language used to express this California versus the federal government sentiment. One article reports Mike Huffington using this language: "Speaking at a quickly arranged news conference in San Bernardino, Huffington said illegal immigration has become such a serious problem that it is time to send a message to illegal immigrants as well as to leaders in Washington that Californians have had enough" (Krikorian and Lesher 1994, A1).

The focus is on California as David and the federal government as Goliath or simply big state versus big government. Columnist George Will (1994) writes one of the most rhetorically powerful articles, indicting the court system for undermining state and local governments. He sees "a pattern of judicial usurpations of state and local responsibilities."

> These usurpations have involved courts supplanting democratic institutions in formulating policies concerning pornography, capital punishment, administration of prisons and mental health facilities and public housing, abortion, school financing and other matters. Proposition 187 concerns not what national immigration policy should be, but what state policy should be regarding violators of national law.

Here, Will suggests that the judiciary, in not acting on behalf of the people, is removed from the problems of everyday life. Further, national immigration policies, because they are made for the nation, cannot address satisfactorily the problems of a given state. Both arguments indict public institutions—the "court" and the "national government"—for not acting on behalf of the will of the people, thus constructing a local-nativist versus outsider-nationalist division.

An article published directly after the election reports Pete Wilson capitalizing on his victories by using nativist themes and reaffirming the rights of "legal" migrants. Wilson says, "What people need to understand is that this issue was never about race or racism. . . . To the contrary, Californians of every race and color and creed voted not just to send a message, but they voted for fairness and for the rule of law" (Stall and Decker 1994, A23). Here, Wilson makes it very clear that there is a "right way" and a "wrong way" to immigrate. And, by labeling the right way "legal" and suggesting the nation-state is founded on "legal immigrants," he constructs a discursive border arguing for who should be on the inside and who should be on the outside. Furthermore, the suggestion that California is made up of legal immigrants also implies that the federal government will somehow be acting illegally if it does not support California in its efforts.[30]

Predictably, after Wilson won the governor's race, one article reports that he wanted to encourage federal legislation similar to Proposition 187. Prodded by the success of his anti-immigrant campaign, Wilson planned to take California's nativism to the national level, following the path of anti–Japanese American nativists in California preceding the decision by President Franklin Roosevelt to incarcerate Japanese Americans during World War II.[31] Ronald Brownstein (1994, A1) writes, "Gov. Pete Wilson, fresh from his resounding reelection victory, proposed Friday that Congress adopt a federal version of California's controversial Proposition 187, which would deny all benefits except emergency medical care to illegal immigrants." Drawing on rhetoric about similar federal legislation, one article describes Newt Gingrich also applying pressure at the federal level: "Gingrich declared that until the borders are secured, the federal government should either excuse states from paying for services for illegal immigrants or pick up the bill" (Shogren 1994).

Much discourse addresses the issue of the state and nation in tension in discussions about the courts and the relationship between voter-approved state legislation and federal court authority. While it was still being decided whether state courts or federal courts would adjudicate Proposition 187, an article cites Assistant Attorney General Charlton G. Holland telling a courtroom that the people of California passed Proposition 187 "by a large margin." Thus, "it should be resolved in California's courts by California judges" (Feldman 1995a, A22). That same article goes on to quote a spokesman for Dan Lungren, who, echoing George Will's words on the matter, "blast[s]" the ruling that the case will be heard in federal court. He calls it "another example of the federal court's lack of respect for a state's right to pass a law without having the over-powerful national government step in and say we're not going to allow you to do that."

In these articles that focus on the state versus federal authority over immigration, there is an underlying mythology of the underdog fighting back against the overweening authority for the right to do as it wishes. And, while some articles say California depends on federal subsidies for education and health, others also show California's dependence on federal protection from "illegal" immigration. Thus, arguments for nativist ideological independence nevertheless acknowledge the dependence California has on federal monies. Therefore, articles also suggest that California needs to send a message to Washington through Proposition 187, even though it ultimately means risking the loss of health and education funds California currently receives. This call for liberation hides the oppressive position taken by the newspaper; despite the editorials' stated opposition to the measure, anti-immigrant discourse ultimately takes a position even more laudatory of the proposition's basic tenets—California nativism and anti-immigration—than discourse of the measure's supporters.

Constitutionality

Other articles about Proposition 187 and the law address the sticky issue of Proposition 187's constitutionality. Articles by or about proponents of the proposition say it is necessary to challenge the 1982 *Plyler v. Doe* U.S. Supreme Court decision making education mandatory for children of undocumented migrants. Thus, anti-immigrant discourse now aims to deny children of undocumented immigrants the right to an education. Since (officially) being born in the United States means one is a citizen,[32] the argument that children (in general) of undocumented immigrants should not receive public education indirectly means a shift in the status of citizenship as well as a shift in the meaning of borders.[33] Specifically, it means a shift in the notion of borders because by ratifying such a law it no longer matters on what side of the border one is born to determine inclusion and membership in the U.S. nation-state.

Harold Ezell, for example, expresses confidence that passage of the proposition will "trigger a court challenge to a landmark 1982 U.S. Supreme Court ruling that stated that illegal immigrant children are entitled to a public school education" (Feldman 1994d, A25). An article summarizing Pete Wilson's reasoning says that he, too, sees the proposition as "a way to provoke a legal challenge" to *Plyler v. Doe* (Weintraub and Stall 1994). Later, another article says that Wilson believes the legal battle to uphold Proposition 187 will end in his favor because of changes in the Supreme Court (Stall and Wallace 1994, A24). The same article reports Wilson's proposal "that the Constitution be amended so that those children no longer would automatically qualify for citizenship."

Articles also focus on proponents' responses to the fact that opponents would challenge the measure in court. But, Ronald Prince (1994a) writes:

> This is a challenge that we welcome. It will force the U.S. Supreme Court to revisit its narrow (5–4) decision of 1982 that required public education for illegals. The Plyler decision was based on circumstances very different from our problem today, where the cost of educating illegal aliens in bilingual programs is much higher than the amount allocated for American citizens.

One article reports a pledge by Dan Lungren, in his capacity as California attorney general, to "strongly defend Proposition 187 against expected lawsuits if voters approve the sweeping anti-illegal immigration measure next week" (Feldman and Ingram 1994).[34] Another article quotes Lungren as saying that even if certain provisions of Proposition 187 are struck down by the court a severability clause still exists to justify its enforcement (Dolan 1994, A1).

Addressing the issue of constitutionality from another vantage point, one set of articles discusses the outrage of some Californians over the notion that public money would be spent to challenge an approved public referendum in court. In these examples, the substantive question of constitutionality is displaced in favor of a local nativist argument, suggesting the will of the majority of voting Californians is more important than the federal Constitution. To spend money and time trying to test the constitutionality of a popular measure adopted by voters thus becomes an irrational act. One article describes the response as "an angry ground-swell of criticism" over the "use of public funds to undo what the measure's backers see as a clear mandate from the voters" (Connell, Shuster, and Rainey 1994, A1). A *Los Angeles Times* editorial argues that public institutions intending to join in the legal challenge should reconsider: "Public agencies would be well-advised to wait and shepherd increasingly scarce tax dollars instead of duplicating existing lawsuits."[35] One article quotes Ronald Prince chastising public officials who join in the lawsuits and encouraging public recall of them. In this article, Prince invokes the "will of the people" as a rhetorical strategy, positioning those opposing the measure as against that will. Paul Feldman and Patrick J. McDonnell (1994b, A18) write:

> Prince, for one, is suggesting the recall of public officials who have voted to take part in anti-187 lawsuits, even though Prince and other sponsors of the measure have long acknowledged that it would not take effect until a flurry

of lawsuits was ruled upon. "The will of the people should be obeyed and it is too often thwarted by special interest groups," Prince said. "It doesn't make sense for elected officials to sue the people. They should be listening to the people."[36]

Similarly, an article quoting Wilson also contains a call to the people's will. Wilson says, "Neither the U.S. Constitution nor the federal courts should be misused so as to prevent citizens from deciding that illegal immigrants should be treated differently than those who have entered this country legally. . . . The patience of Californians will soon wear thin if their will is not carried out" (Feldman 1995a, A1). In both of these examples, those opposing Proposition 187 position citizens against the initiative, as if to suggest that Proposition 187 is anti-citizen and a threat to citizenship.

Other articles focus on the court's arrogance in challenging public referendums. George Will (1994) writes, "This is the familiar non sequitur by which imperial judges turn courts into legislatures: What-ever the judges deem unfair or unwise must be unconstitutional." He writes further:

> Chief Justice Warren Burger, dissenting and joined by Byron White, William Rehnquist and Sandra Day O'Connor, noted that "the court [majority] makes no attempt to disguise the fact that it is acting to make up for Congress" lack of "effective leadership" regarding immigration. The court, he said, was attempting "speedy and wholesale formulation of 'remedies' for the failures—or simply the laggard pace—of the political processes of our system of government."[37]

In addition to questioning the role the federal government should play in addressing immigration in California, this discourse about the Constitution and about the alleged misuse of public funds to challenge a voter initiative constructs a dichotomy between California nativist desires and "government's" (in this case those filing cases in court) dis-reputable and costly challenge to that will. Wilson's statement that "the patience of Californians will soon wear thin" suggests a personal under-standing of how nativist Californians feel, thus constructing himself as sympathetic empath and protector and those who would stand in the way of Proposition 187's implementation as somehow un-Californian.

Immigration and the Individual

While pro-Proposition 187 discourse centers on the nation as divided from other nations and on the identity of the United States (especially with regard to federal versus state jurisdictions); it also centers on the relationship of the individual to the state. Thus, it addresses the issue on nation, state, and individual levels. Specifically, pro-Proposition 187 rhetoric focuses on the familiarity versus strangeness of others, good and bad people, and protests. In each of these ways, subjectivity and citizenship are understood in relation to the state.

Familiarity versus Strangeness

Articles that discuss proponents of the proposition address racial and national differences as a way of arguing for a wary attitude toward immigration. Immigration is said to have changed meaning from early in U.S. history to the present: What was historically the "arrival" of easily assimilated and familiar immigrants to the United States has become an invasion of aliens. Patrick Buchanan (1994) writes, "Ethnic militancy and solidarity are on the rise in the United States; the old institutions of assimilation are not doing their work as they once did; the melting pot is in need of repair. On campuses we hear demands for separate dorms, eating rooms, clubs, etc., by black, white, Latino and Asian students. If this is where the campus is headed, where are our cities going?" Thus, according to Buchanan, the historical narrative of immigration, which necessitated the assimilation of immigrants—the giving up of one's culture, values, ideology, and politics—in order to fit into the dominant U.S. frame had somehow become a narrative in which those who immigrate bring too much of who they are with them. This shift, of course, corresponds with the post-1965 shift in racial identity of immigrants.

Underneath Buchanan's article, in the same feature box, appears a black and white political cartoon by Chip Bok (1994). In it, two genderless figures stand in front of a building, apparently leaving it. On the door behind them appears the phrase "U.S. Citizens only." Above it reads "Public School." A bubble indicating the words spoken by one figure reads, "We'd be a burden to American Born Taxpayers here. Let's go join a gang." Knowing the *Los Angeles Times* has, through its series of editorials on the issue, challenged Proposition 187, readers might be tempted to read this cartoon as an argument against the Proposition, because, in words similar to those used in articles quoting opponents, the measure would "throw teenagers out of schools and onto streets, where they would join gangs and become delinquents." But, because of the cartoon's close proximity to Buchanan's column, an ironic reading is more appropriate. Thus, the comment "We'd be a burden to American Born Taxpayers here. Let's go join a gang" is actually an implicit critique of the language of the measure's *opponents;* it implies that the argument opponents used—that, if Proposition 187 were to pass, children without education would become juvenile delinquents—is illogical and even possibly racist.[38]

Good/Bad Immigrant

Other articles representing the relationship between the individual and the state make a distinction between "good" (former) and "bad" (current) immigrants, not unlike Wilson's view of "right" and "wrong" ways to immigrate. These articles discussing proponents of the initiative, such as Pat Buchanan, also find it difficult to draw a correlation between early twentieth-century migrants and contemporary migrants. Using the very same language Pete Wilson uses to describe how Californians will react to court appeals of the proposition's passage, James Coleman (1994) writes, "Proposition 187 will deny this criminal class benefits that are *wearing thin* for those of us who pay for them—and thereby discourage them from coming altogether" (emphasis added). Coleman continues:

> The truth is that the history of humanity has seen the ownership of land change hands countless times and that it is counterproductive to speak of it being stolen. Ellis Island, moreover, is the very symbol of legal immigration: people struggling to do whatever was necessary to be legal residents of this country. And I have yet to figure out any connection between today's illegals and the stolen Africans of yesteryear.

In a similar construction of "good" versus "bad" immigrants (it is worth noting that abducting African people for enslavement is regarded here as an acceptable immigration path), Greg Krikorian and Dave Lesher (1994, A30) quote Michael Huffington as saying, "But something has changed. In recent years, the problem of illegal immigration has grown beyond previously imaginable proportions. Our hospitals, our schools, our prisons are overflowing. It's time to send a message to those illegal immigrants who disregard our laws and take advantage of our government's misplaced generosity." In general, then, newspaper articles about Proposition 187 in the *Los Angeles Times* make a distinction between good immigrants and bad immigrants. The implication is that prior migration periods were legal ones but migration today is largely illegal. What is not openly discussed in these articles is that early twentieth-century migration was largely from Europe and migrants were largely white people; the migration to California today is largely from the Third World and migrants are largely people of color. Thus "good" and "bad" are racially circumscribed and state-specific adjectives.

Protests

Articles by or about proponents of Proposition 187 represent protests and protesters of the measure by criticizing what opponents say, as well as objecting to the opponents' strategies of persuasion. For example, one article quotes Ronald Prince as saying opponents of Proposition 187 turn a legal issue into an emotional one, arguing from pathos rather than logos (Feldman 1994h, A17). Another article discusses objections to emotional rhetoric. Amy Pyle (1994c) writes, "Backers of Proposition 187 say that peppering lawsuits with emotional stories such as Barbara's is a clever but dishonest tactic to influence public opinion." One article cites Harold Ezell discussing what the opposition said about a boy who died because of lack of health care resulting from Proposition 187. Ezell argues in the article that the use of the child's death as a strategy by those opposed to the measure is wrong: "I think it's outrageous that the no-on-187 people used this tragedy as a way to vent their anger against the will of the people" (Romney 1994).

In addition to criticizing the use of pathos as a strategy, another article cites Harold Ezell's challenge to Proposition 187 opponents for saying the measure is racist. Ezell says, "This is a legal issue, not a racial issue.... And the conduct of these people today suggests anarchy. I was invited here to speak ... and they come in and acted like a bunch of animals" (Enriquez 1994a, B4). An article citing Dana Rohrabacher makes a similar point. Rohrabacher says, "The charge of racism is a tactic of intimidation that doesn't work anymore.... It's meant to close out honest debate. This initiative isn't about racism. It's about whether foreigners should be coming here depleting the scarce resources of Americans" (Miller 1994).

Other articles blame those who protested Proposition 187 for producing false images of what passage of the measure means. For example, in an article by Paul Feldman (1994i), Ronald Prince is quoted as saying, "187 has had no effect at all on public health care yet.... If there's a misperception of such a prohibition, I'd look more at the misinformation campaign of our opponents [before the election] trying to incite that fear." Prince continues, "There were so many lies spread about this that it's understandable there could be some confusion. But the people to look to for responsibility for that are the people who spread those lies and deliberately encouraged it for political gain because they knew they weren't true and they wanted to frighten the public.'" In another article, Feldman (1994a, A23) summarizes Alan Nelson, who in addition to being past INS chief and Proposition 187 co-author is also a Sacramento lobbyist for FAIR (Federation for American Immigration Reform), as saying "that opponents of the measure are guilty of racism for painting a picture of anarchy in the streets once illegal immigrant children are expelled from public schools and colleges."

This article also blames protesters for inspiring racism against Latinos.[39] Jesse Laguna (1994) writes, "The hostile tactics of those fighting the initiative, the boast by many Latinos that 'we won't overcome, we will overwhelm' and the encouragement of young Latino hot-heads to take back the Southwest, Texas to California, by armed force, can only lead Americans to suspect all Latinos of being a potential fifth column." Here, Latinos are constructed negatively as being associated with protest. Thus, a criticism of protest ultimately becomes a criticism of Latinos; yet protest is depicted as un-Latino-like and is blamed for inspiring negative public views of Latinos. Protest becomes evidence of a "fifth column," meaning that despite the fact that there are no doubt citizens among those protesting, the inference that Mexicanas, Mexicanos, Chicanas, and Chicanos will "take back the Southwest" articulates a fear of publicly airing differing views—protests—and the actions for which those protests call. This is a criticism not only of the multiplicity of views held and spoken within any given context but also of protest itself. Some even go so far as to say that people should not protest against racism by calling attention to it, suggesting that protests against racism in fact promote racism.

Two articles celebrate individuals who stood up against collective protest, one who opposed Proposition 187 and one who supported it. Tony Perry (1994) reports that a young man who was kicked and beaten by his fellow protesters during an anti–Proposition 187 rally "when he prevented other demonstrators from burning an American flag was presented with a U.S. flag ... by a San Diego congressman who supports Proposition 187." A second article quotes Joel Wachs, a proponent of the proposition, who planned to challenge the Los Angeles City Council for having taken a stand against it. Paul Feldman and James Rainey (1994a, A38) write, "Wachs said he will press the City Council today to reverse that stand and 'not take that activist position. That is what the public is really angry about, seeing their money used to try to overturn their action. That is what the public sees as an arrogance.'" Both articles celebrate an individual who stands up against collective protest. The fact that the individuals have differing perspectives on Proposition 187 does not undermine the general questioning of protest they represent.

James Coleman (1994), who reports having supported civil rights in the 1960s, challenges anti–Proposition 187 people generally for deciding to protest this measure. In a somewhat lengthy passage, he writes:

> There are people (including some members of the Los Angeles Board of Education) who have sworn that even if voters pass this law, they will not uphold it. These Proposition 187 opponents say they are the new civil-rights fighters. As one who was tear-gassed during the 1960s, I resent the comparison. In the '60s, we were trying to get America to treat Americans like Americans. Illegal aliens have no right to be treated like Americans. Unless they are willing to do what immigrants have done for decades—enter and remain legally—they have no right to our bounty.

As a whole, articles by or about proponents of the measure chastising protesters argued not only against the way protests were conducted but also against the protesters themselves. Protesters waving Mexican flags are treated with hostility befitting the (internal) enemy. And, those who question the constitutionality of laws and protest the assimilationist history of immigration are, for the most part, dismissed out of hand.

Articles on Proposition 187 in the *Los Angeles Times* that depict proponents of the initiative reveal that nativist rhetoric in this campaign struggles to define what it means to be a Californian, to describe the unique experiences of Californians that account for policies that go against the larger nation, and to clarify the need to maintain particular definitions of the border, the flag, the nation, the citizen, and the immigrant in order to maintain a uniquely California culture.

At the same time all of the arguments opponents use against Proposition 187 are also appeals for California. Some raise the specter of a giant federal government working against Californians, others of the unjust legal system so ensconced in its own elitist, detached practices it is unable to relate to the real problems affecting society. Whatever the argument, being a Californian is central to all of this discourse.

Moreover, in a strict rhetorical sense, who would not want to be for California? Who would want to be against California? While by no means are we suggesting this appeal to California nativism is controlling or determinant, we do suggest that those who protest against Proposition 187 are in somewhat of a discursive bind. Could protesters argue that they are simultaneously *for California* but *against Proposition 187?* Is being for Proposition 187 an act of California patriotism? Furthermore, given the history of California—a product of U.S. and Spanish colonialism, a land inhabited first by Native Americans, later by Spanish and Mexican immigrants, and now by transnational, multiracial communities—is it possible to be pro–immigrant rights, pro-immigration, and anti-exploitation and simultaneously be a Californian today? These questions suggest the uneasy problematic that pervades the discourses of nativism represented in the *Los Angeles Times.* These questions about labor, power, memory, culture, history, identity, colonialism, and resistance necessarily maintain an antagonism that goes well beyond simply being for or against a single ballot initiative. These are the very antagonisms that most strongly confront Mexican Americans. Indeed, they cut to the core of what it means to exist in contemporary culture.

4

Opposition and Complicity
in the *Los Angeles Times*

Representations of immigration issues are found in arguments made by or about opponents of Proposition 187, just as they are found in arguments made by or about proponents. But whereas California nativism grounded proponents' claims on the measure, a deep ambivalence appears in opponents' claims. The ambivalence is due in part to the positions the *Los Angeles Times* took with regard to what it means to be an immigrant and what it means to be a Californian.[1] The ambivalence is complicated; as demonstrated in Chapter 3, the *Los Angeles Times* printed commentary by proponents of the measure that was at times hostile and racist, even while the newspaper took a position against Proposition 187. Furthermore, the *Times*'s discourse was in favor of immigration control, Wilson's re-election, and California's fight with the U.S. government to provide compensation to the state for its losses resulting from "illegal immigration."

For the *Los Angeles Times*, opposing Proposition 187 does not equate to opposing anti-immigrant rhetoric and, thus, is not equivalent to a pro-immigrant stance. In fact, the *Times* was clearly anti-(undocumented) immigration. This anti-immigrant rhetoric is coded within the discourse—that is, while the paper might not appear on the face of things to be anti-immigrant, its overall perspective clearly is. For example, in its editorials the paper attempts to deracialize immigration (e.g., to see contemporary migrations from Third World countries as similar to early twentieth-century migrations from Europe),[2] but in the process it rearticulates and thus reinforces the province of government and the law in adjudicating migration claims as well as differentiating between "good" and "bad" immigrants along racial lines. In part, it develops this position by scapegoating undocumented migrants.[3]

Given the theoretical setup of this book, some might expect this chapter, which focuses on anti-187 rhetoric, to concern outlaw civic discourse. However, as we argue in Chapter 1, outlaw civic discourse is in effect an empty cell: As soon as an outlaw vernacular discourse begins to emerge as a civic discourse, it necessarily dissolves into a dominant civic discourse either because its logic is accepted or because it is ideologically disciplined and therefore no longer challenges dominant logic; or, it remains outlaw vernacular discourse. Additionally, arguments against the proposition, especially as found in the *Los Angeles Times*, often work along the same logical, dominant lines as those for the proposition, calling for already existing logics to be put into play or to adjudicate disputes within already existing institutions (i.e., articles argue for the elimination of undocumented immigration but come at it from different directions). Hence, pro and con arguments often reify the same cultural logics and goals. In this chapter, then, we show that even while arguing against Proposition 187, the *Los Angeles Times* nevertheless reifies dominant ideology by relying on common stereotypes of undocumented immigrants and people of color, helping fuel the fire of an overall hostile discourse for all immigrants and people of color, and contributing to a discourse of laws and institutional authorities. Thus, the newspaper takes a position that allows for a reconstruction and reinforcement of dominant logics.[4] In short, while arguing against adopting Proposition 187, the *Los Angeles Times* uses discourse that acts against undocumented immigrants and therefore, indirectly, against immigrants in general. Further, the *Los Angeles Times* discourse represents government officials as authorities with *ethos*, thus framing expertise as objectively measured and politically nonbiased.

To illustrate the shared dominant logic of proponents and opponents of Proposition 187 in *Los Angeles Times* articles, this chapter, like Chapter 3, is organized into the following sections: Immigration and the Nation, Immigration and U.S. Law, and Immigration and the Individual. So, while some subthemes recur and others are unique to discourse by or about opponents, the major categories remain the same. Furthermore, the central concern in both contexts is the state itself—not the immigrant, not the citizen, and not even immigration. After analyzing the discourse in these three sections, we conclude with an assessment of the *Los Angeles Times*'s anti-187 position, its reliance on conservative sources for oppositional claims, and its anti-(undocumented) immigrant position.

Immigration and the Nation

As with articles that address the arguments of proponents, those mentioning opponents' arguments created a discourse focusing on immigration and the nation through discussions of the border, the Mexican flag, and contagion. They also address alternative solutions to the immigration problem.

The Border

Some opponents argue that stronger border control will take care of the problems Proposition 187 is supposed to solve and hence can act as an alternative (rather than a supplement) to the proposition; like proponents, opponents argue that the border needs to be strengthened, to be made less porous. For example, the *Los Angeles Times* in its editorial section consistently argued for a stronger border and praised President Bill Clinton's plan to employ one thousand more Border Patrol agents. An article by Sam Enriquez (1994c) cites James Stewart, a member of the Mid-San Fernando Valley Chamber of Commerce who opposed Proposition 187: "We know we have an illegal immigration problem. But the solution is to do a better job at the border."

Peter H. King (1994b) offers a view of the border as a site of political ambivalence, suggesting the U.S. government purposefully fails to enforce border control, something that must be done if they are serious about solving the "immigration problem." Hence, he writes, "This has been [the Border Patrol's] implicit marching orders: Close the border a little, but never close it all the way; create an appearance of control, but not enough to discourage all the workers." Further, in a picture accompanying an article about Kathleen Brown's campaign for governor, Brown is seen standing at the border while arguing that Wilson is using the issue to get elected (Wallace 1994). The picture and argument ironically point out the ubiquitous nature of "the border" in both pro and con arguments. Regardless of the position taken, the general argument is that the border needs to be strengthened, to be made less porous.

The use of the border argument here posits the border as a "leaky" problem that must be closed off, just as in representations of arguments for Proposition 187. This argument is represented in such a way that "the border" is said to need strengthening (solidification) if it is to be a solution to the "immigration problem." This discourse reifies immigration as a problem augmented by the border's porousness.

The Mexican Flag

Like the border, the Mexican flag evokes questions of national sovereignty. One article suggests that the anti–Proposition 187 movement may be tarnished by its connection to the Mexican flag. While proponents of the proposition described the flag as a symbol of infestation of the American body, opponents expressed concern that displays of the Mexican flag are counterproductive. This concern is summarized in the following question: "How can the symbols of another nation successfully appeal to U.S. patriotic citizens?" As Patrick J. McDonnell and Robert J. Lopez (1994b, B8) point out:

> Some feared a sea of Mexican flags and brown faces in Downtown Los Angeles could only reinforce voters' concerns about a state that has experienced a dramatic—and, to many, extremely unsettling—demographic shift since the 1980s. "Some people felt that the more visible we are, the more difficult it may become to beat this initiative," noted one Latino activist.

This example defends people waving the flag, but still the flag is discussed in negative terms. Another article instructs readers to look past the flag to see the people behind it, thus avoiding the real issue of the symbolism of the flag itself. The article reads, "Look beyond the Mexican flags in the newspaper photographs. There! That young girl, barely 15, speaking with such passion about an issue that hit close to home. Disproving the myth that Generation X lacks political soul, she is the answer to the dreams of scores of Latino grandmothers" (Navarrette 1994, M6).

The *Los Angeles Times* ran articles arguing that displaying the Mexican flag antagonizes pro–Proposition 187 forces and produces argumentative grist for the opposition. In one article, Sandy Banks (1994) writes: "The flags were intended as a show of pride by people who felt their Mexican heritage under siege. Yet among non-Latino voters they were widely interpreted as a symbol of anti-American defiance, of suspicious allegiance to a foreign land—a lightning rod that dramatically increased emotional support for the measure." Patrick J. McDonnell and Robert J. Lopez (1994b, B8), in an article that they say provides a "practical standpoint" given by "independent observers," quote Sherry Bebitch Jeffe, a political analyst, as saying, "In the cold reality of politics ... the pictures that went out on the front pages and on television may have well energized proponents of the proposition." Finally, Daniel M. Weintraub (1994, A30) writes, "The margin against Proposition 187 among the participants might have been even greater except for an angry backlash against the tactics of the initiative's opponents. Protests involving high school students and rallies in which demonstrators carried the Mexican flag have angered several of these mainstream voters and soured them on the opposition's campaign."

The support for flag waving is simply placating. The discourse acknowledges the need for popular symbols "of Mexican national identification and pride" (David G. Gutiérrez 1999, 483) but nudges those who display the Mexican flag to recognize it as a counterproductive strategy that should be abandoned. Thus, whether in the quoted words of protesters themselves or in the words of writers for the *Los Angeles Times*, flying the Mexican flag is represented as having a negative impact on the campaign against Proposition 187. Indirectly, such articles support U.S. patriotism and defense of ideals of nationhood by representing the Mexican flag as a symbol of invasion. The subtext is the assumption that the flags represent the people of an/other nation, not the United States, and as such should not be used to make claims for membership within U.S. society.

Contagion

Contagion, as David G. Gutiérrez (1995, 72) argues, has been a theme in anti-Mexican discourse for the past century. Like stories in favor of the proposition, those by or about opponents of Proposition 187 represent undocumented immigrants as a long-standing threat to the health and security of the nation. Even while attempting to support "illegal immigrants," such arguments position the same immigrants as a health threat to the national body if Proposition 187 is allowed to pass.

An early article provides a synopsis of this overall perspective: Proposition 187 opponents "envision an ill-educated underclass of youngsters roaming the streets prone to contagious diseases and drawn to crime, posing constant hazards for citizens and other legal residents" (McDonnell 1994f, A12). Howard Chang (1994) reiterates the overall point and implies that the proposition could limit the potential to assimilate new migrants (yet another contagion):

> The undocumented and their children would remain among us in spite of Proposition 187, but with less education and health care. Therein lies the most perverse result of Proposition 187: It would create an underclass of illiterate and impoverished residents, deprived of basic skills, including English-language skills necessary for the integration of immigrant children into our society and our work force. This underclass would create new risks to public health and new breeding grounds for crime and thereby threaten the welfare of all Californians.

Multiple articles published between late August and early November 1994 (e.g., Ibarra 1994; King 1994b; McDonnell 1994f; Scheer 1994a) repeat the idea that Proposition 187 would create a "subclass" or "underclass" of undocumented immigrants, and a situation in which unvaccinated immigrants would spread disease and illness throughout the country. For example, Patrick J. McDonnell (1994f, A12) writes, "Hundreds of thousands of illegal immigrant workers handle food in restaurants and fields." Hence, McDonnell constructs a world in which every restaurant in California serves food potentially "handled" by diseased workers.

Threats of invasion are common within discourse opposing the proposition on both a literal and a metaphoric level. In one instance, prior to a rally against Proposition 187, leaders are quoted as saying they want to keep "brown faces in the background" during the protest, so the protest will not appear to be a political takeover (McDonnell 1994a). Further, those most critical of Proposition 187 employed the invasion-contagion discourse as a threat. Carlos Fuentes (1994), for example, says the takeover has already occurred: "Conflict is inevitable unless a kind of political education takes place very quickly in the minds of countries that have colonized and exploited and plundered the Third World for 500 years and are suddenly absolutely surprised that the Third World comes back to them." Fuentes's article is worth pausing over in order to consider the unspoken premise of immigrants "haunting" those who colonized them. Such a premise reinforces the invasion metaphor, this time making it seem possible, indeed inevitable, that a Third World invasion of the First World is about to occur.

The overall image created in the anti–Proposition 187 discourse depicting immigrants without hospital care as infectious reinforces particular racialized perspectives on immigrant bodies and thus effectively evokes possible solutions of expulsion. While on the face of things the discourse is anti–Proposition 187, it nevertheless is also anti-immigrant. Logically, one must ask, "How is it possible to be anti-immigrant and not be for Proposition 187, given that the most popular expression of anti-immigrant sentiment at that time was to support Proposition 187?" But, the pro-187/anti-immigrant contradiction appears far less contradictory when one takes into consideration the fact that many of those who opposed Proposition 187 called for harsher legislation, hence "one upping" Proposition 187 supporters. Thus, the bottom line was: "Who could produce the most effective anti-immigrant proposal?"

Alternative Solutions to the "Immigration Problem"

Many articles suggest that there are better ways to solve what they agree is an "immigrant problem" than to pass Proposition 187. These solutions often are calls for a more pervasive panoptic, surveillance society. This discourse reinforces the notion that immigration is a problem and requires a solution but that Proposition 187 is not the correct solution. Many major public figures, including Bill Clinton, Jack Kemp, and William Bennett, opposed Proposition 187 but argued for greater enforcement and for more stringent penalties for offenders of U.S. immigration laws.[5] For example, in an echo of the invasion language of Carlos Fuentes, California senator Dianne Feinstein is said in an article to have begun "loudly arguing early last year that unless tough steps *are* taken to control illegal immigration, there *will* be a nasty backlash against all immigrants" (Skelton 1994a). The underlying assumption is that the application of control is a necessary solution here. Immigration is an *a priori* problem; thus the question whether it is a benefit or a harm is moot.

In addition to arguing for creating a "beefed-up Border Patrol," one article cites Ernie Gustafson, who proposes that "federal agencies, including the INS, should streamline their rules governing legal immigration" (Ramos 1994b). Others suggest cracking down on employers who hire undocumented workers (Scheer 1994a). In one article, for example, Robert Scheer (1994b) writes:

> There are already plenty of state and federal laws and regulations that are constitutional and that, if enforced, would make undocumented labor much less attractive. If the governor was serious, he would crack down on agribusiness, whose profits are directly dependent on the exploitation of undocumented labor. But those same profits bankroll his campaigns, so it's easier to

make children the target. In 1986, Congress increased fines and jail penalties for employers of the undocumented, but the law has never been enforced.

Scheer sarcastically suggests a solution to the "border problem": "So you want to get tough on illegal immigration? Then seal the border and crack down at airports. Require everyone in this country—man, woman or child—to carry a foolproof identity card and mandate jail time for any employer who hires someone not in possession of such a card. Then you're talking."

One article summarizes gubernatorial candidate Kathleen Brown's suggestion that multiple actions be taken to address the "problem" of undocumented migrations, such as "adding 1,000 Border Patrol agents at the border, toughening employer sanctions, creating tamper-proof identification cards and deporting illegal immigrants who commit felonies to serve their sentences in their native countries" (Wallace 1994, A27).[6] Others advocate reform of the INS, enforcement against those who use fraudulent immigration documents, and "stepped-up efforts to ensure that those here illegally do not find work" (Brownstein and McDonnell 1994, A26).[7] A *Los Angeles Times* editorial ("Error" 1994) makes several recommendations:

> better border management; continued economic development in the "sending countries" to ease the social pressures that push their citizens to come here illegally; bilateral negotiations with the Mexican government to permit the orderly cross-border movement of temporary workers into agriculture and other industries in which they are needed, a change that would relieve a great deal of stress on our southern border; and a tamper-proof Social Security card that would permit U.S. employers to have an almost foolproof way of knowing the citizenship status of its workers.

Other suggestions include making "it harder for employers to hire unauthorized workers" and terminating "the few remaining federal benefits that illegal immigrants now qualify for, such as school lunches and food for pregnant women" (Feldman and McDonnell 1994b, A48). In these discourses, though they all oppose Proposition 187, immigration is clearly represented as a problem to be solved and immigrants are clearly the "them." In fact, many of these suggestions, such as denying food to pregnant women, are at least as punitive as Proposition 187, perhaps more so.

Articles that suggest some other mode of enforcement to solve "the immigration problem" encourage, for example, increased surveillance and control, making it difficult for workers to get work. All of the suggestions, if implemented simultaneously, would yield a police state. Thus, a stated anti-Proposition 187 position allowed discourses that reflect an even more radical suspicion and rejection of migrant peoples than does some of the discourse favoring the proposition. These articles construct the nation as potentially in danger because of undocumented immigration. They also racialize that danger by portraying those with "brown skin" carrying "Mexican flags" as the ones most likely to "infect" the larger population with their "diseases."

Immigration and U.S. Law

Articles representing arguments for the proposition focus on federal law, while articles representing arguments against the proposition tend to focus on California state laws and the criminalization that could be a result of the passage of Proposition 187. Regardless of the focus, however, the arguments here help reify dominant understandings of immigrants and dominant processes of decision-making.

Legal/Illegal

In general, articles in the *Los Angeles Times* unreflexively use the terms "legal" and "illegal" immigrants. While this occurs throughout the discourse on both sides, we do not list every example here; the practice is simply so pervasive that comprehensively accounting for this theme would require taking on an entirely different project from the one we have conducted. Nevertheless, we do include one example here, and we refer to the use of the terms "illegal" and "legal" throughout our discussion of the discourse when we think it might be helpful.

Opponents and proponents of Proposition 187, as well as the *Los Angeles Times*, generally use "illegal" to refer to undocumented migrants and "legal" to refer to documented migrants.[8] While some articles do challenge the use of the term "illegal immigrant," they nevertheless do not challenge the usefulness of "illegal" to describe undocumented migrants. For example, in one article Paul Feldman (1994g, B8) describes a speech Jesse Jackson gave on Columbus Day in which he calls Columbus an "illegal alien" without documents. Using this phrase tends to legitimize use of the related phrase "illegal immigrant" and reinforces the overall assumption that the lack of "legitimate" documents allows for a metaphoric racial and cultural genocide in response.

Juvenile Delinquents

Discourse about juvenile delinquency evokes apocalyptic images of social destruction and chaos, heightening fear and nervousness surrounding immigrants. Some discourse constructs children of undocumented migrants as would-be criminals[9] by focusing on the ways that Proposition 187 would push many children onto the streets and into a life of crime. For example, Robert Scheer (1994b) writes, "Even more mischievous is the proposition's goal of tossing out an estimated 300,000 kids, from kindergartners to high school seniors about to graduate." In the narrative implied by this statement, only public education keeps children off the streets and out of jails. Schools intercept juveniles before their incipient criminality leads them down a path of personal and social destruction. One article quotes Cardinal Mahony as having said that, if Proposition 187 goes into effect, "We'd have several hundred thousand youngsters, not getting educated, on the street, drawn to gangs and crimes" (McDonnell 1994d, B4).[10] For Mahony, there is a causal relationship between being uneducated and out of school and entering a life of gangs and crime. This link is central to the discourse of criminality, which contains the underlying assumption that those who are uneducated will ultimately become criminals. One article quotes Pat Dingsdale, president of the state's Parent Teacher Association, using this enthymematic reasoning: "This would put children out on the streets and quite frankly, we know what happens with dropouts" (Feldman 1994d, A25). Stephanie Chavez and Sandy Banks (1994, A24) quote Augie Herrera, a school principal, making the same link: "We have to educate these young people. . . . We have to teach them what we want them to learn here or they will learn what they think they need to know in the streets."[11]

Within these articles is a discourse of gross paternalism in which references to "we" assume the need for in loco parentis logic—the state stepping in to take care of children because their parents clearly are unwilling or unable to do so. Drawing on long-standing racist images of the irresponsibility and depravity of people of color, such logic presumes parents will do a poor job of taking care of their children and that as a result the children will then become "wards of the state." More specifically, in constructing the problem as a deficiency of care and hence locating it in the realm of domesticity, the discourse is gendered specifically to be an indictment of mothers, who are depicted as incompetent;

relatedly, the responsible state, in its guise as father and better parent, logically must be allowed to assume custody of the child. The discourse also assumes the innate criminality of children needing to be tamed, lest their true character is allowed to be expressed without proper parental guidance and control.

Personal testimonies are among the many approaches used to discuss the negative impact Proposition 187 would have on students. Such a rhetorical approach uses pathos to emphasize longing for the fictive ideals of democracy and to turn attention away from the complexity and messiness of material life.[12] Stephanie Chavez and Sandy Banks (1994, A24) quote a student named Carlos, "an illegal immigrant from Mexico who has attended public schools for four years and wants to become an immigration attorney": "School is what can make my dreams come true. . . . It is my only way to improve myself, stay out of gangs. If I can't go to school, I won't be able to become anything in life." Another article quotes an undocumented migrant mother as saying, "I don't know what I would have done without [school district officials]. . . . They're the reason my son, although he has problems, is not on the streets in gangs or doing drugs" (Richardson 1994, B2). These articles posit a causal link between not being in school and eventual criminality. Through reference to the personal, they also imply that even trustworthy migrant informants verify the fact that migrants are prone to depravity without state parental tutelage. In this last example, the ethos of the parent who knows and acknowledges the incipient criminality of her child ("although he has problems"), lends credence to the larger racist construction.[13] The entire construction finds fault with the parent—diminishing her capacity for supervisorship of her own child—and recenters the state agent as a superior ward of migrant children.[14]

Only after the theme of juvenile delinquency has become an established part of the discourse against Proposition 187 does the *Los Angeles Times* cite political figures who are opposed to the measure testifying that delinquency is a key argument. For example, one article reads, "In explaining their opposition to the proposition, Clinton and Feinstein emphasized two oft-cited potential impacts: an increase in crime by those youngsters denied schooling and left on their own on the streets, and a spread of disease by immigrants who would be unable to obtain immunizations and other health care" (McDonnell and Lesher 1994, A23). As the vote date nears, the argument that Proposition 187 will produce criminals of immigrants becomes more pronounced and more specific. One article reports, "In a last-chance appeal for voters to defeat Proposition 187, Los Angeles County Sheriff Sherman Block and top prosecutors from Los Angeles and San Francisco charged that barring up to 400,000 undocumented students from school—as the measure calls for—would result in a substantial crime increase" (Pyle and Feldman 1994a).

A Big Brother Police State

Rhetorics about immigration and U.S. law that are anti–Proposition 187 focus also on the enforcement of U.S. immigration laws and argue that Proposition 187 will lead to greater police control through surveillance and paramilitary activities. One function of this book is to report themes regardless of our opinion of them. In this instance, we do not object to arguments against surveillance and a police state. We do object, however, to the reliance on institutional authority and logics in the arguments used to oppose the measure.

Ironically, even as some discourse by opponents of the legislation makes the case that enforcement options other than Proposition 187 should be used to curb immigration, much discourse argues that increased spending on enforcement technologies necessary to implement the measure is impractical. As Patrick J. McDonnell (1994f, A12) writes, "New procedures would be required to verify the status of the more than 5 million public school students in the state and at least as many parents—some of whose whereabouts would undoubtedly be unknown or difficult to track." Additionally, opponents saw the increased role educators and hospital personnel would play in immigration enforcement to be "Big Brother"-like,[15] an "expansion of government authority" (Brownstein and McDonnell 1994, A26).[16] Indeed, one of the main arguments against the proposition was that it would cause educators to scrutinize students in their classrooms and hospital personnel to question people seeking medical treatment about their legal status and to turn them away if they did not have the proper documents. Attorney General Janet Reno makes such an argument in an article in which she is quoted as saying: "It doesn't make sense to turn school teachers and nurses into Border Patrol agents. It doesn't make sense to kick kids out of school or not to give them immunizations" (Ostrow 1994, A6). Sam Enriquez (1994c) quotes James Stewart voicing the same sentiments when explaining why he voted against the measure: "We didn't feel that requiring medical and educational personnel to be INS cops was appropriate."

School personnel in particular would play a role in the surveillance of students. Robert Scheer (1994b) calls it "a 'snitch on kids' measure." According to this argument, school personnel would question and refuse to enroll students, encourage students to turn in their parents,[17] and burden already overworked INS personnel with even more papers. Carl Shusterman (1994) writes:

> Proposition 187 would force school districts to refuse to enroll students who could not produce papers proving their legal status. Even children who are citizens would be forced to turn over information to the state about the immigration status of their parents. All suspicious information would be turned over to the local INS office, where already overworked investigators would have to dig through piles of paperwork in search of illegal aliens.

Justifiably, many articles describe the fear that teachers will become immigration officers. As Stephanie Chavez and Sandy Banks (1994) write: "The measure would require school officials to verify the citizenship of students—a provision that has alarmed teachers and generated opposition from the state's professional education organizations. Currently, schools collect data only on whether students are native English speakers; they do not ask about legal status." Peter King (1994a) even goes so far as to suggest that Proposition 187 "would require schoolteachers to round up undocumented children for deportation."

Not surprisingly, teachers became more active in protesting the role Proposition 187 would ask them to play, that is—becoming extensions of the INS.[18] Paul Feldman (1994h, A16) writes, "A spokeswoman for the California Teachers Assn., which has raised the specter of its members being turned into snitches if required to report suspected illegal immigrants, said the organization is contributing $350,000 to Taxpayers Against 187." Newspaper reporter Amy Pyle (1994a) writes that teachers signed pledges not to enforce Proposition 187 because they felt the legislation "would shatter the essential bond of trust between teacher and pupil." Pyle goes on to quote Steve Zimmer, a teacher at Marshall High in the Los Feliz area, who says, "It is more of a crime to enforce this than to break the law."

Some articles focus on the effect such aspects of Proposition 187 as the elimination of the protection of refugees would have on the INS's area of responsibility (Feldman 1994h). Brian O'Leary Bennett (1994) voices his concern with this part of the legislation, saying: "Certainly, turning our schools, businesses and hospitals into INS battlefields is not the answer."

The lack of control over law enforcement, the expanding role of the INS, and the potential harm to refugees was only part of the fear the newspaper portrayed. Indeed, articles suggest enforcement of Proposition 187 would lead to a sort of police state.[19] Paul Feldman (1994f, A3) reports that conservative think tanks, such as the Alexis de Tocqueville Institution, the Reason Foundation, and the Heritage Foundation signed a statement opposing the measure. He writes, "Proposition 187, the conservative analysts said, would 'promote government intrusion into the lives of individuals' and eventually create a hostile environment for legal immigration." Carlos Fuentes (1994) takes the notion of a police state further when he writes, "And it is both humanly and politically aberrant because it makes targets of schoolchildren and snoops and witch-hunters of teachers and health workers. It is going to create a kind of McCarthyite police state of extreme danger." Kathleen Brown began calling the measure, "Snoop or Snitch," in response to proponent's nickname for it, "Save Our State," or "S.O.S."[20]

A variation of the "police state" theme appears in articles that use the image of "Big Brother." One article indirectly challenges opponents of the measure, noting that Dan Lungren would not be willing to prosecute teachers who failed to turn in students (Stall and Weintraub 1994, A10).[21] In an excerpt focusing on Michael Huffington, Greg Krikorian and Dave Lesher (1994, A30) write: "Similarly, Huffington said he was not troubled by arguments that the measure portends a 'Big Brother' future for California—one that, in [Jack] Kemp's words, would 'turn teachers and nurses into agents of the INS.' Arguing that proof of citizenship hardly constitutes a police state, Huffington said he had no qualms about requiring people in this country to display identification before receiving public services."

The *Los Angeles Times* editorial staff calls attention to unwanted government intrusion as well ("Proposition 187" 1994): "Proposition 187 supporters admit that some of the measures are Draconian—for instance, state and local agencies would be required to report 'apparent illegal aliens' to immigration authorities.'"[22] Ron Unz (1994), author of Proposition 227, English-only legislation eliminating bilingual education in public schools and passed by California voters in the November 1998 election, opposed Proposition 187. Comparing 187 to incarceration of Japanese Americans, Unz argues, "Having schools encourage

small children to inform on the status of their parents has heavy total-
itarian overtones; even the Soviet Union abandoned this practice after
Stalin's death."

After the election, the court halted implementation of Proposition
187, but some articles said people feared Proposition 187 was already
being implemented in hospitals and schools. In fact, the newspaper
carried an article about Julio Cano, whose parents did not seek medical attention for him because they feared being deported (Ruben Martinez 1994).

These articles are replete with examples of the fear of government
surveillance and intrusion. However, despite the critical nature of the
discourse, anti-proposition discourse itself tended to rely on government institutions and logics, as well as, ironically, calling for greater
enforcement of already existing anti-immigrant mechanisms. These
arguments do not challenge the possibility of increased surveillance of
the state at the border; they attend only to the most sensationalistic elements of surveillance: education and health care. And, arguments against
unwarranted state intrusion inadvertently draw on politically "conservative" arguments against "big government," suggesting that the effect
of the state policy, itself designed to combat federal irresponsibility, will
inevitably lead to greater government intrusion. Further, as in the example of Janet Reno, even while arguing against the police state that could
result from the passage of Proposition 187, at least in this example,
assumptions about the inherent criminality of juveniles not in school
subtended arguments against unwarranted state surveillance, thus maintaining stereotypical assumptions about Mexicana, Mexicano, Chicana,
and Chicano children. Nonetheless, this "positive" theme arguing
against a police state is somewhat of an aberration within anti-Proposition 187 discourse.

Immigration as Economic Cost/Benefit

The discourse against 187 also addresses a need for federal compensation for the economic shortfalls of the state of California resulting from
"illegal immigration," and hence, like the discourse of proponents, at
times reduces immigrants to economic "cost"/"benefit" units rather
than focusing, for example, on the grounds for group and community
membership.

The general argument by opponents is that undocumented migrants
are a boon to California, and that should Proposition 187 pass, not only

will undocumented workers leave, but because California schools and hospitals are subsidized by federal monies, these services for all Californians will be threatened.[23] As Patrick J. McDonnell (1994f, A12) writes:

> Moreover, the analysis found that the proposal could put at risk billions—perhaps as much as $15 billion—in federal funds now provided to California for health, education and welfare programs. This is because of conflicts between the measure's provisions and federal privacy, non-discrimination and procedural requirements. U.S. Education Secretary Richard W. Riley has already indicated in writing that the proposal would endanger federal education money.[24]

Stating budgetary concerns, a large number of articles include criticisms of Wilson for "forcing the hand" of the federal government. Bill Stall and Dave Lesher (1994) write: "The governor, facing a Democratic challenge from state Treasurer Kathleen Brown, has fought without success to get the federal government to honor its commitment to reimburse California for the cost of such services, estimated at from $1.8 billion to $3 billion a year. . . . And he predicted that passage of the immigration measure would reverberate in Washington and elsewhere with the same force as Proposition 13, the property tax initiative of 1978."

Further, one article reads, "But the state could lose billions in federal funds and be forced to spend hundreds of millions to find, expel and, presumably, deport immigrant students and then to fight countless lawsuits—including a big one with the federal government because 187, targeting 'suspected illegals' on what amounts to racial and ethnic grounds, is almost certainly unconstitutional" (Flanigan 1994). Another article makes the point that testing the constitutionality of *Plyler v. Doe* will not bring money to California: "Even if the measure passes and is upheld by the U.S. Supreme Court, which Wilson has predicted would occur, there is no mechanism either in the initiative or at the court's disposal to force the President and Congress to appropriate money to California" (Stall and Wallace 1994, A24).[25]

A key editorial ("Error" 1994) in the *Los Angeles Times* chastises Wilson for supporting Proposition 187 but then goes on to argue for his re-election over Kathleen Brown and, furthermore, praises him for demanding that the federal government pay California back for lost border control revenues. Also, it justifies California's expenditure to restrict immigration, and it supports the border. The editorial reads:

The federal government, asleep at the switch for years, is at last putting resources on the border; Gov. Pete Wilson, though horribly wrong to endorse Proposition 187, has been right to pound on Washington's door, along with many members of the California congressional delegation, demanding more federal aid to address a problem that is fundamentally a federal responsibility: international border control.[26]

An article published 5 November 1994, reports that President Clinton agrees that the federal government bears a share of the responsibility for California's immigration costs and that he would work to make amends. This position rests on an anti–Proposition 187 platform in order to call for economic support of anti-immigrant activities. The article reads: "Clinton made a pitch to precisely those voters, saying he agrees that California has 'borne an unfair burden in the cost of illegal immigration.' His Administration, Clinton noted, had increased spending on the Border Patrol and on aid to California to offset some of the costs of immigration. He conceded, however, that Washington does 'need to do more'" (Lauter and Broder 1994, A23). This acknowledgment of responsibility by the federal government for California's "illegal immigration problem" indirectly assumes that in fact there is a "problem" and looks at immigrants in economic terms, drawing attention away from the racist and punitive nature of Proposition 187. An anti-immigrant posture is so linked to the identity of being a Californian, it is almost as if one could not deny that immigration must somehow be bad for California. Thus, while Clinton opposed passage of Proposition 187, here he articulates an overall sympathy with those who think California is unduly overburdened by the costs of "illegal immigration."

Constitutionality

Articles focusing on those opposing Proposition 187 quote opponents as saying it is unconstitutional on several counts. While the proposition was indeed eventually found to be unconstitutional, we point to this theme in order to stress the way the arguments by both proponents and opponents rely on constitutional arguments and on grounds of *litige* rather than of *differend*. As a result, these arguments ultimately reaffirm the legitimacy of the government to resolve matters of immigrants and immigration. In other words, immigration becomes a matter of nation or state arbitration, rather than a conceptually contested discursive construction.

Some articles make general arguments about the measure's unconstitutionality.[27] Patrick J. McDonnell (1994f, A12) writes: "On a practical level, even if Proposition 187 passes in November, it could be years before its major provisions are enacted, if ever, because of conflict with state and federal laws, constitutional protections and court rulings. Implementation could largely depend on protracted legal battles." One article calls Proposition 187 an unconstitutional "scheme" created by politicians to challenge judiciary decisions (McDonnell and Feldman 1994a, A35). An editorial ("Brave" 1994) comments that the co-directors of the think tank Empower America "essentially called the ballot measure what it is—an unconstitutional and nativist reaction to a complex problem, a misconceived measure that carries the potential to spread poison elsewhere and undermine the very spirit of democracy in this country." Roger Mahony (1994) points out, "Most provisions of Proposition 187 are now widely recognized to be unconstitutional, in violation of privacy and eligibility laws and completely impotent to change immigration laws." Patrick J. Buchanan (1994), who favored the initiative, nonetheless quotes Al Hunt of CNN's *The Capital Gang*, who called the proposition "an outrage," adding "It is unconstitutional. It is nativist. It is racist." Buchanan goes on to refute Hunt's charges.

Some articles by and about opponents of the initiative defend the 1982 Texas *Plyler v. Doe* decision.[28] Howard Chang (1994), for example, writes: "The unfairness of punishing children for circumstances beyond their control is obvious enough: The injustice of such policies led the U.S. Supreme Court to declare in Plyler vs. Doe (1982) that depriving undocumented children of free access to public schools violated their right to 'the equal protection of the laws' guaranteed by the Constitution."[29] Carl Shusterman (1994) reiterates that point in a summary of the Supreme Court's ruling: "Penalizing the . . . child is an ineffectual—as well as unjust—way of deterring the parent."

Robert Scheer (1994a) draws a parallel between Proposition 187 and legalized segregation. He writes: "I did not care to dwell on the fine points of Mississippi's system of segregation as compared with Alabama's. I just knew in every fiber of my being that segregation was wrong, that it rots our souls to have a class of people live among us who are denied their essential humanity. Surely the courts will once again determine that segregation is unconstitutional." Here, he articulates a blind faith in the perceived objectives of the law.

After the election, lawsuits were filed, and one article reports that a lawsuit cited the state's intrusion into federal rights over immigration as a primary issue. Paul Feldman and James Rainey (1994b, A18) write, "A fourth lawsuit before Byrne on Wednesday, filed by the ACLU and a coalition of civil rights groups, charges that the sweeping ballot measure unlawfully ... denies constitutional rights by terminating benefits without legal hearings and by encouraging discrimination against people who look or sound foreign."

In response to proponents of the proposition who argued that the constitutionality should be tested, President Clinton was quoted as saying, "I don't think as a matter of practice it's a good thing to condition an election referendum, much less other elections in California, on a measure that even the supporters say is unconstitutional" (McDonnell and Lesher 1994, A1).[30] Further, Adela de la Torre (1994) compares Pete Wilson to Adolf Hitler in his efforts to step up the enforcement of the measure before the courts decide its constitutionality.

> On Nov. 9, 1938, Hitler's Nazi regime officially sanctioned the destruction of Jewish shops and synagogues, a major step forward in his drive to solve the "Jewish problem" in Germany. On Nov. 9 this year, Gov. Pete Wilson announced his executive order to immediately enforce provisions of Proposition 187 affecting the health of the most vulnerable of the Latino community, pregnant women and the elderly. Wilson could have waited until the courts clarified the law; but, no longer a moderate, he has acquiesced to the right wing of the Republican Party, which demands not justice but tyranny, which values rhetoric over reason and which seeks to destroy rather than to build.

As the election neared, articles about the constitutionality of Proposition 187 began to appear almost as if to say, "I told you so." At least eight organizations vowed to file lawsuits to block implementation of Proposition 187 at the state and federal levels (Feldman and Connell 1994), including the California Medical Association, the Los Angeles–based National Immigration Law Center (Feldman 1994j), Superintendent of Schools Delaine Eastin, and the City of Los Angeles (Feldman 1994e).[31] As discussion about the pending court reviews began, even before the election, reports were given about Proposition 187's constitutionality, one of which says that while education clauses would be found unconstitutional, those affecting health would not (McDonnell and Feldman 1994b). The same article reports that the legislative council felt the measure would "fly in the face of the California Constitution" and furthermore that the state supreme court "deemed education a 'fundamental interest,' entitling all children to primary and secondary schooling" (A14). That same advisory panel found that federal health, social, and education subsidies to California would be threatened by the initiative (A1).

After the initiative passed, articles about the constitutionality of Proposition 187 began focusing on the court. For example, Carla Rivera and Paul Feldman (1994, A22) write, quoting Supervisor Ed Edelman, "Granted, when an initiative passes, the voters have spoken, but they may have spoken in an unconstitutional way." Another article reads: "Some officials maintain that they have a moral and constitutional duty to protect the rights of all constituents, particularly children and the needy. Los Angeles Councilwoman Jackie Goldberg argued that lawmakers, in keeping with their oaths of office, had to file suit to defend the principles of the U.S. Constitution" (Connell, Shuster, and Rainey 1994, A22).

Following this, an article published 17 November 1994 reports that Judge Marianne Pfaelzer issued a temporary restraining order "blocking immediate enforcement of the sweeping initiative's bans on non-emergency medical, educational and social services for illegal immigrants" because these portions of the Proposition 187 "may conflict with federal statutes and the U.S. Constitution" (Paul Feldman and James Rainey 1994b). An article published 23 November indicates the court would ban most portions of Proposition 187 (Feldman and Rainey 1994c). Then, on 15 December, an article appeared that discusses Pfaelzer's striking down several parts of the measure (Feldman and McDonnell 1994c).

Articles by and about opponents of the proposition that question the measure's constitutionality or focus on its conflict with *Plyler v. Doe* or on the cost of protracted legal battles characterize immigrants in terms of legal and illegal status, represent immigrant youth as potential criminals, and address the potential for a Big Brother–like state were the measure to pass. None of these articles questions the legal system itself or the very idea that the discussion could raise the issue of the universal right to migrancy. Instead, the concern is over what will happen legally and economically if Proposition 187 passes. Appeals to law provide a convenient distance from the issue, as if the courts will magically solve a social catastrophe. The entire debate comes to focus on how the courts will adjudicate the matter. Hence, as this overwhelming body of discourse indicates, a large portion of the arguments against Proposition

187 legitimize both state and federal governments as arbiters of how and where human beings will live. In the end, the oppositional discourse supports the government's right to exclude particular subjects in order to protect the interests of others.

Immigration and the Individual

Articles about immigration and its influence on individuals put forth arguments that posit the measure's targets as innocent and vulnerable people or that say the measure differentiates on the basis of race and that today's immigrants are similar to those in earlier period of U.S. history. Some suggest that people will not seek services if the measure passes, while others focus on the immorality of the measure.[32] Collectively, the articles construct undocumented workers as weak in comparison to government power and irrationally fearful of government intrusion. Ultimately they reproduce the standard *mythos* of immigration that the United States is a nation of opportunity.

Targeting Innocents

Articles by or about opponents of Proposition 187 represent the measure as scapegoating the most vulnerable in society. This paternalistic approach highlights and therefore reproduces the notion that the government is strong and that undocumented immigrants and their children are weak. It is a rhetorical call for agency in response to self-helplessness, once again undermining the role of Mexicans as agents and leaving action to be taken only by non-immigrants. One article cites Cardinal Mahony who, speaking in Spanish, tells members of a Latino Catholic conference that the "economy is not going to be remedied by adopting punitive measures against those with little or no political power: the poor and immigrants" (McDonnell 1994d, B1). Another article summarizes Los Angeles mayor Tom Bradley as saying that it "is not fair to turn the children of illegal immigrants into scapegoats by ejecting them from public schools and denying them vital health services" (Feldman 1994b). Yet, another article reads: "It is clear that Prop. 187 is not about improving the future of Californians. It is about criminalizing the voiceless and most vulnerable" (Cassyd et al. 1994). Columnist Peter King (1994c) writes: "They drafted a ballot proposition that would require schools and hospitals to report any suspected 'illegal' Kindergartners. Pregnant mothers.

No matter. No papers, boom, out the door." And, in their report on Kathleen Brown, Bill Stall and Dan Weintraub (1994, A3) write, "State Treasurer Brown decried Wilson as a bully who had taken aim at a vulnerable, politically unpopular segment of society in supporting the immigration initiative."

One article constructs people from Latin America as vulnerable and innocent, suggesting that Proposition 187 would mandate inhumane conditions for them: "However unintentional, Proposition 187 subtly attacks the dignity and humanity of a defenseless people (particularly from Latin America). It encourages those who would equate illegal status with being stupid, lazy, even criminal. Proposition 187 would treat these immigrants more severely than felons. Even the worst thugs housed in our prisons get vaccinations" (Bennett 1994). Ironically, while this article decries the depiction of "people particularly from Latin America" as "stupid," it invokes instead another, equally demeaning and agency-robbing stereotype of them as "defenseless." Paul Feldman (1994g, B8) quotes the Los Angeles Urban League president, John Mack, as saying: "This is anti-Latino, anti-vulnerable people. . . . If you talk about closing the borders to Latinos, the same rule applies to closing the border to Haitians."

Some articles focus on the vulnerability of children. As Howard Chang (1994) explains, "Perhaps the ugliest aspect of the current wave of immigrant-bashing is the tendency to lash out at the innocent children of undocumented immigrants." George Ramos (1994b) makes the connection between childhood and innocence directly when he quotes a former INS agent as saying, "It's a political opportunity for these people. It will solve nothing. It will take the innocence of children and make them the scapegoats of a failed policy."[33]

The construction of immigrants as children—in part by focusing on literal immigrant children and in part by depicting immigrants as "vulnerable" and "defenseless"—infantilizes all immigrants by implying that they lack the power to have any effect on their own lives and that the always-successful government should find a way to end its exploitive practices. Such discourse may also, indirectly, draw on a controversial assumption that the "[Anglo] West has won" and that those who were beaten have no power to effect change. This strategy constructs and reaffirms power relations in such a way that changing roles and expectations is not considered a potential response to either Proposition 187 or current migration practices.

Many articles distinguish between child and parent. For example, some articles that distinguish between "legal" and "illegal" portray children as "vulnerable," "innocent," and "legal," whereas parents, who have a choice, are "criminal" and "illegal."[34] Citing *Plyler v. Doe* as justification, one article reads: "Proposition 187 aims primarily at hurting children, who are not the ones who make the decisions to come here or to leave. The folly of punishing children for their parents' decision was recognized in a 1982 Supreme Court ruling that held a very similar Texas law unconstitutional. Penalizing children, the court held, 'is an ineffectual—as well as unjust—way of deterring the parent'" (Scheer 1994b). As Scheer further suggests, "It's a punk's game to beat up on kids."

Another article quotes a student distinguishing between child and parent. Simon Romero (1994) quotes a fourteen-year-old: "It's not my fault my parents are here illegally.... If they have to leave, what am I going to do?" This persuasive strategy of quoting a child attesting to the ostensive illegality of his parents relies on the fact that the overall offensive claim (that the parents are "illegal") is uttered by the person about whom the claim is made: the son (who suffers because of his parents' "illegality"). Similarly, Amy Pyle and Beth Shuster (1994, A1) quote Henry Romero, a tenth grader from Belmont High School who testified in front of the Los Angeles City Council, as saying, "It is not fair to take education away from the kids." Other articles represent kids as being treated like "pawns" (Nalick and Feldman 1994) and "political issues" (Mahony 1994). In the distinctions between parents and children, parents are portrayed as consciously "breaking the law" and children are constructed as separate from their parents and therefore of a different (potentially redeemable) class. The responsibility for change lies with the parents, who are constructed as being alone responsible for their "illegal" status. Such a construction further criminalizes parents and provides justification for any impending prosecution against them.

What is important here is not so much that children are not constructed as guilty but that distinguishing them from their parents serves the need to find someone responsible for what is constructed as unquestionably a crime. Furthermore, if the children are valorized as in need of protection, by extension any discussion of immigrants as in need of protection by implication infantilizes them. And, since children are in need of protection, their parents must not be protecting them. This point is particularly clear in articles that link the immigrant children to particular types of worker immigrants.

For example, some articles focus on the children of female domestic workers. Here, women and children are linked—both are potentially "duped" by the ever-absent father. Robert Scheer (1994a) writes: "How dare we deny education to the children of women who clean our homes and raise our children? . . . How dare we deny medical care to those who harvest our crops, clip our lawns and golf courses, bus our dishes, wash our cars and every night leave spotless the very office towers whose top executives support the governor behind this mean proposal?" Here, the long list of back-breaking tasks does not articulate immigrants' agency and humanity but instead infantilizes them.

The Representational Politics of Public Aid

Another theme in the rhetoric against Proposition 187 describes the effects of the proposition on individuals and communities that will not seek help from social service agencies. This assumption, too, constructs the immigrant subject as infantile, vulnerable, and, furthermore, irrational and strange (unfamiliar). These articles represent undocumented migrants as fearful of medical and other social services (code: they are irrational); as willing to deny themselves such services (code: must not really need them); and as reacting strangely to a system that provides such services (code: because such handouts are not provided in their [backward] home countries).

For example, one article argues that the measure will erode the community trust necessary for proper police protection. Patrick J. McDonnell (1994e, A28) quotes a thirty-year-old mother of four from Mexico: "To me, police are here to protect us, not to ask us about our documents. . . . People will run away from police if they start asking for papers.'" Another article observes that people have become afraid to call the police under any circumstance. For example, Carla Rivera and Paul Feldman (1994, A22) write, "Estelle Chun of the Asian Pacific American Legal Center of Southern California said her agency heard from an undocumented Korean woman who was afraid to call police—for fear of being reported—even though her husband had beaten her." Including the last detail not only constructs a negative image of immigrants (the abusive husband) but uses that image to heighten the pathos in the Korean woman's Proposition 187-produced fear.

Others cite a threat to the education process, particularly distressing because of the central role of education in the tale of the "good" immigrants working to better themselves. For example, Lisa Richardson

(1994) writes, "But students have to trust teachers and faculty enough to tell them that their families are hungry or without clothes, and jeopardizing that trust, officials say, threatens the bedrock of the educational process in Lennox" (B1–B2). Richardson cites a student who says to her: "If teachers told on us, how could we trust [them] anymore? . . . Or if they told on, like, your parents, then you wouldn't want to come to school" (B2). Another article recounts a school administrator's distress over a twelve-year-old girl who wondered whether she was still allowed to go to school: "As an educator, my friend has seen drug abuse, child abuse and classroom neglect. Still, he told me, in a voice choked with emotion, this was his most painful experience yet" (Navarrette 1994, M1). Further, Deborah Sullivan (1995) reports that students are considering not going on to the university because they fear deportation.[35] Immigrants are also represented as being uninformed and having an irrational fear of seeking public medical aid (at a time soon after the vote) when the proposition was not being enforced. This fear is made evident in reports from Los Angeles hospitals and clinics of declines in patient numbers. For example, Carla Rivera and Paul Feldman (1994, A22) write, "From South Central to the Eastside, hospitals and clinics in Los Angeles began reporting declines in patient numbers in the wake of the proposition's landslide victory."[36] Ruben Martinez (1994) first called attention to the most dramatic story of the effect of a person's not seeking medical help because of fear of the authorities when he wrote about Julio Cano, a twelve-year-old who died from "acute advanced leukemia" after not receiving treatment. Martinez describes the father, an undocumented immigrant, who "tells us from the shadow of his fear that the family didn't take Julio to a public hospital because of Proposition 187—the specter of the *migra* leaping out and tearing the family apart. Instead, they decided to save up money to take him to a private clinic. He didn't make it."

Martinez addresses those who voted for the proposition when he writes, "You may not have directly caused Julio Cano's death. But by transmitting your concerns through a measure drafted by a vicious minority, you did help to create the atmosphere of fear that he and his family, and hundreds of thousands of other families in California, now live in. There are likely to be many more cases like Julio's before the fate of 187 is decided in the courts."

Morality

Unsurprisingly, stories about the opposition to Proposition 187 make general pleas to morality. Appeals based on morality, many of which invoke the church, God, transcendent values, and notions of a higher truth to support their claims, are central to colonization discourses (e.g., those that justify missionary incursions to "aid" "innocent," "vulnerable" colonized people). What is most problematic about this discourse in the *Los Angeles Times* articles on Proposition 187 is that those who agree with the anti-Proposition 187 position that priests and others who appeal to morality take may not recognize the religious basis of the appeal and the related construction of the legitimate power of the Church (as well as those who use moral claims, in general). Furthermore, moral appeals are uncompromising and inconsistent with appeals to pragmatic decision-making, practical reasoning, and various logical arguments.

Many articles argue that the moral problematics of Proposition 187 outweighed other considerations. For example, Doreen Carvajal and Gebe Martinez (1994, A1) quote Father Richard C. Kennedy as making the following comment about Proposition 187: "I won't be mincin' words on this one. I haven't worked out what I'll say, but I'm going to make it clear. Proposition 187 is immoral. . . . This thing is completely godless." The use of dialect here combined with an appeal to an anti-intellectual position ("I haven't worked out what I'll say") constructs a "person on the street" persona for the priest that strengthens the validity of his belief that the Proposition is "godless."

Articles report that Proposition 187 is seen as testing the "ethical standards of [patients'] confidentiality" (McDonnell 1994f, A1), and that it is "a devastating assault on human dignity" (McDonnell 1994f, A12, citing Cardinal Roger M. Mahony), "malevolent and misguided" (Howard Chang 1994), "humanly and politically aberrant" (Fuentes 1994), "the worst moral disaster for our state since the internment of Japanese Americans" (Unz 1994), " 'senseless' and 'unjust' " (Schwartz 1994, M6), "immoral, unhealthful, and unworkable" (Feldman 1994g, B1), "immoral" (McDonnell 1994c, quoting Enrique Hernandez Jr.), "inhumane" (Merl and Feldman 1994), "an affront to the dignity of man, woman and child" (Fineman 1994b, A13, citing Armando Calderon Sol), and "morally bankrupt. . . . [It] pushes the button of emotional bigotry, and attempts to place blame on a defenseless group of people for the ills of the state" (Benites 1994). Such appeals to ethics, dignity, and morality forego appeals to reason, argue opinions based on transcendent versus pragmatic grounds, and tend to mask what are otherwise simply assertions and opinions.

Some comments focus on the role of the church in protecting morality.[37] Doreen Carvajal and Gebe Martinez (1994, A16) quote Father Miguel Urrea, the pastor of Christ the King Church in San Bernardino as saying:

> I just said that it's very clearly stated as a church that we should not be concerned if people are documented or undocumented. If we do, we're losing our whole perspective of why we are priests. This is a humanitarian issue. Are we supposed to say, sorry, we can't take care of you because you don't have papers? Stand there and bleed to death?

Roger Mahony (1994) writes, "There are numerous reasons—especially those grounded in basic moral and ethical principles of our religious heritage and tradition—why California's Catholic bishops oppose Proposition 187." Quoting the California Association of Catholic Hospitals and the Catholic Health Association of the United States, Paul Feldman (1995b) writes, "[We] have a moral obligation as Catholic institutions to provide medical care to all persons, regardless of citizenship." Others make the case that the special dictate of doctors necessitates moral responses to such legislation (Shuit 1994, A27, citing Ralph Ocampo). Comments also criticize Republicans for immoral behavior. One article, quoting the executive director of the Civil Rights Network, reads: "We feel the Republican Party is trying to scapegoat the Latino and immigrant community for their own political gain, and that's immoral. People are being hurt by it, and these companies need to pay the price" (Feldman and McDonnell 1994a, A36). Robert Scheer (1994c) focuses on Pete Wilson: "Wilson's championing of Proposition 187 represents a profound moral failure. Whatever his and the proposition's fortunes in this election, Wilson's career now bears, indelibly, the mark of shame."

Such appeals to the church and to medical doctors' credos reproduce a "morality" that has been used throughout history to justify destructive ends, such as the enslavement of African peoples, the attempts to eliminate Native American peoples and their religions and culture, and the denial of a woman's control over her body's reproductive functions. We are not only saying that the means of these appeals do not justify the ends, however. We are also suggesting that (in this case) accepting such appeals to morality, simply because they happen to be made on behalf of migrant people, reproduces the logic, ethos, and power of such appeals (in general). Consequently, such appeals can potentially be used with even more force, more conviction, and possibly, even more legitimacy in the future supporting causes that are not ones critics of Proposition 187 would want to support.

Familiarity versus Strangeness

Another theme concerns the ethnic and national representation of immigrants. Articles about opponents of Proposition 187 concentrate on how the measure leads people to distance themselves from those who look foreign. While Proposition 187 certainly would have legal effects on all immigrants, it ultimately portrays the immigrant in racialized terms, pointing almost solely to Mexicana, Mexicanos, Chicanas, and Chicanos. According to one article, "Critics see proponents' efforts as Big Brotherism run amok, an invitation to official harassment of the 'foreign-looking'" (McDonnell 1994f, A12). Similarly, Al Martinez (1994) writes, "Just as they've always done, the humans are looking around for people to blame who, though members of the same species, aren't quite like them. So they look to the other side of the line." Robert Scheer (1994c) makes a similar claim: "When the economy starts to crumble, our tolerance for those who are different evaporates. . . . Historically, in this country as elsewhere, the easiest target is the stranger. Strange by color, religion, language, country of origin—the 'other.' Two years ago, the target of opportunity was the welfare mother. Today, it's the illegal immigrant." An article cites Vice President Al Gore as saying, "Throughout American history and throughout world history, you will find examples of people who are bereft of ideas, who have failed at governing . . . coming up with the strategy of scapegoating groups that they can characterize as different or outside the group they're appealing to" (Stall and Weintraub 1994, A10). These examples intensify the effect of difference, unfamiliarity, and vulnerability of immigrants in order to argue that those who are strange deserve protection rather than discrimination.

Ruben Navarrette Jr. (1995), too, sees fear of difference behind support for Proposition 187:

> [Proposition 187] was also about too many Latinos being too visible on too many streets in too many California cities. It was also about fear and shifting demographics and Los Angeles resembling Tijuana. It was also about which undesirable element was going to public school with your children or sitting in hospital waiting rooms. And it was also about immigrants as eyesores.

Articles that focus on protesters construct visual difference by making clear protesters' sensitivity to the issue of strangeness. In doing so, they solidify the cultural meaning of "brown faces" as equivalent to undocumented immigrants and reify racism based on fixed phenotypical characteristics. Patrick J. McDonnell (1994a) writes:

> Asked about the campaign to defeat Proposition 187, one leading Latino activist heavily involved in the effort responded, "We're keeping the brown faces in the background. . . ." In an effort to appeal to the voting majority, anti-187 forces have de-emphasized the involvement of Latinos and immigrant-rights representatives in the mainstream campaign targeting the hearts and minds of white suburbia. Instead, spokesmen such as Los Angeles County Sheriff Sherman Block have taken center stage to bolster the case.

Commenting on a march that received much negative publicity because people carrying Mexican flags took part in the demonstration, Patrick J. McDonnell and Robert J. Lopez (1994a, A14) write:

> Many in the anti-187 coalition—including mainstream Latino groups such as the Mexican-American Legal Defense and Educational Fund—argued that a massive march barely three weeks before the election was a bad tactic, and attempted to scuttle the event. Several Latino activists privately expressed fears that a sea of brown faces marching through Downtown Los Angeles would only antagonize many voters.

In both of these examples, articles construct visual difference by pointing to the fact that *even those protesting the measure* are concerned that showing a "sea of brown faces" negatively impacts their case.

Good/Bad Immigrant

Another theme suggests there is no difference between early immigrants and contemporary ones; nevertheless, as the preceding section illustrates, there continues to be a deep ambivalence over immigration. Thus, even appeals to fight against scapegoating contemporary immigrants stress the need to curb "illegal immigration." That is, multiple articles criticize the idea that immigrants are "bad" by positing the historical need for hard-working immigrant labor and by placing the blame elsewhere, such as on bad employer practices. Nevertheless, the discourse of the good immigrant ultimately reifies the immigrant as an economic cost/benefit to the state, implying the possibility of a bad immigrant who does not benefit society economically.

For example, Robert Scheer (1994a) writes, "The governor can't be serious about stopping illegal immigration. If he were, he would see to it that TIPP [Targeted Industrial Program Partnership] had enough money to field more than the 30 inspectors who are expected to enforce labor law throughout the entire state. And he would stop casting immigrant workers, rather than employers, as the villain of the piece." Ron Unz (1994) argues that undocumented migrant workers are a boon to the state: "Turning hundreds of thousands of our hard-working, tax-paying, minimum-wage gardeners and nannies into prison inmates at a cost of tens of billions of dollars hardly seems a sensible means of solving our state's budget problems." Brian O'Leary Bennett (1994) goes so far as to suggest that immigration is an inherent good, part of the "American Dream." He writes:

> Millions possessed of such 'will and heart to get here' are here illegally. While it would be unfair to suggest that Reagan advocates illegal immigration as a vehicle, he was reminding us in the metaphor he loves most that immigrants are innately beneficial to America, notwithstanding legal status. After all, there is no human difference between a legal Vietnamese refugee and an illegal Haitian or Mexican.[38]

K. Connie Kang (1994, B4) cites Quynh Tram Nguyen, a refugee to the United States, discussing the benefits migrants provide and argues, "Nguyen, a Vietnamese who came to California legally as a refugee in 1984, says it is unfair to dismiss the contributions of newer arrivals to the state's work force—even if they are in the country illegally."

Each of these examples addresses immigrants who provide something useful but does so by constructing immigrants as pawns of government and big business. "Good" immigrants, that is, are without agency, but, for that reason, without the pressures of government and big business they might not be so productive and thus would be "bad" immigrants.

An editorial in the *Los Angles Times* ("Brave" 1994) praises hardworking contemporary migrants when it refers to a warning "against alienating hard-working and entrepreneurial immigrants" that Governor Pete Wilson ought to take to heart. One article comments on the role education plays in entrepreneurial success. Sam Enriquez (1994b, B1) writes, "For years, CSU [California State University] schools have been the fast track for undocumented students bright and ambitious enough to escape the low wage drudgery endured by their immigrant parents."

Personal testimony is used to support the view that undocumented migrants, given the opportunity, can be successful in the United States. Enriquez (1994b) introduces Vladimir Cerna, a high school sophomore who "asked that his real name be used" and comments that Cerna's "decision to shed anonymity reflects the deep sentiment that Proposition 187 has aroused among those who did as they were told, rejecting gangs and drugs and welfare in favor of the historical and well-worn path to success in America" (B7). Enriquez sees Cerna as "the sort of student whom high school counselors always remember—a poor kid but bright, someone who gets into trouble early on, straightens out and makes it to college" (B1). Another article cites personal testimony supporting undocumented migrants:

> Some who came to vote spoke of spouses and parents who had crossed the borders, of aunts and uncles who fear Proposition 187 in a real way. "Personally," said Barbara Velasquez, "I know too many people who are illegal. They are good people. Hard workers. They want to educate their kids. I know one mom who has five kids and all of them are straight-A students. What will happen to them?" (King 1994d)

A personal testimony of the "American-ness" of undocumented migrants also appears in an article by Diane Seo (1994, A26), who writes: "Luis, a Cal State Los Angeles junior who is here illegally, said he would have to withdraw from school if he is forced to pay the higher fees. 'The feeling I have is that we're not wanted,' he said. 'People want us to have low incomes and seem afraid of us succeeding.'" In another emotionally appealing personal success story, Ruben Martinez (1994) writes,

> From what I know of him, Julio [Cano] was far more American than any anti-immigration media barker. For me, he was the American dream incarnate. A brilliant student, he rapidly learned English and was tutoring his more recently arrived cousins from Latin America at his Orange County junior high school. He had all the makings of a kid who would overcome the risks of the inner city to make his parents' hardships in coming to America worthwhile. Julio Cano belonged here because Julio Cano was California's future.

Personal stories play a significant role in articles discussing opponents of Proposition 187, particularly those published on 10 and 11 November. One story introduces a deaf woman who praises education; in other stories people talk about the sweet taste of their new citizenship. Like stories that distinguish between good and bad migrants, stories that elicit the strongest empathetic responses focus on children who live the

American Dream but are not themselves U.S. citizens. Like their parents, they suffer racism and they work hard, they do not lie and cheat, but also they do what their parents could not, such as go to school and work to be successful. Personal testimonies tend to direct attention to the potential for individuals, through an "American success" *mythos*, to overcome obstacles. Indirectly, such an approach not only constructs a "bootstrap" narrative that focuses on the economic potential of immigrants and implies that if immigrants are not doing well it is their own fault, but it also directs attention away from social conditions circumscribing the lives of immigrants. Additionally, personal experience may suggest that these "good" immigrants are the exceptions and that there are (many more) "bad" immigrants.

Protests

Many articles discuss activists and their protests against Proposition 187, making distinctions between good and bad protesters. While articles by or about proponents see protests only in negative terms, calling protest "un-American" and representing protesters as being emotional and having ideas that are not rational, those arguing against 187 construct protestors both negatively (e.g., alienation of voters) and positively (e.g., cultural pride).

Articles by opponents that stress the negative aspects of protests focus on the large marches that took place against Proposition 187 (McDonnell and Lopez 1994a estimate one protest to have been larger than any protest in the 1960s); others express concern about the "physical look" of those protesting, in particular the skin color of the protesters and the effect the number of protesters might have on readers. One article that expresses sensitivity to the way protesters appear, suggesting they will have a negative effect on onlookers, for example, uses the same water metaphor Patrick Buchanan (1994) uses when he describes a "sea" of Mexican flags: "Some immigrant advocates sought to postpone the march, underlining divisions within the advocate ranks. Their fear: A heavily publicized sea of Latino faces would only further alienate many undecided or wavering voters." Hence, this representation of protest suggests that the protest itself may appear to mirror what is feared by proponents, the "flood of immigrants" (McDonnell 1994a).

Many articles reporting on student walkouts undertaken in Los Angeles County to protest Proposition 187 see this form of protest as only counterproductive. For example, Amy Pyle (1994b) writes, "A student walkout across Los Angeles County planned for Nov. 2 touched off debate Tuesday among Proposition 187 opponents about whether cutting class is the best way to protest the possibility of diminished access to public education." Pyle quotes Maurice Miranda, president of the United Neighbors of Temple-Beaudry, a Los Angeles neighborhood, as saying, "It's very dangerous, a walkout of the kids." Another article quotes a member of Taxpayers Against 187 as saying: "We do not believe this educates the voters about the problems of 187—we believe it distracts them. . . . We encourage kids to stay in school—that's one of the things this is all about" (Shuster and Johnson 1994). Additionally, Paul Feldman (1994f, A31) quotes Bruce Cain, a professor at the University of California at Berkeley, as saying that the walkouts are "probably a break for the pro-187 people. . . . It would be very easy for everybody to become fixated on the events and sort of ignore the issues." Each of these articles rejects the protest because it undermines a central aspect of the Horatio Alger narrative: education. Thus, they may be anti–Proposition 187 but they nevertheless are entirely commensurate with dominant logics that assume there is a right and a wrong way to be an immigrant.

The articles that see the benefits of protests emphasize the value of displays of cultural pride. Antonio H. Rodriguez and Carlos A. Chavez (1994), for example, write:

> Can't these politicians understand the affirmations of cultural pride that their racist attacks have produced? Their denying the significance and the implications of the movement that spawned the march is a gross underestimation of how personal the political issue of Proposition 187 has become in the Latino community. . . . The response in the Latino community has been increasing solidarity. Sunday's march was a manifestation of that. While it was but a single event, it demonstrated the surging unity for self-defense and survival that Wilson and Proposition 187 have unwittingly promoted.

Among the articles that find value in protests are those that praise the Los Angeles County student walkout, also on the grounds of solidarity. For example, Al Martinez (1994) writes, "I was impressed by the march last Sunday, but I'm an emotional kind of guy, easily moved when I see members of the same species celebrating their small differences by banding together for a common good." David E. Hayes-Bautista and Gregory Rodriguez (1994) echo that sentiment in an article that reports, "Many credit the activism inspired by Proposition 187 with birthing a new political consciousness among Latinos, driven in large part by immigrants." The author of another article praises students for inspiring pride in him. Art Torres (1994) writes, "I will reach out to the young people in this state who showed me during the campaign year what truth and conviction are all about."

Ruben Martinez (1994), in his article about the death of Julio Cano, also praises student protest:

> Many young people like Julio walked out of class and attended rallies against 187 because they were offended by the charge that they and their parents had come to America to take rather than give; they were insulted by the insinuation that immigrants were freeloaders. And, in the epitome of hypocrisy, they were called 'criminals' by the very people who lured them here with the promise of jobs in the first place.

These celebrations of protest as expressions of cultural pride do not address the social challenge to government structures inherent in the protests. Furthermore, they are much less common than are articles that criticize the protests. More often, articles by or about both proponents and opponents, as well as editorials in the *Los Angeles Times*, construct protesters negatively, making a point of stating that protesters overestimate numbers at rallies, that protesters themselves fear that the "brown faces" among them may be off-putting to audiences, and that children protesting may "send the wrong message." The consistently derogatory construction of protest in the *Los Angeles Times* implies that while disagreement with a measure is fine overt protest is too extreme a response.

Analysis

The rhetoric of Proposition 187 in the *Los Angeles Times* very often uses the same argumentative strategies whether discussing proponents or opponents of the measure. One strategy is the use of synecdoche, a substitution of a part for the whole. Specifically, children—the subjects perhaps of stories about their being thrown out onto the street or about their unfairly taking up seats in California classrooms—stand in for all undocumented people, who, because of their overall vulnerability and helplessness, need the paternalistic hand of the state to guide them. The connection between children and all undocumented people follows from a pattern established early in colonial U.S. history, when rulers and society generally constructed Native Americans, then African Americans, then immigrant peoples generally as noncitizens lacking intelligence, unable to govern themselves, and as needing civilization to be freed from heathenism. Every invocation of the terms "children," "kids," and "juveniles" might point to, and effect, the understanding of all undocumented people as misguided and in need of tutelage and other forms of paternalistic authoritative control.

Another key element of the rhetoric of immigration in discourse for and against Proposition 187 is citizenship, about who belongs and is included in a society, what kind of member of a society a person will be, what benefits of citizenship will be offered to some and not others, and how those who do not belong and are not members ultimately will be treated. As the world moves toward transnational global capitalism with large transnational corporations no longer existing as single corporations limited to a particular nation-state—such as Xerox, RCA, Chrysler, ITT, IBM, and Eastman Kodak (see Lipsitz 1998, 55—anxiety about citizenship and belonging become recurrent parts of national discourse. Thus, the discourse suggests belonging should be determined by status: "illegal" status means one does not belong; "legal" status means one does belong. In essence, the rule supersedes the reasoning behind the rule.

More and more, what many understand to be fixed rules and laws about what constitutes citizenship may not be relevant. Citizenship may not be a bounded and determinate status but instead may be a quite indeterminate, incommensurable, and inconsistent notion bounded only by countervailing rules, approaches, and contestations of rhetoric. Thus, every discussion of citizenship is fraught with contradictions. For example, regardless of citizenship status, waving the flag of any nation as a form of protest would seem, on the surface, to be a legitimate form of political expression; certainly it falls within the constitutionally protected area of free speech under U.S. law. But, because Proposition 187 is about restricting health, education, and welfare for non–U.S. citizens, what role does waving a Mexican flag in particular play? How are we to make sense of and then judge the rhetorical arguments and strategies associated with using such a symbol? And on what grounds can one determine the efficacy of an argument when the very rhetorical premises, as stated by proponents, that the United States is experiencing a takeover and, as stated by opponents, that voters fear a takeover, seems to be represented by the waving of Mexican flags on "U.S. soil"? The role the *Los Angeles Times* plays in producing information about these arguments reproduces dominant logics.

We're Against Proposition 187; We Really Are

Early on in the news coverage of the issue, the *Los Angeles Times* ran editorials encouraging readers to vote against Proposition 187. On 2 October 1994, it ran the first of five pre-election and five post-election general editorials. Entitled "Proposition 187 and the Law of Unintended Consequences: Anti-Immigrant Initiative Would Deny Medical Care, Roil Schools and Make Snoops Out of Teachers; Is This What California Wants?" this editorial laid the groundwork arguments for the *Times*'s overall opposition to the measure. The editorial begins by depicting "illegal immigration" as a serious problem. It states: "Proposition 187's understandable appeal is based on the assumption that we have to do something about illegal immigration. We certainly do. And this proposition would certainly Do Something. But what it would do is not something California should want to happen." The editorial goes on to discuss the economic boost undocumented workers provide. For example, it states, "Think of all the work—from home repair to garment manufacturing—that keeps marginal businesses profitable and allows new small firms to open." Moreover, the editorial introduces what became a mantra within Proposition 187 rhetoric—"The lure is jobs, however ill-paid, not welfare"—then explains how Proposition 187 poses a "public health threat." It states, "A major and vital goal of public health care is to keep the problems of even the sickest and most destitute individuals from becoming a danger to the rest of the population."

The editorial makes a gesture toward education as a means to protect the public interest against another prominent threat in contemporary public discourse: gangs. It states: "So it is in the public interest to make sure they become well-educated and acculturated to American life. . . . It's no wonder so many law enforcement officials are vigorously campaigning against Proposition 187. By tossing kids out of school it's virtually an unintended but effective gang-recruitment tool." Here, the threat of gangs is powerful enough to become entirely displaced from the media's typical cognitive leap of connecting gang members to non-immigrant African American people. The next set of issues in the editorial questions the surveillance strategies schools would take, the cost to California, and state versus federal authority. It ends by arguing that Proposition 187 may, because of litigation contesting it, cost more money than do illegal immigrants; however, it also argues that renewed racial tolerance would benefit the California economy. The ultimate argument is: "Racism costs," but the reason racism should be challenged is to better the economic interests of the United States through its globalization of capital: "In an era when California businesses increasingly look to Asia and Latin America for new markets, this state doesn't need such ethnic division. Vote 'no' on Proposition 187."

While the editorial argues for a "no vote" on Proposition 187—and this is a relatively consistent approach throughout the editorials as well as many other articles in the *Los Angeles Times*—it simultaneously argues, albeit inferentially: (1) "illegal immigration" (itself a propositional argument worth contesting) is a problem that needs a solution, (2) exploitation of underpaid workers is beneficial to the California economy, (3) "citizens" should worry about the dangerous diseases undocumented immigrants might give them, (4) citizens should train undocumented people to accept the values of their host culture through education, (5) (migrant) children will necessarily exhibit criminal behavior without proper paternalistic education, and, finally, (6) further colonization of the market economies of the United States' geographical neighbors would produce national economic strength. These six points make clear that, despite the editorial suggestion of a "no vote," the ideology of the *Los Angeles Times* further marginalizes the subject position of migrant people, distinguishing and differentiating them from what is conceived to be the mainstream.

The arguments in this first editorial provide a snapshot view of the larger rhetorical strategy of the *Times*. In arguing against Proposition 187, the editorial relies on certain assumptions about difference, that "alien" peoples have fewer human rights than citizens and therefore must be treated differently according to U.S. law. Additionally, the editorial relies on specific assumptions about difference that reproduce, in large part, the racist logic of the dominant culture. The editorial does precisely what racist logic intends: in its opposition to social change, it reinscribes the racist assumptions of the state, even while on its surface it implies such assumptions remain in question.

Conservative Supporters Are Our Friends

Even though two former INS officials, Alan Nelson and Harold Ezell, helped author Proposition 187, the *Los Angeles Times* builds its case by regularly citing INS and other government officials who opposed the proposition. By citing the state officials opposed to "illegal immigration" and to Proposition 187, the newspaper depends on the counterintuitive strategy of providing as a witness a person who, because of his or her political and professional position, would be expected to defend the proposition. This strategy creates an interesting moment when the ethos of the "governmentality" (Greene 1998) and its practices and policies colonize oppositional spaces only to rearticulate that ethos back within the realm of objectivity. As a result, in the *Los Angeles Times* articles, only objective folks like INS officials can speak authoritatively on the issue of Proposition 187; and they are very often given the final word.

Conservative governmental authorities who are opposed to Proposition 187 litter the rhetorical landscape.[39] Their opposition is reflected in the titles of many articles run in the *Los Angeles Times* between 19 September and 28 October 1994. These include: "Prop 187 Foes Get a Boost from an Unlikely Ally"; "An Initiative Even Conservatives Can Hate"; "LA Police Panel Joins Foes of Measure"; "Kemp, Bennett and INS Chief Decry Prop 187"; "Business Leaders Attack Immigration Measure"; and "U.S. Justice Official's Memo Assails Prop 187." One INS informant, Carl Shusterman (1994), for example, argues that a crackdown on employers of "illegal immigrants," a tougher Border Patrol, and modernization of "an antiquated record-keeping system" in the INS would help deter "illegal immigration." Thus, he argues that reform should take place within an all-powerful INS; hence, immigration moves from being a public issue to an internal public relations problem for the INS. Also as a former trial attorney for the Los Angeles INS office, Shusterman draws on generic criticism of Proposition 187 to make his argument but ultimately, because he sees his solutions as superior to those of others, concludes by fetishizing greater policing, punishment, and efficiency in the system of surveillance than is even at the moment possible.

Another official appears in the article entitled, "An Initiative Even Conservatives Can Hate: Prop 187: You don't have to be a liberal to oppose the dehumanization of illegal immigrants." The *Los Angeles Times* presents the heart of its strategy here. Brian O'Leary Bennett (1994) begins his article by quoting Ronald Reagan's "city on a hill" speech. Bennett, former chief of staff to Representative Robert K. Dornan, a Republican from Garden Grove, then says: "I don't condone law-breaking. I don't believe that illegal aliens are entitled to most social benefits. But meat-axing essentials like medical care and education, as this initiative proposes, is unsafe, morally suspect, politically shortsighted and culturally separatist." He continues, "However unintentional, Proposition

187 subtly attacks the dignity and humanity of a defenseless people (particularly from Latin America)." In arguing against Proposition 187, Bennett says: "Abortion supporters have successfully confused and so far persuaded Americans that the unborn are not 'legal' persons. The result has been the destruction of 26 million babies in their mothers' wombs." Like the editorial that shifts the conversation to "gangs," this article opposes Proposition 187 yet simultaneously scapegoats women generally and transfers the social anxiety surrounding immigration to social anxiety about reproduction. Bennett appeals to what he calls "fundamental rights" and encourages conservatives to consider immigration a federal matter, arguing that if Proposition 187 passes, children will be the main victims: "We will see spring up among us a generation of ignorant and troubled children who, lacking our common language and political and social ideals, will evolve into a huge, parallel underclass." Before ending, he draws on his "Irish-American Democrat grandfather," who was an immigrant, and then concludes by saying, "Certainly, turning our schools, businesses and hospitals into INS battlefields is not the answer. The border is where our fight ought to be." Again, the INS and border patrol remain the ultimate arbiters and seats of power—a locus where war metaphors are given practical manifestation.

In the process of arguing against Proposition 187, Bennett also argues that "illegal aliens" are law-breakers, that undocumented immigrants should be excluded from some social benefits, that morality should be our guiding principle, that Proposition 187 is akin to abortion, that "fundamental rights" are paramount ones, that victimization of children is inherently more troublesome than victimization of adults, that acculturation to a unified political agenda leads to more effective public policy, and that a racial issue can simply be understood through the model of white ethnic relations.

This particular rhetorical strategy within the *Los Angeles Times* of relying on conservative government figures—sources with institutional legitimacy and power—to make arguments against Proposition 187 has important implications. First, it prevents a viable rhetoric of resistance from emerging within the newspaper in response to Proposition 187. Conservative rhetoric thus saturates the discursive terrain, while simultaneously implying that a balanced or even liberal position is being presented. Hence, it is really no surprise that Proposition 187 passed, despite the *Los Angeles Times*'s "opposition." Second, the governmental agent becomes an ironic figure who ostensibly should support anti-immigrant legislation and who, because of this "authority," speaks as an expert on the issue as a member of the opposition. Battling immigration makes one an expert on immigration legislation—even legislation that makes immigration less likely. The INS official plays hard politics with a soft heart and utters a matter-of-fact ideology for handling public issues.

Anti–Proposition 187 and Anti–Undocumented Migrants

Some of the most insidious political effects in the *Los Angeles Times*'s rhetoric about Proposition 187 grew out of the rhetoric of "so many law-enforcement officials . . . vigorously campaigning against Proposition 187."

The U.S. government initially defended immigrants by opposing Proposition 187 but ultimately supported other legislation that made immigrants' lives more difficult. Like the *Los Angeles Times*, Clinton opposed Proposition 187 but believed something had to be done about the burden the United States, and in particular California, carried because of massive numbers of undocumented migrants. In this capacity, Clinton asked California voters, after the proposition was voted in, not to scapegoat immigrants and supported the court's stalling of the measure. Key Republicans Jack Kemp and William Bennett also spoke out publicly against 187 (e.g., Brownstein and McDonnell 1994). Yet, in February 1996, Clinton signed a bill cracking down on businesses employing undocumented workers by denying them government contracts ("Stiffer Punishment" 1996). And, nearly two years after opposing Proposition 187, Clinton signed into law a nationwide welfare bill with wide-ranging economic, welfare, and education restrictions on immigrants. He promised to increase Border Patrol surveillance along the U.S.-Mexico border, and early in September 1996 he ordered missiles be launched at Iraq for its unsympathetic, military response to the migrant peoples, the Kurds. As Clinton said to justify the air strikes, "When you abuse your own people . . . you must pay a price" (Mitchell 1996). According to a similar cultural logic, this launching of missiles closely followed the 2 July 1996 opening of the blockbuster Hollywood film *Independence Day*, in which the elimination of the alien m/other ship was completed with dramatic finality. In short, not unlike the rapid shift in California governor Pete Wilson's politics—from pro-migrant work early in his term as governor to anti-"illegal immigrant"—Clinton moved, without having to provide a public rationale for shifting positions, from vituperating California's governor for basing his campaign on Proposition 187 to supporting larger wide-ranging national measures for welfare reform that in some respects essentially implemented on the national level an even harsher Proposition 187. Clinton's strategies mirror on a national level those of the *Los Angeles Times* at the state level in constructing a campaign against Proposition 187 that relied on the villianization of undocumented migrants.

Ultimately, the *Los Angeles Times* does not oppose Proposition 187 so much as it reaffirms certain humanistic tenets. This discourse claims the terrain of liberal, human discourse in the process of saturating that domain with a conservative, surveillance-focused, and nationalist rhetoric. Surveillance by the INS takes the place of the U.S. military presence worldwide in the post–Cold War era as our protectors, and the *Los Angeles Times*, contributes to that by making INS figures into heroes who do the hard work of surveillance along the nation's borders. They are themselves "bandits" of the state, willing to enforce state boundaries, make the hard decisions, and ultimately err on behalf of national security. The passage of California propositions 209 (ending affirmative action) and 227 (English-only legislation banning bi-lingual education), and the nation-wide bipartisan welfare bill are a natural extension of making the border police the protector of the state. This Cold War politics constructs immigrants as new national enemies. These new enemies take the place of a stable Soviet Union; they follow naturally from a continuing colonialist project in the name of liberal humanist morality.

5

Complicity and Resistance in Vernacular Discourse

The dominant arguments and themes we discuss in chapters 1–3 on the rhetoric of immigration in news media are very much in keeping with the findings of other studies of the rhetoric of mainstream media. Much media studies research of the rhetoric of mass media has been able to locate "hegemonic" or "dominant ideological" themes, arguing that, while mass media present images and narratives that imply that real social change has been made, in fact the very same ideologies that media purportedly transcend actually continue to be perpetuated in media texts.[1] Our findings that argumentative discourse both for and against the proposition share common logical assumptions about nation, law, identity, citizenship, and race, thus, is consistent with and adds to this body of work on mainstream discourses. Nevertheless, to study just these mainstream, or what we call here "civic," discourses is not sufficient to an understanding of the discursive negotiations surrounding Proposition 187 that take place at more local levels of culture—vernacular sites.

While researchers have conducted many examinations of civic discourse to determine what kind of messages and information reach larger publics, there has been surprisingly little research on "vernacular" sites where "local" conversations about issues of political importance take place (Ono and Sloop 1995). The value of vernacular spaces is not to be underestimated. For example, as Robin Cohen notes

(1997, 26), "In the age of cyberspace, a diaspora can, to some degree, be held together or re-created through the mind, through cultural arti-facts and through a shared imagination." As such, vernacular discourse provides a site for a case study of the development of "resistant" dis-cursive strategies that can illustrate the difficulties encountered in devel-oping such strategies. It is a rich area that can illustrate the complexity of media culture and of culture generally, as well as of the dynamic rhetorics surrounding significant social issues.

In this and the following chapter, we discuss vernacular discourse—discourse by, for, and about local communities. Our discussion is based on an examination of e-mail messages posted to an e-mail distribution list devoted to defeating Proposition 187 before and after voters passed the measure. The list, "187-L: Resisting and Organizing Against Prop 187,"[2] began operating as a forum for those interested in challenging Proposition 187 to discuss strategies of resistance, issues pertinent to anti-immigration legislation, and "news items" dealing with immigrant issues. While the list by no means provided the only space for vernac-ular discussion of these issues, and while it is exclusive in the sense that it is limited to those who have e-mail access and are aware of its exis-tence, it does provide a space in which activists and others opposing Proposition 187 and anti-immigration issues in general and concerned with issues related to social change and politics were able to develop strategies and create arguments that countered Proposition 187. More-over, because any subscriber could add comments to the discussion, it provided a space for a wide range of issues pertinent to immigrants, to self-defined leftists, and to many others.

We examined 558 posts from 21 November 1994 to 16 March 1996.[3] One of us was on the list during this entire period. We focused on the extent to which strategies articulated in discourse varied from those used in the dominant media, what form those strategies took, and the logic such strategies drew on to take politically challenging and resis-tance stances. In this chapter, we examine three major sets of strategies that emerged:

Dominant Logics: posts drawing on themes in mainstream media dis-course characterizing immigrants as prone to disease and as eco-nomic units, focusing on the courts and the legislature as sites for conducting social change, focusing on issues of constitutionality, and calling for reform of existing institutions.

Diffusion of Purpose: posts focusing more on coalition building than on immigration issues, posts altogether unrelated to Proposition 187, and posts discussing conservative and progressive politics and legislation.

Textual Poaching: posts of news reports from the popular press, posts of templates of letters and telephone scripts for would-be activists, posts and reposts of articles in Spanish, and media education posts.[4]

Ronald Greene (1998, 27) has called for renewed attention to the way rhetoric contributes to "the act of government." He suggests that a materialist project should examine how governing institutions "represent, mobilize and regulate a population in order to judge their way of life" and points out that one way in which governing is possible is through rhetorical practices. Chapters 1–3 focus on the ways in which mainstream media news reports on Proposition 187 construct a rhetoric of "government" at the national and state levels; this chapter and the next address the way vernacular discourse constructs it at a more local, nevertheless, geographically wide-ranging one. In particular, this chapter focuses on the way in which vernacular discourse may in certain instances be complicit with the overarching logical assumptions produced within dominant discourses. Thus, despite the significant differences between dominant and vernacular media, the common language of dominant logics and discourses provides a degree of complementarity in their purposes, practices, and effects.

While outlaw forms of resistance can be found within the discussion on the distribution list and make up the subject of Chapter 6, in this chapter we primarily study discourse resistant to Proposition 187 that works on the grounds of legislation or commensurability (and, by implication, govern-mentality), rather than the *differend*, and hence reproduces the logic of dominant culture even while attempting to resist it.[5] That is, this discourse works through the logics of current state institutions and apparatuses rather than logics that are not coincident with them. We suggest that although much of the discourse resisting Proposition 187 works within the logic of dominant discourse, there are ways in which the list does disrupt, through various types of textual poaching, dominant representations of immigration issues, at the very least in terms of the weight and skepticism given to the coverage of various elements of immigration issues in dominant media. Hence, this chapter focuses on the complicity of much resistant discourse, while simultaneously noting some of the ways in which even those arguments that use the logic of dominant culture and society can work to change that logic.

In the first section, we suggest that much of the vernacular discourse countering Proposition 187's supporters is problematic to the degree that it replicates the meanings by which "immigrants" and "immigration" are understood within dominant civic discourse, in terms of both metaphorical description and legal prescription. In general, those upset with Proposition 187 who were willing to challenge it on this e-mail list generally forwarded ideas based on the political system as it currently exists. Thus, for example, a pro-immigrant stance is not necessarily equivalent to a stance against exploitation, racism, or violence. Regardless of its challenges to dominant judgments of immigrants and immigration, this strain of vernacular discourse (that is, what we would refer to as "dominant vernacular" discourse) tends to reify the grounds on which public understandings are made. In this sense, we suggest that the arguments against Proposition 187, along with arguments for Proposition 187, "create the conditions of possibility for a governing apparatus to judge and program reality" (Greene 1998, 22). As almost any thesis about the operations of hegemony would posit, when the rules of governmentality and judgment are agreed to on the level of mass culture, the battle for ideological control is, in large measure, already over.

Furthermore, while a great deal of early discussion on the list focuses on boycotts and protests related to the "voter's decision" on the proposition, the general tendency on the list is to move from discussions of specific arguments over Proposition 187 to more general issues of anti-immigration legislation (e.g., border patrol issues, quotas) and, as time passes, to a more generalized set of liberal issues (e.g., union issues, freedom of speech). While such postings generally have at least indirect ties to immigration issues, they also encourage a less "activist" discussion and a move toward general information distribution. In a sense, without the driving force of the particular issue of Proposition 187, the distribution list comes to resemble more and more a group that disagrees with the general tenor of political attitudes but nevertheless is willing to work within governing rules, logics, and often institutions to make minor adjustments rather than to reconceptualize whole structures.

This is not to say, however, that the picture we paint is one of complete despair; indeed, limited, tactical resistance never completely collapses. While the vernacular discourses we study are for the most part complicit in that they represent dominant logics and grids of judgment, the distribution list community also makes creative use of the materials available to it in using, constructing, and attempting to change a worldview. Hence, for example, when an article from a national newspaper is "poached" and placed on the list (with or without commentary by the poster), readers get a different sense of what is important and what is given priority in national news. In this way, an identity is created among all the community in terms of worldview knowledge. David G. Gutiérrez (1995) points out that members of the diaspora and government actions against the diaspora create the conditions under which a similar and unified identity is created. Out of necessity (because they are threatened by government policy), members of the diaspora create a survival identity and worldview out of the fabric laid out to hold them in check. When members of the list supply templates for letters to government officials and corporations, they allow for more efficient political action from list participants, even if this action works within existing judgmental logics. Thus, while what we are labeling dominant vernacular discourse reifies some of the logic of dominant civic discourse, it also, like all arguments from positions of the (discursively) marginalized, illustrates evidence of resistant and creative uses of "dominant civic" media products.

Dominant Themes

Greene's thesis on the materiality of government focuses on an overdetermining disciplinary logic and set of practices he finds operating in social institutions. Drawing on both Greene and Jean-François Lyotard, we might say that when resistance is based on litigation rather than the *differend*, governmentality is as much a product of government's "subjects" as it is of social institutions. While most of the discussion on the 187-L list occurs after the passage of Proposition 187, that which occurs before passage and that which focuses directly on legislation regarding immigration uses familiar metaphors and tropes concerning disease, economic value, the law, and reform.

As in much of the dominant discourse, in the vernacular discourse, we find a pervasive metaphor of contagion associated with undocumented immigrants—a persistent representation of immigrants as disease-carrying hosts. For example, an American Civil Liberties Union (ACLU) news release on the list notes: "Proposition 187 could be called the 'Communicable Disease Act of 1994' said Mark Silverman of the Immigrant Legal Resource Center. 'This law not only hurts immigrant families, but is a prescription for a public health disaster for all Californians" ("News").[6] Similarly, a letter forwarded from the Florida Immigrants Rights list observes that "Governor Pete Wilson and the legislators and citizens supporting Prop 187 have failed to see what most health care providers are seeing: the potential for a rising rate of epidemics . . . for tuberculosis, for sexually transmitted ailments and for other infectious diseases" ("Aftermath").[7] Even in a resolution by the Oakland School Board announcing that the board would refuse to comply with Proposition 187 regardless of its legal status, one of the reasons listed for noncompliance is based on this disease metaphor ("Oakland School Board votes on 187"). In the dominant civic discourse, immigrants are represented by those against Proposition 187 as potentially bringing epidemics to the United States. Here, in vernacular arguments against Proposition 187, such discourse suggests that, if the proposition passes, undocumented immigrants will be denied proper health care, leading, necessarily, to the spread of disease.

In making their arguments about disease, resisters are drawing on a construction with a long history in U.S. society. As Susan Sontag (1990, 61–62) writes:

> Authoritarian political ideologies have a vested interest in promoting fear, a sense of the imminence of takeover by aliens—and real diseases are useful material. Epidemic diseases usually elicit a call to ban the entry of foreigners, immigrants. And xenophobic propaganda has always depicted immigrants as bearers of disease (in the late nineteenth century: cholera, yellow fever, typhoid fever, tuberculosis).[8]

Some might say the proponents of Proposition 187 have defined the issues; we would say resisters accept existing dominant logics as the grounds on which to dispute the measure. As such, the discourse highlights and reifies an attention to health care, and the representation of a diseased and contagious immigrant naturally follows. As Steven Perry (1983) notes in his study of the infestation metaphors in Adolf Hitler's discourse, the logic of the disease-infestation metaphor narrows the policy options that are imaginable. Just as Hitler's infestation metaphors led "naturally" to policies that demanded the elimination of the Jewish population, if immigrants are understood to be part of an infestation, their removal is necessary if the body politic is to be saved.

A second theme emerges within the discourse focusing on economics and labor. Robin Cohen (1987, 142–43) posits that in contemporary capitalist culture, immigrants act as "new helots" or as a reserve army of labor for those nations with large accumulations of capital.[9] When the economy requires it, the U.S. nation-state encourages migrants, whether documented or undocumented, to work in low-wage jobs. At such times, not only does migrant labor facilitate the efficient function of the economy but the availability of labor helps keep wages lower than would be normal. Moreover, during periods of economic growth, there is little discussion of the economic cost of immigrants—legal or illegal—to the state or to individual workers. However, during periods of recession, when external labor is not required, familiar arguments are raised time and time again concerning the impact of "illegal" labor on the state and on its citizens.[10] Such arguments construct immigrants as exhibiting criminal traits, evading taxes, and exacting a huge cost on the social body. Such arguments say that immigrants make "exorbitant claims on welfare, medical services and housing [and] provide a cultural threat to mainstream North American values and deprive US workers of jobs" (Cohen 1987, 187). Cohen (1987, 127) notes that these arguments have historically (and consistently) underestimated the economic cost-benefit ratio of migrants by overestimating services received from the state and underestimating taxes paid to it. More important, however, he echoes Juan Ramón García (1980, 23) in suggesting that such arguments metaphorically reify the notion that everyone—both immigrant and "legal" citizen—can be seen as an economic unit of labor to be exploited (or not) rather than as human beings with universal rights.

Indeed, in the case at hand, rather than argue against the "cost" argument made by those in favor of Proposition 187 (i.e., undocumented labor results in California's failing economy because of extra costs associated with providing immigrants with education, health care, policing, etc.), several postings counter proponents' arguments by showing how immigrants actually contribute to the economy and are in fact essential to the economy; thus, both arguments frame the issue of immigration in terms of which position—for or against Proposition 187—yields more capital.[11] For example, one poster notes that "states are suing for these 'costs' as if to say that undocumenteds haven't contributed to their economies (a fallacy). Of course, undocumenteds contribute in the form

of sales taxes, property taxes, etc." ("Unfunded Mandates"; see also
"Florida 187"). However, one article implies that while immigrants are
an economic boon for the middle class, they are detrimental to less
skilled and less educated laborers, including "blacks and earlier immigrants" ("Impact").[12] Elsewhere, immigrants are represented as "primarily hard workers, creators of wealth *for US businesses*" ("Florida
Immigrant"; emphasis added).[13] Further, after pointing out that supporters of anti-immigration policies often note the costs of illegal immigration incurred by individual states, one poster comments that these
same people never mention the taxes paid by undocumented workers
each year: "According to official California records, the undocumented
immigrants pay state income taxes, state sales taxes, state and local property taxes, state vehicle licenses and registration fees, state excise taxes,
state gasoline taxes, state lottery revenues, and local sales taxes" ("Undocumented"). Finally, another article points to the "informal economy" that exists in which undocumented workers work on a cash basis,
supporting an undiscussed part of the U.S. economy; the post thus suggests the necessity of such an economy ("REASON").

In these posts and similar ones, resistance to the argument that immigrants are an economic burden rhetorically turns immigrants into an
economic benefit—more specifically, into workers who produce wealth
for U.S. businesses and the state. Thus, when discussed in terms of economics, the primary construction of immigrants is as essential elements
of the labor process, as valuable economic units. Hence, immigrant
work should "count," on the one hand, because it adds to the economic
prosperity of the United States, but it should not count, on the other
hand, because it detracts from that same prosperity. By equating immigrants solely with economic value, "worth" changes as the result of
changes in the U.S. economy (i.e., when cheap farm labor is needed,
immigration has positive value; when economic times are bad, immigration has negative value). In such equations, economic cost-benefit
analysis supersedes more complex questions about immigration generally, such as the absolute right to migrancy. Both arguments rely on a
definition of "citizenship" that means "one who contributes capital,"
thus suggesting that those who do not "contribute capital" are not (acting like) citizens. Regardless of how one views the economic status of
undocumented immigrants on the U.S. economy, supporting either of
these diametrically opposing positions—"Undocumented immigrants
are a boon for the economy" or "Undocumented immigrants are a drain

on the economy"—means one upholds the system of governmentality such reasoning represents.

A third major theme that emerges within the discourse concerns matters of legality. Posts on the list that call for legal help and reinterpretations of the Constitution, as well as legal justice, rely on existing definitions of citizenship or "legal" immigrant status. Such calls primarily seek help in aiding undocumented immigrants' desires to work within the United States, helping fight proposed policies that could hurt the status of immigrants, or helping immigrants work directly toward citizenship.

There were sixty-four posts concerning the law, the courts, and legislation. Careful description of all of these posts and their themes is beyond the purposes of our study; hence, we have listed exemplary posts rather than every post using a given theme. The posts we list include discussions of legislation that places more restrictions on how immigrants receive loans ("AAW"; "Perm"; "Speech"), updates on bills, acts, court decisions, and other legislation affecting immigration in various legal contexts ("1995-05-3"; "Anti-immigrant legislation"; "Asian Law"; "DV96"),[14] legislative updates on the status of Proposition 187 ("Legal Notice"), announcements of legislation in other states that is similar to Proposition 187 ("Fla. Prop 187"; "NY Community"; "OREGON"; "Re: need info"), and discussions of legal action that can be taken against Proposition 187 ("California Summer"; "FL convention"; "Frontline"; "Greetings"; "Pressuring").

One post ("Sonoma Co") includes a draft document on strategies to stop the proposition. Strategies suggested in the post include countering Proposition 187 with a ballot initiative, getting people to vote, getting people to become naturalized citizens, supporting citizenship courses, organizing voting drives, and providing voter education, as well as organizing boycotts, strikes, and work stoppages. Another post ("Immmigrant [sic]") forwards an article by the Prairie Fire Organizing Committee protesting federal legislation it says works similarly to Proposition 187. The post discusses the problem and says such legislation "constitutes a human rights emergency." It then encourages participation in a hunger strike in front of the San Francisco Federal Building and encourages people to send faxes and telephone messages to Senators Dianne Feinstein and Barbara Boxer.

What is significant about these challenges is that each operates on the assumption that the battle against anti-immigration should be waged

on the level of legal challenges (litigation), in effect legitimating and justifying laws and the legal system as a site for adjudicating political claims.
Hence, while such legal challenges might be successful, identifying their
usage as a route for reform places the reading of one's identity within
the U.S. legal structure. Such arguments strengthen the link between
identity and legality. As Maurice Charland (1987, 133) points out, if
identification is "logically prior to persuasion," one's willingness to be
identified within a legal structure severely limits what actions can be
taken to challenge the state producing the legal structure. In this case,
identifying with the legal system provides one with a pre-established
identity in relation to the United States, reinforcing a national view. As
such, appeals must be made on grounds commensurate with existing
U.S. law (and legal systems), rather than on challenges to that system
itself made on the basis, for example, of appeals to universal rights or
to transnational migrancy. Again, rather than being an insistence that
the current system is itself incommensurable with their vision of reality, this is an insistence in which rights are commensurable with U.S.
law, in effect constructing U.S. citizenship and its legal constructs as
having universal legitimacy. To be within litigation is to be legitimate;
to refuse to engage such legal rights and arguments is to be illegitimate,
an outlaw. As a result, the potential force of some logics of outlaw judgment are ignored.

Each of these metaphors—disease, the economy, and the law—works
on the grounds of those who favor Proposition 187 and those who
respect (or are at least willing to follow) existing legal structures in general. But perhaps even more interesting are several documents that
argue directly on the grounds of the constitutionality of Proposition 187
by taking up the terms by which the courts arbitrate constitutionality.
While such arguments can be powerful because they offer rhetorical
reinterpretations of the Constitution, immigrants, and Proposition 187,
we should be careful to note the ways in which building such arguments again equates "rights" generally with "Constitutional rights."
For example, an ACLU representative is quoted as arguing that "Proposition 187 shreds the US Constitution and the protections guaranteed
to people within our borders. This country is founded on equity and
law, not prejudice and suspicion" ("News"). Later, a person who had
been assisting a state commission on civil rights notes that list members had no need to worry about the implications of Proposition 187
because "the entire initiative is unconstitutional as an attempt to usurp

the federal government's exclusive authority to pass laws affecting immigration" ("187's"). Indeed, one post details how English-only legislation flies in the face of the Constitution and ends by saying, "This ought to give hispanics some encouragement ... the Bill of Rights (including the First Amendment) IS working for them" ("9th Circuit"). Again, we are not suggesting that arguing against the proposition on the grounds of its unconstitutionality has no benefits—it obviously does to the degree that it removes or changes the law. However, if such an argument is made in conjunction with arguments concerning economics (labor value) and health issues, the ground is established for a battle within existing dominant civic language and this might have much more severe repercussions than might be imagined at first glance. Indeed, in the previous quotation, we see an endorsement of the U.S. government's ability to provide the very meaning of resonant ideographs— "labor," "citizenship," and "rights"—an endorsement that justifies the current social structure. Thus, the entire question of immigration makes sense only in relation to *U.S.* immigration policies; immigration comes to be understood as a national, as opposed to an international or transnational, concern. As a result, space is limited or closed for arguments outside of the logic of legal/illegal, clean/dirty, healthy/diseased, economic benefit/cost when the meanings and the rules are of the dominant understanding.

While such arguments offer different interpretations of the meanings of "immigrants" and different definitions of their value, they ultimately reaffirm the legitimacy of their value and meaning within the parameters of "governmental" discourse. As Iain Chambers (1994, 37) notes, logics in which opposition and resistance simply mirror and invert the language of oppression do little to challenge the systems that are producing the problems.[15] Hence, the disease arguments link immigrants with disease metaphors; the economic arguments reaffirm valuing humanity based on economic worth; and constitutional arguments reaffirm the Constitution as the grounds on which arguments concerning legitimacy must be made. As Richard Sandbrook (1982, 218) argues concerning the problems with uncritical acceptance of populist or vernacular discourses: "It does not reject the dominant value system.... It thus fosters only protest against a corrupt, nepotistic and self-interested political class, not concerted political action to control or reshape institutions." For Sandbrook, if vernacular logics reify the dominant values, they simply leave us in a space in which the same ideas (here, health, economics, law) function regardless of who is in power. While there may be times and situations in which we want to reaffirm the base of such binarisms, being aware that we are doing so leaves a much more powerful space for knowing the implications of doing otherwise.

Diffusion of Purpose

In the days and months immediately following the passage of Proposition 187, several protests, marches, and boycotts were planned in and around California to demonstrate that the case against the proposition would not end with the vote.[16] While working within the logic of governmentality, such arguments and actions provided a specific focus for action and mobilization, implying that activism as a *telos* is not sufficient for social change.[17] During the course of our study, however, the interest of the list seemed to shift from a specific focus on Proposition 187 to posts about coalition building around immigration, to articles altogether unrelated to Proposition 187, and finally to general protests against conservative politics. It is important to emphasize that this shift is simply a tendency we noted within the discourse, not a linear fact. As the politics that were being argued against became more general, the list as a space for resistant identity and potentially incommensurable understandings of rights and direct material action was lessened.

While not always chronological, in general, the information that appeared on the list moved from specific information on Proposition 187 to a focus on immigration. Two key posts provide evidence of this shift. One post by the Asian Pacific Islanders Against Proposition 187 announces that the group is changing its name to the Asian Pacific Islanders for Immigrant Rights and Empowerment ("API-FIRE"). Another post contains a call from Grace Napolitano, a member of the California Assembly, for informal meetings with constituents to discuss issues of immigration in general in the aftermath of the passage of Proposition 187 ("June 22"). Examples of the move from Proposition 187, specifically, to immigration, generally, include posts on immigration information, anti-immigrant legislation, immigrant rights ("8-27"; "BOOK"; "BORDER CRISIS"),[18] border issues ("6 DAY"; "MARCHA"; "Network"), police brutality ("A CALL FOR JUSTICE!"; "Orange County"), the "English Only Bill" ("Bilingual Ed."; "English First"; "English-only Update"; "Denver"), HIV/AIDS ("Migrants against HIV/AIDS"), and the Welfare Reform Act ("Immigrants' Right").

Other posts, however, do not discuss Proposition 187 or immigration in detail, if at all, and instead are simply about activism. For example, the Center for Campus Organizing sent out a general call inviting people to subscribe to a list of campus "activist" e-mail lists, listing such topics as "Economic Conversion," "Right-wing trends," "Anti-Racism," and the "Young Feminist Network" ("CANET"). They also sent out a post for a job position for someone "committed to expanding progressive activism on college campuses nationally" ("Jobs") and a call for interns ("UCP"). Many posts on activism call for even more peaceful protests than, for example, civil disobedience, itself a "peaceful" strategy. Others call for direct and strategic actions. And many frame arguments in terms of national identity versus universal rights. These posts might use Proposition 187 or immigration rights as starting points, but the underlying focus is on "doing something." These include articles on activism and leadership ("May 2"), a panoply of immigration issues ("Aug 5"; "First"; "FREEDOM SUMMER"; "Oakland: Anti-187"; "Petition for Affirmative Action"; "SFSU"; "R&R's"; "Sonoma March"; "UNITY 95"), racism generally ("Latino Law"; "Re[2]: Cultural"; "Racist Remarks"), affirmative action ("AFFAM-L"; "Boycott of American"; "June 24"; "LA Office"; "OCT. 12"; "Students & Community"; "UC Faculty Statement"), Pete Wilson ("CALL TO ACTION"; "Seattle Protests"), labor and union activities ("AFL-CIO"; "HERE"; "LA Justice"; "LABNEWS"; "Lafayette Park: Fax"; "Two"; "UFW summer internships"; "World Bank's"), activist rights ("New FBI"), hate crimes ("Asian Hate Crime"), Asian American studies ("MAASU Spring Conference"), ethnic studies ("Columbia U takeover"), freedom of speech ("Internet"), e-mail activism ("REPORT: Prop 13"), the minimum wage ("Help"), the garment industry ("Organizing Training"), police abuse and harassment ("Moratorium's Position"), politicians ("Nader"), Chicanos ("25th"), the environment ("1-800 to Congress"; "Environmental Justice"), and global issues ("InterAction").

Some posts focus on conservative stances or legislation, such as the Contract with America.[19] The arguments in these posts assume a general criticism of anti-immigration if they have anything to do with immigration at all. Rather than directly organizing activist labor, then, these posts, two in particular, relate to or call for action against conservative politics. In response to a comment cited internally within the post saying, "the Republican-Controlled congress will try to pass 'Contract With America' in jan that includes denying numerous social services to permanent residents and Legal immigrants," one of these posts responds, "This has been the subject of much posting on a list of soc.cul-ture.* newsgroups in the past week. I suspect a mailing list will get cre-ated in the next few days ;-)" ("Re: Contract"). Another post encour-ages people to combine individual efforts around larger demonstrations "against the proposed Federal, State & City budget cuts," saying, "It may be time to build support/unite around many issues rather than just one issue ("Re: May 1"). Thus, these posts, most of them against the Contract with America, respond to what some posts refer to as the "far right agenda" in general ("1-800 number"; "ACT NOW!"; "ALERT: Leahy"; "Apr 9"; "Buchanan's Bigoted Statements"; "ENDORSERS"; "'ethnic humor'"; "Istook"; "PROGRESSIVE"; "Re: anti-immigrant show"; "Save Hightower"; "Slim"; "Unity Time"; "White House says").

When the general level of information here loses its original ties to Proposition 187 and anti-immigration, the focus of the discussion moves from the concerns of immigrants and those affected by immigration dis-course (e.g., Mexicanas, Mexicanos, Chicanas, and Chicanos in Cali-fornia) to more general concerns dealing with conservative legislation. We do not mean to claim that either general protests or protests and actions against specific policies cannot lead to legal and policy changes (either through galvanizing a coalition against a vast array of specifics or though a more general electoral shift akin to the one that brought Republicans to power in the U.S. Senate and House in 1994). However, this new focus provides a dispersed politics of disagreement rather than a specific challenge to the institutional logics and procedures used to adjudicate claims. That is, while the general tone of anti–Proposition 187 arguments may have worked within the dominant discourse con-cerning immigration and legal rights, these dispersed arguments may further the reification of governmentality and, given their more gener-alized disagreements, provide less space for direct action on the grounds of litigation. Such posts contribute to their taken-for-grantedness as a means of conducting social change, thus reinforcing the limited param-eters in which disputes may be addressed.

Rather than a counterdiscourse that engages the issues or assump-tions underlying positions on immigration, the more general the issues become (i.e., the further removed from Proposition 187), the more the argument is assumed rather than articulated. In this case, the univer-salization of issues leads to a less effective community in producing counterlogic discourses.

Textual Poaching

While the general thrust of many of the arguments investigated here works on the grounds of *litige* (commensurability), still there are productive effects to some of these arguments. Indeed, claiming that these arguments are completely complicitous would not only be wrongheaded but also insensitive to those making the arguments. The arguments studied here, while reproducing the general worldview of dominant civic discourse, often do so by producing a different vision of the prominence and hierarchy of particular information. The area addressed on the 187-L list provides a discursive map with a different legend and with different features than one finds in civic discourse.

One feature of this different map is poaching, the most resistant of the three kinds of dominant vernacular discourses we found on this list. Poaching involves reframing texts that do not initially center a group's concerns so that those concerns are effectively centered. It entails rethinking the world in terms that, while potentially incommensurable with existing discourses (i.e., they could be outlaw discourses), are more often reworkings of existing discourses using generally commensurable logics. If we take the imaginative fan reinterpretation of the television program *Star Trek* as an example (as so many other scholars have done), we realize that even if *Star Trek* could be reworked in such a way that a focus on humans, for example, is displaced (e.g., if the Borg were victorious over the Federation),[20] such a reading might fail to address the similarities between the Federation and the Borg. Further, when fans poach *Star Trek* in such a way that changes remain within some existing logic (e.g., while *Star Trek* fans may indeed alter the gender of those in power or play with various sexual attractions, gender and romance remain organizing principles), the general hierarchy of power often remains largely the same. In the 187-L list, we encounter multiple ways in which those who poach also argue positions on immigration that are commensurable with existing logics and institutions. In doing so, they change the emphasis of the prominence of particular discourses in the general cultural conversation but do not upend existing logics. In looking at some of the ways in which this poaching takes place, we want to indicate the power of such poaching in rearticulating conditions, while simultaneously noting its limits.

Like the general discourse on the list, "reposts" of news items from newspapers, other news groups, or even non-mainstream news texts tend, like posts in general, to move from a focus on Proposition 187 to a dispersed focus on immigration generally (e.g., "70 IMMIGRANTS"; "1995-06-23"; "[AP] Larry Gerber").[21] They show a concern with immigration and universal rights beyond California, indeed very often outside of the United States. Some posts focus on sweatshops, some on personal narratives. In general, the posts appear to rely on a general faith that increasing information available to readers (i.e., education) will lead to social change in the same way that generations of relatives of immigrants who see education as a means toward advancement and, quite possibly, social equity might also see education as the principal means of social transformation.

There are a large number of reposts of news reports from dominant newspapers (e.g., "[51] REPORT"; "Anti-immigration movement"; "Californias" [sic]).[22] Indeed, a cursory reading of the posts indicates that perhaps the most common are those that are simple repostings of news stories that have run in large city newspapers or on wire services that serve these newspapers (these reports are often taken straight off news source Web pages). The reports range from Associated Press and Reuters news services to ones copyrighted by individual newspapers such as the *New York Times*, the *San Francisco Chronicle*, the *Boston Globe*, and the *Los Angeles Times*. The topics of the articles range from exit polling after the vote on Proposition 187 ("PROP187 ELECT") to an interview with a student named Eric Garcetti about protests at Oxford against the proposition ("LA TIMES") to reports about legislation in Germany meant to deport Vietnamese, who are reportedly "a source of violent crime" in Germany ("Germany").

While we discuss the discourse from these newspapers in chapters 1–3, what we are interested in here is the way the reposting of these news articles acts on a list dedicated to resisting Proposition 187 beyond merely providing information about it. On one hand, there is little about reposting that could be called "poaching" in the sense of transforming the preferred meanings of a given text. On the other hand, the existence on this list of reposted articles, out of their original context, is not simply an extension of dominant civic discourse. Rather, texts are being smuggled from one reading context into another: from civic newspapers into the vernacular space of a distribution list.

Certain assumptions about the usefulness, trustworthiness, and credibility of news information are communicated through textual poaching from civic discourse that may imply an "informed" liberal and "uninformed" conservative dialectic. Hence, while the articles are not overtly reworked by anyone on the list (although this might be done by individual readers or groups of readers after the posting), the simple act of placing the articles on the list is itself a reworking of the prominence of information on each reader's landscape. That is, being reposted on this list not only brings the article to the attention of readers who normally would not have seen it (e.g., they do not receive the primary newspaper or they skipped over it) but also gives prominence to the news report by taking it out of its initial context and posting it on its own. Moreover, given that readers of the news group are also reading a variety of other posts regarding immigration policies and protests, their interpretive framework and skills regarding the posts are already altered simply by their being part of the news group. That is, the reader's interpretive frame is more likely to be slanted toward a tactical reading of an article. Hence, one way in which dominant arguments are reworked is simply through reposting.

Nevertheless, we should be careful to remember that reposting always has reifying effects. Here, in reposting the news report, the posters are implicitly endorsing the news report itself as having something "factual" to tell readers. That is, while readers may be skeptical of the "reporting" of dominant news or may indeed be skeptical about any factual reporting about immigration issues, the unquestioned, uncommented-upon posting of news articles seems to offer the news report, at least in part, as something to be trusted. At the very least, such repostings do not actively encourage a questioning of the "authenticity" of dominant news services and imply that only posts not obviously favoring one's political position need be considered.

Perhaps more to the point for those interested in poaching are those instances in which a news report is followed by or preceded by comments by the poster that provide commentary or give an interpretive framework. Such posts have a number of different appearances. Some implicitly endorse the information as factual (and therefore endorse the news source) while simultaneously making it clear that the "facts" themselves are not beneficial to those who are attempting to counter anti-immigration measures. For example, after a repost of an Associated Press (AP) article suggesting that hate groups were guilty of bombings in the United States, the submitter of the post adds: "Scary stuff from AP news" ("Hate"). In contrast, there are posts that ask readers to be skeptical of the news information contained in the report. For example, in a posting of U.S. Census statistics on racial breakdown in the United States, the poster adds, "But don't ask me how they determined these figures" ("More U.S."). Similarly, following a *San Francisco Chronicle* report on the rising number of undocumented immigrants moving to Arizona, there is a disclaimer that reads in part: "These articles are forwarded from assorted sources throughout the Internet. No attempt was made to verify the accuracy of the information presented. The readers should make their own conclusion" ("[SFC] Arizona"). In such posts, while the information is not necessarily undermined, the reader is encouraged to question it.

Other posts directly indicate the problematics of news reporting and offer routes of political activism for readers. For example, after a reposting and discussion of a *Time* magazine advertisement that draws a parallel between bilingualism and child abuse, the poster provides information about how to contact *Time* to complain ("TIME"). Similarly, after providing the text of an anti-immigration advertisement during an ABC television news report, the poster provides the addresses of programmers at ABC to whom one should write as part of a protest of the advertisements ("ABC").

Perhaps more interesting are those repostings of news reports that provide the reader with a strategy for connecting the information in the news story with other social issues pertinent to the list. For example, at the top of a post that is almost entirely a reprinting of a *Boston Globe* article concerning English-only bills, the post asks readers of the list to resist this "Proposition 187-inspired bill" ("Re: National"). Although bilingual education and bilingual bills are discussed on the list, this post directly articulates a link between Proposition 187 and all bilingual legal issues. Similarly, after a reposting of an *Arizona Republic* news report on neo-Nazi attacks against immigrants, the submitter of the post adds: "In case you are wondering, Arizona's legislators failed to pass a 'hate crimes' statute last session. Many speculate the bill failed to pass because the law included crimes based on sexual preference" ("More News"). Now again, while the link between issues affecting "underrepresented" people might be a logical or common one, here we see a link between neo-Nazi attacks on immigrants and a general antihomosexual attitude on the part of legislators in Arizona. In one sentence, the editorial comment provides a link between neo-Nazis and legislators, as well as between the concerns of immigrants and of homosexuals. Further, in a reposting of a news report about militia bombings of federal buildings, the poster notes that the people responsible for bombing federal buildings are "out of the right wing 'militia' movement which is based on an anti-federal, pro-gun platform, the logical extension of the Contract's [with America] extremist attack on children and the poor" ("Rightwingers"). The comments go on to connect militia attacks with Newt Gingrich and the new right. Again, an articulated link is drawn between one group of people and specific activities that otherwise would not necessarily be combined, and again, if accepted, the link provides a context for reading all future reports about either the new right or the militia. While certainly not poaching in the overt sense of "rewriting" stories, each of these reworkings of news items does provide new articulations and reading strategies—contexts for reading, emphasizing certain "frames of intelligibility" (Hall 1997).

Another somewhat more assertive act (in terms of dominant vernacular discourses) is the posting of template letters or telephone scripts for contacting legislators about anti-immigration laws or corporations who have either supported anti-immigration candidates or have anti-immigration policies of their own (either overtly through campaign donations or subtly as interpreted by critics in advertising themes). For example, drafts of letters are offered that are addressed to Dianne Feinstein about Proposition 187 ("Feinstein"), to the U.S. Senate in general about the Personal Responsibility Act ("Immigrant Rights"), and to Grace Napolitano of the California State Assembly in support of AB 81 and AB 83, two bills that protect workers from anti-immigration harassment ("Action Sheet"; "Anti-enslavement"). And while several other templates appear that deal with immigration issues,[23] just as on the list in general, as we move temporally away from the passage of Proposition 187, the types of templates or telephone scripts offered change from general anti-immigration issues to welfare reform and then to more loosely connected issues, such as the activities of students in high school newspapers ("PHONE") and calls for a county commissioner in Indiana, described as racist, to resign ("Stop"). Hence, again, while such templates provide a route of action for readers, they work along two lines: They continue to work within the existing "governmental system of discourse" (fighting laws rather than fighting the system of arbitration), and they eventually become more general, less specific to Proposition 187 or to immigration and thus mirror the change in the list as a whole.

Reposts of articles from the Spanish-language press and from Spanish speakers are generally reprinted without any comment or with only a short introduction in English stating the article's topic (e.g., "Coordinadora 96: Regarding"; "[CSPM]"; "[JORNADA]"; "Los"; "[OPINION"; "Prensa"). In such posts, we see a move that, while reifying the legitimacy of a news source, calls into question the dominant language used to discuss anti-immigration issues—English. The posting of articles in Spanish may also act as a symbolic threat to those who cannot read Spanish. It may symbolize a lack of access for those who cannot read Spanish to knowledge about what is happening in the dominant press and government and may suggest that much larger changes (e.g., the displacement of those currently in power) are on the horizon. The language itself is incommensurable with dominant discourse, regardless of the article's content, for those who do not speak or read Spanish. Just as Jean-François Lyotard (1985) calls on the metaphor of "language games" in discussing the incommensurability of different forms of judgment, here the language itself provides a sense of the incommensurable and of what the dominant language may do for Spanish speakers. It may lead to reflection on positions of power constructed by authorial language relations.

Given the history of migrant labor within the United States, posting in Spanish is a meaningful act. As Robin Cohen (1991, 42–43) points out, Henry Ford "made language training [English] in his factories compulsory; this was but a part of the training his immigrant workers had to undertake to obtain citizenship." Ford, of course, is not the only employer to have pushed for assimilation through English as a way to make migrants "citizens" in both the legal sense and the ideological sense of speaking the language of the employer. A preference for one language, cultural form, or expressive mode over another moves migrants both literally and ideologically into "dominant civic" logics; indeed, in Ford's case, into a particular mode of capitalist production. As Ella Shohat and Robert Stam (1994, 191) write in their book *Unthinking Eurocentrism*, "English, especially, has often served as the linguistic vehicle for the projection of Anglo-American power, technology and finance." The inability to use Spanish or hybrid languages as one wishes is in and of itself a delegitimation of the subject position of the Spanish-speaking worker. As Gloria Anzaldúa (1987, 59) notes: "Until I am free to write bilingually and to switch codes without always having to translate, while I still have to speak English or Spanish when I would rather speak Spanglish, and as long as I have to accommodate the English speakers rather than having them accommodate me, my tongue will be illegitimate." While posting in Spanish to a group that does not make the poster "accommodate" by learning English does not by itself end a particular culture's sense of what is legitimate knowledge, it is a very clear threat to dominant ways of speaking and a very clear statement of ideological exclusion.

In addition to providing material for repostings, dominant media outlets also provide a means for activists to broadcast their concerns. While a look at the discourse on 187-L cannot get at the actual consumption and usage of mass mediated news by list members, it can illustrate how activists employ mass media forums for their own "tactical" agendas. Such forums as press releases and news coverage are obviously commensurable with the existing structure to a degree that they reify the dominance of those forms of the master's tools, but they can also be coercive to the degree that their reposting alters the media landscape.

For example, a post entitled "Good Luck: Get on TV while you're at it" provides those protesting Proposition 187 and other anti-immigration issues a draft of a student media guide. The poster notes that "the impact of any event . . . can be greatly enhanced by the media. A small forum attracting 30 people can reach 3,000 people if you can convince your campus newspaper to send a reporter. . . . A good rule of thumb is to spend about 10% of your organizing time on attracting press" ("Good"). The remainder of the document provides some specific actions such as "10 days before your event, mail a press advisory to any weekly papers" and "Two days before the event, call everyone who got the press release to confirm your event." The poster recommends that press releases be written in language so clear "that your aunt or your grandfather would understand what you were trying to accomplish."

The point here is to make sure that a group's arguments work within the existing structures on "their" schedule, along "their" lines of thought, in "their" language. Translating into existing understandings rebolsters those understandings, since those familiar with existing practices get used to not having to work to understand new logics. Again, it is not a matter of this being a tactic that does not promote discursive change; it most certainly does. However, it is a tactic that promotes change within existing logics rather than working to alter those logics. As Lyotard might say, it is taking one's own ideas, in one's own language game, and translating them into the phrase regimes of the dominant press, hence rendering one's own ideas commensurable with those of dominant logics. A similar tactic can be seen in suggestions for how to educate the public on how immigrants are economically beneficial to the U.S. economy ("AAAS") and other general informational strategies regarding Proposition 187 ("Information"; "Western"). In each case, the emphasis is on the use of dominant media in the language and logic of dominance.

A final interesting example of this type of mass media effort is the Coordinadora 96 Statement, put forth by the California Regional Meeting of Coordinadora 96/Campaign 96 as a press release and part of a "media education" posting. The statement, which we quote here at length, works by co-opting the logic and wording of the Preamble to the United States Constitution.

> We the People of the United States, in Order to form a more perfect Union, establish Justice, insure domestic Tranquillity, provide for the common defense, promote the general Welfare, and secure the Blessings of Liberty to ourselves and our Posterity, do ordain and establish the following as Universal Constitutional Rights for the United States of America:
>
>> Human and Constitutional Rights for All;
>> Equal Opportunities and Affirmative Action;
>> Public Education for All Children;
>> Preserve and Expand Public Health Services;
>> Citizen Police Review Boards;
>> Labor Law Reform and $7.00 per Hour Minimal Wage;
>> Citizenship Now and Extend the date of Eligibility for Amnesty
>>   ("COORDINADORA 96: CALIFORNIA")

What is so interesting about this document is not just the use of the wording of the Constitution (after all, the co-optation of the United States Constitution or Declaration of Independence is a traditional genre of protest in itself).[24] It is that after taking the words of the Constitution as if to establish something new—to "constitute" something new—the demands are either ones that could already be in place or are ones that are simply minor reforms in existing law. For example, the statement does not question the existence of a below-poverty-level minimum wage, it simply demands that the minimum wage be raised (slightly). What such a document leaves in place is, again, governmental ways of thinking. In these documents, we see wording that reifies the way in which the dominant discourse "holds us still" in order to investigate us. When the minimum wage is simply something to be argued over, when review boards can be put into place for existing police forces, we are in most ways allowing the workings of such institutions to remain intact with only minor adjustments. The structure of governmentality remains the same.

Commensurability and Governmentality

In an essay that examines racist ideologies and the media, cultural critic Stuart Hall (1981) discusses the complicated representational issues surrounding the production of even leftist critical media texts. A co-participant in the production of an antiracist television show, *It Ain't Half Racist, Mum,* Hall demonstrates in his study that racism is embedded in contemporary culture and that historical issues such as colonialism and immigration play a profound role in people's everyday lives. Key to the contemporary phenomenon of race are ideologies, which "tend to disappear from view into the taken-for-granted 'naturalized' world of common sense" (32). Because they largely work unconsciously, ideologies enter unreflectively into our everyday practices, as well as into the day-to-day functioning of institutions. Thus, throughout our lives and through our various daily practices, ideologies come to have material effects.

Hall's ideas here are important to our case study, because despite the overt attempts by many posts to counter Proposition 187 and issues and policies seen to be like it, the practice of ideology through the rhetoric of posts, and hence the governmentality implicit even in anti-racist, pro-immigration discourses, are not, here, fundamentally challenged in any substantive way. Vernacular media, such as the posts we study here, are powerful places where ideas about immigration and race, as well as, say, gender, class, and sexuality emerge. And, because they are powerful, simply examining the stated positions taken by various posts, say, against English-only legislation, is insufficient to demonstrate the complexity of ideology, government, and cultural logics. As Hall writes, "The task of a critical theory is to produce as accurate a knowledge of complex social processes as the complexity of their functioning requires. It is not its task to console the left by producing simple but satisfying myths, distinguished only by their super-left wing credentials" (35–36). As he suggests, one way to address complex topics such as race and immigration ideologies within media would be to make "visible what is usually invisible: the assumptions on which current practices depend" (47). It is also to recognize that there is no single solution, that each attempt at a solution is conditioned by the circumstances in which the critique and challenge is made, and that multiple approaches to challenging the now reified nature of race and immigration ideologies will be necessary.

In the case of immigration issues and citizenship rights, we have a clear example of logics and laws that help constitute "citizens," "noncitizens," and ways of governing them. Discourses about Proposition 187 are material practices that help affirm a discourse of governing and of the constitution of citizens and noncitizens, of what labor and value does, and does not, count. However, what we also see when we investigate rhetorics of resistance (such as 187-L) is the way the materiality of governing discourses, located in governmental institutions and pseudo-governmental institutions (e.g., mass mediated reproductions of state logic), is strengthened by any argument on its own grounds. Those who attempt to resist governmental practices by working within both the institutions (newspapers, laws, and peaceful protests) and the discourses of government (e.g., using the "disease" metaphor and individuals as economic units) in part reestablish and reify the very systems that are being challenged. While this observation is not meant to be a completely pessimistic account of the power of discourse, it is meant to point out the way in which arguing with discourses on the very grounds of governmentality and materiality produces a situation in which one is "always already" pulled into governing logics in order to take part in the conversation.[25]

Perhaps, however, this will not be true for long. Ronald J. Deibert (1997, 177–201), an international relations and media theorist following current research on the ontology/epistemology of the Internet and digital communications, clearly expects a slow transformation over the next several generations from the modern sense of individuality and the nation-state to a stronger sense of identity being dispersed among multiple transnational identities.[26] However, as Deibert notes, there are at least two concerns in such theorizing. First, if one expects changes such as a cause-effect relationship between the Internet and identity, one is sure to be surprised by the lack of an obvious, visible transition. Indeed, such changes are intergenerational rather than intrapersonal: While international digital communications may set up conditions under which such epistemological and ontological changes could take place, these changes can emerge only gradually. In the present, he notes, people's epistemologies will work along familiar lines and familiar log-ics, as this chapter illustrates.

Second, as Deibert notes, "If there is one clear 'winner' in the hyper-media environment, it is the collective interests of transnational capi-tal. The modern subordination of economics to politics has been dra-matically reversed by this change such that the core values of most all states are now defined in terms of the interests of capital" (206).[27] Again, if there is space for optimism in changing people's understandings of their identities and their "rights," we are battling ideological constraints that maintain our understandings of "self" within existing knowledges and are faced as well with ramifications of transnational corporate cap-ital. In that regard, the key to changing logics lies in the hands of the changing needs of capital for workers in different areas and is not as much of a rhetorical battle as we would wish.

In the end, rhetorics of commensurability have only so much lever-age to work with and are greatly constrained by tradition and capital. However, if we are looking for a change in "constitutional" discourses at the level of "primary identity" in regard to issues of migration, per-haps finding those incommensurable logics (outlaw discourses) that already work toward rethinking such issues at the universal rather than the national level, and raising interest in them as points of identifica-tion, can aid the critical and political task. We turn next to this task.

6

Outlaw Vernacular Discourse: Thinking Otherwise

n rethinking "migrancy" theories, Robin Cohen (1991, 56) argues that studies of immigration reform (legal and cultural) have focused almost exclusively on what he calls "visible" forms of resistance. Such investigations have looked rather narrowly at forms of resistance that are most visible to those "in power," such as street demonstrations, labor strikes, or letter-writing campaigns. Cohen goads those interested in actually improving conditions for immigrant laborers to turn their attention to "invisible" forms of resistance—not only to more obvious actions such as sabotage or desertion but also to protests not generally considered resistant in the literal sense (e.g., changing one's religious beliefs, altering one's intake of drugs, and acquiring illnesses that allow one to stay away from the workplace) or to those that are more discursive than physical (e.g., discussions and consciousness raising).[1]

Key to Cohen's conception of "invisible" protests is an ability for critics of immigration policies to see, as he metaphorically puts it, "Babylon as a site of creativity." That is, while the multiple diasporas that led to many "Babylons" are cast in mainstream public discourse as well as many academic treatments in negative terms, Cohen (1997, 4) reminds us that any lengthy period of forced residence in Babylon (i.e., away from where one considers to be the "home" land) provides "an opportunity to construct and define historical expe-

rience, to invent tradition." Hence, rather than see diaspora in a negative light, Cohen wants to re-engage the roots of the word: *speiro* (to sow)
and *dia* (over).[2] In Babylon, a new discourse, a new sense of tradition or
identity can be sown.[3] Babylon is necessarily a place for creativity when
it comes to identity. While it is also a location for "oppression," and critics must be careful to note the ways in which the clash of cultures often
leads to marginalization of those who migrate, it is valuable to understand some of the ways new discourses or identities can be constructed
even in hostile environments.[4] In this chapter, we investigate a particular form of "invisible" protest—e-mail posts in the vernacular mode in
187-L that "think otherwise"[5]—taking care to note the new subject positions such invisible discourses create and the influence of these discourses
on already existing dominant and subordinate subject positions.

To repeat, in addition to providing critical readings of dominant
(civic or vernacular) discourses, one of the functions of critical rhetoric is the articulation of outlaw discourses in civic forums, or at least the
articulation of those outlaw discourses that individual critics most wish
to see available for civic consumption.[6] We identify outlaw discourses
in the form of protest and engage a critical rhetoric that takes a position in relation to these discourses. Because we do not want to see all
of the outlaw discourses become dominant discourses, we note our disagreements with some outlaw posts. We then draw together fragments
of other outlaw logics in order to build and promote a logic that we
would endorse operating at the level of public judgment.[7]

A Critical Rhetoric of Outlaw Discourses

As we argue elsewhere (Sloop and Ono 1997), the term "outlaw discourses" refers to those material and vernacular discourses that emerge
from marginalized communities and work on the basis of *differend* rather
than litigation (i.e., incommensurable logics rather than commensurable ones). While outlaw discourses are articulated, or given voice, by
individuals, we do not refer to individuals but instead to the "logics" of
judgment upon which individuals base their arguments. Not all vernacular discourses are outlaw discourses. As we show in this study, just
because people happen to occupy a particular social position (e.g., an
exploited migrant laborer) does not guarantee that they operate by way
of an outlaw logic or that when they participate in the political they use

outlaw logics. What we are suggesting here is that there never can be a guaranteed equivalence between subject position and ideology.

Critics can help bring particular outlaw discourses to various spaces in which dominant logics operate so that outlaw logics provoke the social imaginary and encourage the formation of other ways of thinking about judgment and justice (Sloop and Ono 1997, 59–65). Thus, the critic recognizes that dominant institutions are not the only participants in the construction of "the public." We take a doxastic view that public discourses circulate, albeit haphazardly; and, no matter in what kind of space (e.g., malls, kitchens, streets, the halls of justice), public discourses functionally produce culture. In taking such a perspective, we recognize the particular contribution made by ordinary people living their lives, because they too "contribute to the production of public knowledge[s]" (Hasian and Delgado 1998, 252).

Stated simply, outlaw logics that by definition challenge dominant ways of thinking and acting create the potential for substantive social change. Challenging immigration laws and practices necessitates the crossing of social boundaries and spaces in the process of envisioning social change. It entails cultivating a care and interest in the experiences of people from radically different social and cultural backgrounds; it also entails honoring and respecting ways of thinking and acting that go beyond one's own. Paying attention to particular experiences and being willing to consider ways of thinking that might initially seem counter-intuitive, ludicrous, absurd, or even threatening are necessary to the critic studying outlaw discourses.

Elsewhere (Sloop and Ono 1997) we argue for a prescribed change in critical orientation toward outlaw discourses, a concept that originates in Jean-François Lyotard's discussion (1988) of the *differend*. As we suggest in Chapter 1, Maurice Charland (1998) offers an example of a judge who makes (Lyotard's "pagan style") judgments that are contingent on situational factors rather than on a legal precedent (i.e., a predetermined language). Charland establishes through his fictional example the need for a system of adjudication to arbitrate between two parties operating within distinctly different language games. A pagan judge ignores judgments that precede conflicts (precedents, laws), instead constructing judgments as a result of the particularities of the conflict itself (Lyotard 1988, 179). Lyotard and Charland both argue that there are times when judgments will be made in the interest of those arguing "outside" of common precedent and times when judgment will support those taking a position based on precedent. In terms of the actions of cultural-rhetorical critics, both would have the critic "bearing witness to the *differend*" (Lyotard 1988, 142), continually pointing out the contingency of all judgments and the incommensurability of various logics rather than arguing for the validity of any one claim.

It is here that we part ways with both Charland's and Lyotard's positions. Rather than always "bearing witness to the *differend*," we would see this case, or any other case of judgment, as an opportunity for a given rhetorical-cultural critic to act as a champion of a particular outlaw logic "as if" it were universally valid, even while simultaneously acknowledging its temporal and logical contingency. While Lyotard does not want judgments made based on legislation as a rule preceding judgment, we see the dominant logics, themselves, as a kind of precedent. Thus, we wish to look for logics that challenge those dominant logics and to promote them. That is, in that those arguing a case do not hold their own positions to be contingent language games (e.g., in Charland's example, the Mohawk people "know" the land to be sacred; the courts "know" the primary function of land is to be owned and used) and in that outlaw arguments (here, those of the Mohawk people) could spark a social imaginary that, if enacted, could be an improvement on current logics (at least in the mind of the critic), we argue that the function of the critic is at times to cease "bearing witness to the *differend*" and to bear witness to a contingent logic as if it were universal, as if a particular outlaw logic were Truth with a capital *T*, as if all judgments should be made the way the Mohawk peoples' judgment operates.

Because many public arguments are made on the basis of "truth" value rather than on the basis of being a "better idea" for a given situation, many people will not be willing to settle for bearing witness to the *differend*, or to a pagan judge who never considers the "truth"-fulness of particular claims even when granting the legitimacy of their position. Hence, the role of the critical rhetorician is to bring selected voices and logics to the fore, if indeed the critic views as necessary the implementation of such logics in dominant civic culture. Taking the perspective just elaborated, the critic's question becomes: Will the logic of the outlaw discourse make for a better system of judgment than the current one, and, if so, how can I help bring it into being?[8]

In chapters 2–5, we look at the arguments and implications of dominant civic discourses—those arguments in mass mediated outlets that fit within the ideological logic of "governmental" discourses—and of dominant vernacular discourses—those discourses that resist dominant judgments but do so in a logic that reaffirms or reifies the logic of dominant decision-making (litigation). Dominant vernacular discourses, as we show in Chapter 5, can work defensively even as they are resistant; they often respond to arguments on the playing field of dominant logic, staying within the logic of litigation. In this chapter, we investigate outlaw vernacular discourses—those discourses that operate on a logic of the *differend* or incommensurability with dominant logics, disagreeing both with the passage of Proposition 187 and with the very legitimacy of the grounds on which it could potentially be judged. Thus, this is not simply a question of whether or not the proposition is "constitutional" but is instead a question of whether or not the U.S. Constitution should be the basis for deciding such a question. Just as the Mohawk Indians in Charland's example see little value in fighting a court battle concerning the ownership of land that cannot be owned, especially using the rules and language of the court to do so, here (in some cases) there is no need to discuss the economic "value" of immigrants and their labor when their economic value is irrelevant to the question of what it means to be migrant.

A few final observations before we discuss outlaw arguments: First, since outlaw discourses are incommensurable with dominant discourses, there can be, and indeed are, multiple outlaw discourses. The space of "blocked opportunities, hostility from others ... seems to create an advantageous sociological ... ethos in the ethnic group concerned" (Cohen 1997, 101), making the marginality of the migrant's space into a productive arena, although not necessarily a consistent one across all migrant groups. Further, these multiple outlaw discourses often contradict one another at different points. Outlaw discourses do not necessarily overlap because they differ from dominant logic any more than Spanish and Cantonese intersect because they differ from English. Hence, while we investigate several examples of incommensurable discourses, our own writing, our performance in this critical act, to some degree creates a single logic behind these discourses or separates them from one another as different. That is, we are picking up the residue of living, changing logics and codifying them here, giving uniformity through a reading of various outlaw logics.

Second, as the preceding chapter suggests, most 187-L posts operate through a discourse of "dominance" or "governmentality" because they generally have the most "intuitive appeal." Hence, the examples of outlaw discourses we cite are almost by definition "minor" discourses[9]—the majority of arguments on the list are indeed based in dominant logic.

Finally, while it is the task of the critical rhetorician to bring vernacular outlaw discourses to the fore, making sure that such discourse in effect is spoken in "civic" spaces, the very idea of an "outlaw civic" discourse is transitional. That is, as we argue in Chapter 1, once an argument is brought into the civic realm, it is either rejected or "disciplined," or any portions of its logic that are persuasive become part of the dominant conversation.[10] Hence, an outlaw discourse that is brought into civic spaces (in part) becomes a part of dominant logic. Indeed, this is the political purpose behind a critical rhetoric that attempts to bring outlaw discourses forward, and to do so in a way that is most effective in civic spaces. A successful outlaw logic must change the way normative judgments are made. All revolution is always in the end (in part) rhetorical; history books as well as official institutional papers will document a conception of the rules that revolutions have effected. Outlaw discourses that have been "accepted" discourses become (in part) a part of the logic of dominant discourses.[11]

Outlaws at War: Us and Them

Identification, as Kenneth Burke (1969) reminds us, is always simultaneously divisive and unifying. The dominant vernacular and dominant civic discourses we investigate in previous chapters, for example, constitute a world in which, regardless of an individual's reasons for supporting or condemning Proposition 187, they continue to have a rhetorical union, an identification, at the level of the nation (i.e., while individuals may disagree on Proposition 187, they agree to use the legal means provided by the United States and its legal structure to solve their disagreement). Identification unifies discourse at the level of the nation-state; outlaw discourses either provide identification in reaction to the nation-state (e.g., we will give up citizenship to create an entirely new nation and a new citizenry) or provide identity at a level that transcends the nation as the primary level of identification regarding immigration policies (e.g., on this issue, our identity as migrants may transcend any logic entailed by our identity as United States citizens).[12] As Stuart Hall (1992, 310–14) notes, in terms of identity, the world seems to be moving in two directions: One is toward globalization, homogenization, and assimilation; and the other, the one investigated in this section, is toward ethnicity, nationalism, and various fundamentalisms. We sympathize with the call for radical change in the discourse we examine in this section, but its rhetorical practice of rejecting the nation is not a practical means to effect change. Thus, this is not the kind of outlaw discourse we would expect to have the potential to enter and remain in civic spaces and thereby become dominant.

Marouf Hasian and Fernando Delgado (1998) in their study of critics of Proposition 187 suggest that "new vernaculars" include four themes—they "crafted their own narratives celebrating the contributions of immigrants to America," "united around celebrations of 'La Raza,'" "pointed out contradictions in the pro-187 tales," and "offered competing counterhistories of immigration laws" (259). But as Hasian and Delgado note, some of these discourses simply invert the "racial hierarchies" or defend "different essentialisms" in opposing Proposition 187 and "may be unconsciously perpetuating racial stereotyping" (260). Certainly, within our own study of 187-L, most posts do not counter dominant logics. Nevertheless, for example, some posts advocate a notion of citizenship different from and opposed to dominant conceptions of U.S. citizenship. Such arguments disrupt and alter existing systems of judgment and policy by providing both logics and positions that replace, rather than transcend, existing ones.

One post focuses more on race than on immigration to argue against Proposition 187, and thus it shifts the terms of the argument from immigration to race and, in effect, creates a grounding on which future conversations on the subject can take place. It reads: "This message is for those who feel a sense of desperation or utter dismay at the attitudes being fostered in California over the issue of PEOPLE OF COLOR. That's right, it's not just an immigration thing; it is a racial thing" ("Using"). In discussing the proposition not in terms of immigration policy but in terms of racism, the post also shifts attention about potential solutions from a focus on new immigration legislation to the more challenging destruction of a "system" or community that developed the legislation in the first place. The post reads, "I am sick and tired of people constantly advocating reliance on using the system. . . . If the system worked, we wouldn't have to be victimized and treated as second class citizens . . . but it hasn't and will never work" ("Using"). In the logic of this post, a system that could produce such a proposition as Proposition 187 must be so out of touch with a basic conception of civil rights as to be unredeemably beyond reform and thus in need of elimination. This argument necessarily leads to revolutionary logics—a complete wiping away of old subjectivities and judgments in favor of more equitable ones. Since the system has never worked and "will never work," there is little if any need to try to reform it. This position does not allow for compromise and does not see any purpose for a negotiation that allows the continuity of the nation or identities based on the nation as understood in dominant terms. This is not what we would call a productive outlaw discourse.

What is clear in this argument is that the current political and cultural context in which such legislation as Proposition 187 could emerge, a context overdetermined by a history of similar acts, can be addressed only through the overthrow of existing logics and their replacement with revolutionary ones. Such incommensurability cannot be overcome through specific laws or through judgment within the constraints of existing logics in general. The post illustrates this point explicitly by drawing parallels to historical revolutions. After acknowledging that others on the list may see these ideas as "too radical," the poster provides the following parallels, which are similar to those Malcolm X offered in his "Message to the Grass Roots" to justify his political proscriptions against the philosophy of nonviolence practiced at the March on Washington.

> Well, I'm sure the French in 1789 were pessimistic against the elites and they were radical and extreme for bucking against the state. . . . And I'm sure the Cubans in 1960 were pessimistic against the elites and extreme and radical for bucking against the state. But you know what, that is the *only way* they came about change, was through a revolution. That's right, a bloody, dirty, messy revolution. . . . Prop 187 is just the beginning of a long and bloody race war. The GOP and the White elites have fired the first shot. Are you ready? ("Using"; emphasis added)

While others make arguments that at times broach some of the themes raised in this post (see, e.g., "east"; "FOUR WINDS STUDENT"; "Reviving") and call for aggressive offensive political actions, none quite so clearly discusses the proposition in terms of race and none so clearly posits that the proposition is an act of aggression against people of color. As a result, this post does not offer a solution within dominant logics or dominant institutions. Rhetorically, there is no space in which one can both continue to be a member of the existing nation-state and continue to uphold the ideal of "equality," a term that has come to stand in for the collective concerns of constituents of the nation-state. Such a disjuncture between one's personal identity as a member of society and the inability to abide particular interests within that society militates against a solely rhetorical revolution in favor of a more actively physical one. As the poster writes, "If they want to deport us, let's send them back to the hell where the White Devils and all of their demon friends came from" ("Using"). This post articulates an outlaw logic inconsistent with dominant views articulated in mainstream U.S. culture. It states a worldview necessitating a solution that goes well beyond the strategy of reform; in this context, the society is replaced, not simply rethought or reworked. Only those who are separate from the "White Devils" and their friends are constituted as familiar subjects.

What is perhaps most striking about such forms of outlaw discourse is their seeming persistent appearance throughout the history of immigrant discourses. David J. Goldberg and John D. Rayner (1989, 166), for example, cite the words of Teodor Herzl, a Viennese journalist who covered the "Dreyfus affair" (in 1894, a French Jewish army officer was falsely accused of spying for Germany). While covering the trial, Herzl, who later became a key advocate of Zionism, noted, "Everywhere we Jews have tried honestly to assimilate into the nations around us, preserving only the religion of our fathers. We have not been permitted to.... We are a nation—the enemy has made us one without our desiring it.... We do have the strength to create a state and, moreover, a model state." What seems most striking about this is the rhetorical move to note that the "nation" or "people" has been constructed by dominant peoples according to their own interests, those that new migrant groups often experience as oppressive.

In addition to the physical destruction encouraged by this form of outlaw logic, which we consider problematic because it is dissociated from people's everyday experiences and therefore is impractical and rhetorically ineffective, it is also rhetorically problematic in terms of its relationship to the past. Michael Calvin McGee's discussion of revolution (1998, 47) is pertinent to this type of outlaw discourse. McGee distinguishes between revolutionary calls that draw from the existing social fabric and revolutionary calls that simply transcend the social and offer a plan based on a nonexisting set of conditions. In his assessment of revolutionary appeals, McGee emphasizes how closely a revolution draws upon, and uses, discourses of the past. He says that a revolution is a "bad" revolution if it calls for an overthrow of the current circumstances (e.g., government, logic, structure) but does not grow rhetorically out of the existing structures or discourses and does not posit itself as an extension of existing tradition. We share McGee's critique here because we consider this kind of ahistorical call for revolution ineffective. While all "revolution," all change, is necessarily a transformation based on tradition, one type of revolution claims to be liberating itself from the past (e.g., the example in this section), while the other (i.e., the discourse of the next section) builds on it. For McGee, opposed to the "bad" revolution (as seen above) is a "glorious" rhetorical revolution.[13] We view such a revolution as an outlaw discourse influencing the collective imagination and changing key constitutive rhetorics and logics, while appearing to grow out of existing traditions and thus engendering personal commitment to the ideological past, present, and future.

Glorious Outlaws? Redefining Immigration

A second, larger category of outlaw discourses expands notions of citizenship beyond nation-state definitions. These posts include arguments and assertions that, while overtly finding the existing grounds of judgment to be incommensurable with the "proper" bases for judgment, do so on grounds that encourage the adoption of logics of existing "peoples" and logics in a larger identity that transcends existing factional identities. Rather than rhetorically creating or emphasizing an "us" and "them," these discourses create a larger "us," sometimes in the sense of radically contingent identities (as Edward Said [1989, 225] would prefer) and sometimes in terms of fairly stable ones (e.g., children of God). Such discourses encourage people to take new, often oppositional, stances and identities.[14] For example, some articles see Proposition 187 and other policies like it as part of a larger issue of rich versus poor (e.g., "NPC: Resist"; "Student Leader"). Rhetorically, such arguments are made either by pointing out that existing senses of identity have been wrong (e.g., "We need to see each of us as an immigrant rather than distinguishing between citizens and immigrants") or by moving the grounds of judgment to an assumed "higher" level (e.g., "Rather than judging these policies on the grounds of legal rights, we need to think in terms of civil rights"). Both approaches allow traditional identities to continue (i.e., concepts of "immigrants" and "rights") as long as they fit within new policies. In both cases, the outlaw discourses are following what critical theorist Gayatri Spivak (1990, 41) suggests is a general mode of the postcolonial citation: reinscription and reworking of the historical. The postcolonial necessarily reworks the U.S. Constitution and that of others in multiple ways.[15]

More important, the outlaw logic we discuss here is not as clearly planned out and organized a "system" of thought as it might appear in our telling. While all the discourses we investigate provide a rearticulation of the meaning of immigration and stress "immigrant" rather than "citizen" as a primary subjectivity (and hence move away from litigation or civil law to a space outside of existing law, they do not draw on one another in building this subjectivity. In fact, as critical rhetoricians, we are pulling together arguments that have certain levels of disagreements with one another and building a coherent story. While we attempt to remain "faithful" to those differences, we also recognize that our job is to articulate an argument or worldview, "inventing a text suitable for criticism," in McGee's language (1990, 288). Our goal is to build an argument that could potentially bring about productive changes on a wider cultural level.

This outlaw argument, which ultimately can be seen as one that reconfigures immigration (i.e., "We are all immigrants and deserve the same respect, honor, membership, and treatment"), develops through three different strategies. These strategies, which do not often refer to one another (i.e., posters rarely refer to previous posts or arguments on the list), together lay the groundwork for an outlaw understanding of immigration, the illegitimacy of Proposition 187 in general (not just in terms of Constitutionality), and the construction of a single identity rather than the annihilation of existing systems or structures. This argument is built, first, through a discussion of guerrilla theater that problematizes the pragmatics of immigration policies requiring the display of legal identity; second, through noncompliance resolutions that ultimately deny the legitimacy of government (e.g., university, state, and federal government) on questions of immigration; and, third, through arguments that directly reconstitute the meaning of immigration either by elongating immigrant identity over generations or by elongating the narrative of any single person's life beyond the existence of the physical body.

In the first case (and the only one that builds within a single conversational thread on the list), a series of posts follow an initial one in which a student describes "guerrilla theater" performances at the University of Wisconsin–Madison and asks students at other universities to share narratives of their activities and their relative levels of success ("re: 'migra'" #1). One theme that gets repeated and becomes something of a model for activity on some campuses (at least as reported in this 187-L community) is a strategy in which students pose as agents of the INS at various locations on campus (e.g., cafeterias, classroom buildings) and demand to see ID cards from other students as proof of citizenship. A University of Wisconsin student notes that while the tactic met with limited success on his or her campus, the campus security force "misinterpreted the acts" and claimed that the guerrillas were attempting to scare foreign students, and, moreover, the overall reaction of the campus is described as evidence of "precisely this creeping fascism which we were trying to warn the internal community about" ("re: Madison"). The student goes on to argue that when it comes to questions of immigrant rights, there should be no question about whether individuals are foreigners or citizens; there is only a question of humanity. Students at Vassar ("re: 'migra'" #2) and Yale ("re: 'migra'" #1) note their successes and failures with a similar strategy and also note that they are working to make everyone understand that identification procedures are impractical, demeaning, and, in the end, inhumane because they conflate race with nationality (i.e., European immigrants and those of European ancestry are not likely to be "carded"; Mexicanas, Mexicanos, Chicanas, and Chicanos in general are more likely to be). Moreover, a student at the University of California–San Diego reports that while activities on his campus were not successful, the students at Madison should be commended in that they "obviously have brought the issue to everyone's attention and highlighted the reactionary nature of their government and administration" ("re: 'migra'" #3). In all these posts, the students articulate a vision of the current U.S. government and its immigration policies (or potential policies) that acts outside the boundaries of human decency, and they suggest that such policies cannot be tolerated because they violate civil rights regardless of legal status.

The second category of posts focuses on acts of noncompliance in which the legitimacy of normative frames of government is called into question (e.g., "Oakland School Board votes on non-compliance," "UC-Berkeley Campus"). These posts not only articulate the unconstitutionality of Proposition 187, they also express an overall dissatisfaction with and unwillingness to abide by laws in general, through noncompliance resolutions as passed by, or proposed by, numerous medical care workers, University faculty or staff, and local school boards. In a general noncompliance resolution, employees agree en masse that they will refuse to enact any element of Proposition 187 that would require anyone to act as an agent of the proposition (e.g., through checking immigration IDs or reporting illegal immigrants to INS officials). These noncompliance resolutions, more than any other examples of outlaw discourses, offer a mixture of arguments, some operating within litigation and some being incommensurable with it. That is, while those posting noncompliance resolutions often stress that workers will not comply with Proposition 187 regardless of any eventual legal determinations of its constitutionality, they also generally argue that the proposition is most likely unconstitutional (or that the resolution will cost the state a great deal of money). Hence, while they use a logic outside of dominant legal justice as the major argument justifying their decision to disregard legal determinations, they also justify their action by assuming the "unconstitutionality" of the proposition or its economic cost—both arguments that operate "in law."

For example, a member of the Oakland School Board posted a proposed noncompliance resolution before the resolution was passed by the board. While the document contains numerous arguments that function within dominant logic or dominant hierarchies of judgment (e.g., the resolution contains "whereas" statements dealing with disease and health issues, economic cost, and the assumption that the proposition is unconstitutional—all arguments made within dominant logic), the general force of the resolution is that the school board will openly direct its employees not to enforce any part of the proposition (even before appeals courts have decided on its status) on the grounds that the proposition is not in line with their "education mission" and as a result should not be enforced ("Affirmative"). Indeed, after the school board voted to support the resolution, a poster submitted news of its unanimous passage and noted that the Oakland Unified School District is "on record as refusing to comply with [Proposition 187's] terms, no matter what the outcome of the legal battle" ("Oakland School Board Votes for"). In the school board's logic, the mission of educators transcends legal determination of the proposition's validity. While the resolution makes note of dominant logic, its resolve works on the broader justification of the education of human beings. Hence, Oakland School Board members and educators can take the position that if the proposition is unconstitutional, members of the school board are happy to fit within dominant logic; if it is found to be constitutional, their actions will not fit within dominant logic. What is important is that the board is forcing dominant logic to fit their definitions and is not willing to operate on any logical grounds other than its own.

In another case, the University of California Academic Senate unanimously passed a resolution condemning Proposition 187 and refusing to follow its policies. The Academic Senate's arguments work on the same ambivalent ground as that of the Oakland School Board. While the Academic Senate notes that the proposition is being appealed and, hence, cannot currently be enforced, they also assume the proposition will be found unconstitutional. Moreover they too assert that they will not, indeed cannot, comply with the proposition regardless of its constitutionality because its enforcement would "interfere with our responsibilities as scholars and educators," undermining "the relationship of trust between faculty and students on which the University is based" ("UC Santa"). Hence, again, while the Senate assumes their stance will fall "within" the logic of dominant law, their justification is one that places some other system of judgment (i.e., scholarly responsibility, faculty-student trust) as the one standard upon which judgments should be made.[16]

A noncompliance resolution or petition also circulated through the University of California–Riverside. This document more directly argues that Proposition 187 should be seen simply as one element in a system of "overt social control" of people of color that works on the basis of "racial scapegoating" to encourage violence toward, and the exclusion of, this target group: "While couched in non-racial language, Proposition 187 is racialized" ("UC-Riverside"). Hence, in this logic, the proposition is problematic and will not be complied with because it "is part of a broader onslaught against immigrants that threatens to change the basic notion of the United States as a nation of immigrants" ("UC-Riverside"). Here, the notion of the proposition's legal status, or the legitimacy of any single person or group to make a legal decision on similar issues is, if not recognized, then at least not acknowledged—only the logic of those signing the resolution comes into play, and this logic is one that re-members the United States rhetorically as a nation of immigrants, in effect working to reconstitute everyone under the subjectivity "immigrant."

We should be cautious in our optimism about this second category of resistance to the notion of immigration, however. In *The New Helots*, Robin Cohen (1987, 141) notes that although such global concepts as the "Universal Declaration of Human Rights" might allow individuals a "legitimate" space in which to question the moral and legal limits of state policies, the policies put into place through assertions of the "Universal Declaration" are often more limited than previous state policies. That is, while calls to a universal rather than to a state subject forces the state grudgingly to grant concessions, there remains a weeding out process of some migrants who will not be protected under the "Universal Declaration" and, at the very least, a bureaucratic slowdown on granting rights produced by this litigious context. In these examples the actual protection of all students' right to education is circumscribed by an authoritarian statement from the school board or faculty senate. These groups do not give up their authority to have the final say for their constituencies.

Our final category of arguments is illustrated by a turn made in the UC-Riverside resolution to an argument that works against Proposition 187 on the basis of a struggle over the term "immigrant" and, consequently, the meaning of "citizen." While in some sense, of course, all of the documents and arguments concerning Proposition 187 are in part a struggle over "immigrant" and "immigration" as terms, the arguments in this section work on the level of the *differend* because they constitute "immigrant" as universal, rather than positing it as something that needs to be slightly broadened. Hence, in that we are all migrants in either a spiritual sense (i.e., we are all migrants on Earth on our way to another spiritual place) or a temporal sense (i.e., everyone has a heritage that is ultimately located "elsewhere"), or, alternatively, in that no one is a migrant (i.e., if borders are arbitrary, humanity has no identity from which to emigrate or to which to immigrate), "immigration" and each individual must be re-membered. In each of these definitions, the sense of time and identity is elongated—either we must think of ourselves in terms of our generational lineage or we must think of our individual lives in a temporal span that goes beyond physical being. In either case, this elongation of time simultaneously provides an identity that transcends national boundaries and places everyone outside the purview of the nation and its system of government and into transnational, global contexts. Thus, the posts in this category fundamentally challenge normative definitions of immigration and privilege definitions not specifically tied to the nation-state.

Such an argument can be found in a post that suggests that the Green Party's candidate for president in the 2000 election, Ralph Nader, must be forced to address immigration, "which is really the study of international human rights, worker rights, consumer rights" ("Re: Nader"). This claim places international rights above any nation's rules. This argument also works, however, in more complicated fashions in other posts by way of, for example, rhetorical or spiritual discussions of the term "immigrant." For example, the Catholic Bishops of Florida issued a statement that begins by noting that Jesus, Mary, and Joseph should be seen as the archetype of all refugee families who have moved in order to reach a better life. While holding up Native Americans as nonimmigrants, they argue that everyone else in the United States—brought here by force or choice—is an immigrant. Hence, in a time of world interdependence, we are asked to take a careful look at civil rights and human dignity because to do so is to "welcome the strangers who seek only to better themselves and this great nation" just as the Holy Family did ("Fla Convention"). Hence, while the bishops recognize the need for nations to establish policies concerning borders, any such policies must give first nod to the moral and ethical questions revolving around human rights. What Cohen (1991, 106) refers to as "other worldly solutions" (i.e., immigrants' myths and beliefs that their problems will be solved by external force) emerges here through an ontological frame that allows immigrants to be seen, or to see themselves, as legitimate people within a system of illegitimate or immoral laws. A "moral" law must necessarily fit within the parameter of universal rights.

One post that operates within the law nevertheless calls for the law's transformation to a global way of thinking. The post provides information about a San Francisco city voting initiative called the "San Francisco Immigrant Voting Rights Initiative" ("San Francisco"). The text of the initiative is included in the post. Section one reads, "That all noncitizens living in the city and County of San Francisco, and who otherwise would fulfill all other legal requirements to vote except that of citizenship, will be allowed to vote in all municipal elections for Mayor, Board of Supervisors, Board of Election, Community College Governing Board and local ballot initiatives." The initiative's creators are listed as members of the Immigrant Rights Movement. This post calls for voting rights for people who are not citizens and clearly goes against dominant logics and institutions by defining voting rights on grounds other than "formal citizenship," on the grounds of participation in community life. In the process, the concept of "citizen" shifts.

Some posts take for granted a "global" way of thinking. That is, they operate in terms of a larger world society and use phrases "in world terms" (e.g., "Pro-EZLN"). Within this group of posts, some argue for a "world without borders," thus objecting to nation-state citizenship and instead calling for a kind of transnational or global citizenship (e.g., "[BORDERLINES]"). For example, in a short inquiry entitled "Are We Immigrants?" the author identifies the problems of dominant vernacular discourse by pointing out that the terms of the debate have been defined by those in favor of Proposition 187 and as a result, "They have forced us into a defensive position in which we argue that 'immigrants' are an 'overall asset' rather than a 'debit' to the U.S. Fundamental questions such as 'Do 187 type laws assert power or define rights . . . remained unquestioned'" ("Are"). The poster notes that there is no justification for arguments against Proposition 187 on the grounds of dominant discourse because, in brief, we "all have the right to be here" ("Are"). It is impossible and illogical to require "a legislative grant to convey a right which existed prior to legislative enactments. This right is a right with which we are endowed not by government, but by our Creator" ("Are"). In its most limited sense, this post's argument asserts that anyone who was already living anywhere in North America is exempt from immigration policies because Europeans set up borders in North America that do not exist in a transcendent sense. In a wider sense, however, one invoked when the post ends with the phrase, "A LAND WITHOUT BORDERS," universal rights are constituted here as being granted by "a creator" rather than by governments, and hence, the post is arguing that "national" laws do not and cannot have any legitimacy on the constitution of "immigrant." While this document posits two positions that are slightly at odds (dominant logics are faulty, but our Creator [a dominant concept] provides universal rights), in both cases, the United States as an entity has no right to make determinations of immigration because it is attempting to establish boundaries that do not exist at the very broadest levels of society.

Another post questions the legitimacy of nations to define and determine migration policies. A comical post appearing quite late on the list details the actions of "The Mexican caped crusader, 'Superbarrio.'" The post, which is poached from the United Press International wire service, describes how Superbarrio Gomez, garbed in a "wrestling mask, golden cape and red tights," has announced his "symbolic candidacy for the U.S. presidency." Gomez, who (among other things) promises to eliminate the U.S. Border Patrol and the Drug Enforcement Administration, also will "permit free migration throughout North America."

The article quotes Gomez as saying, "We now have the right to intervene in their politics" ("Mexican Hero"). The article also likens the U.S. presidential election to the campaign of Adolf Hitler as führer of Germany in 1936. The article says Gomez had "the endorsement of Superman, Spider Man, Batman and the Power Rangers, among other super heroes." By constructing an imaginary context in which to critique U.S. politics, the post also fundamentally questions the basis upon which governmental U.S. logics operate with regard to immigration.

When Iain Chambers (1994, 133) writes about contemporary migrancy and cultural identity, he posits this state of identity (i.e., that "everyone is an immigrant") as a dominant part of contemporary identity. That is, he notes that "the migrant's sense of being rootless, of living between worlds, between a lost past and a non-integrated present, is perhaps the most fitting metaphor of this (post)modern condition." Chambers is arguing in a sense that in the contemporary cultural condition, the "previous margins now fold in on the center." What we illustrate in this and previous chapters is that while the notion of a universal immigrant identity might be dominant in some "academic" discourse, it still remains something of an outlaw one on the level of public discourse and argument. If we hope to follow Paul Carter's call (1992, 7–8) to disarm "the genealogical rhetoric of blood, property and frontiers," substituting in its place a rhetoric that "stresses the contingency of all definitions of self and the other, and the necessity always to tread lightly," we must be aware that the battleground for making this change is far more constrained on the level of public discourse than it seems to be on the level of academic-critical discourse. As Chambers (1994, 7) suggests, in order to produce the conditions for migrant peoples to "threaten the binary classification deployed in the construction of order," we must be aware that this threat often lends itself to disciplinary discourses that quickly cut off its critical possibilities; both dominant and (some) vernacular discourses work against that threat. The potential for outlaw discourses exists, but their possibility within the academy or in the margins of an e-mail list such as 187-L should not lead us to ignore the caution with which they must be employed in "the public," generally.

Ronald J. Deibert (1997, 157) has noted that one change we can expect in the contemporary media environment is an explosion of transnational social movements "with multiple, overlapping, and often competing interests" that represent the emergence of a "global civil society." While Deibert is concerned that all current changes work in the interests of capital, ultimately he sees the current growth in (and future dominance of) these transnational movements as offering a challenge to modern nation-states in that they provide a diffuse "dense network of social and interest-group activities across territorial-political boundaries." This chapter in some sense provides witness to a variety of potential outlaw logics that indeed work potentially as challenges to national identities, moving toward a more global and more dispersed, often contradictory, set of identities.

In each case investigated in this chapter, we see arguments that not only deny the validity of Proposition 187 within the parameters of the U.S. nation-state but also deny the legitimacy of a U.S. nation-state that could potentially make such a proposition legal. Given its illegitimacy in the realm of various conceptions of rights, a realm that transcends the rights of nations, there is an incommensurability posited between an immigration act such as Proposition 187 and what is "right" in a broader sense. While these posts and arguments sometimes acknowledge that the proposition might well be found to be unconstitutional, the primary argument of each of these documents is that migrant rights outweigh or "trump" governmental legislative rights. The very question of constitutionality is misplaced in this outlaw logic. While the reactions to the passage of the proposition vary from a proposed armed uprising to noncompliance resolutions to an imagined "land without borders," in every case a higher right is posited. In accepting the subjectivities implied by any one of these documents, the reader must shed his or her subjectivity either as a U.S. citizen or as an immigrant in exchange for a more inclusive subjectivity (e.g., universal, North American). This, in essence, sets up a *differend* in legitimacy between their new subjectivity and the rights of U.S. lawmakers and policy makers. While we certainly applaud this expansion of a legitimacy of a right outside of boundaries and while we applaud the way in which such arguments force a rethinking of the moral authority of law and legislation, we acknowledge the problematics of some of the arguments implied within these moves (e.g., Where do civil rights end and begin? What is the effect of having religion brought into the story?). Nevertheless, while outlaw discourses will always have their own problems, when we listen, we are forced to rethink our own assumptions, and this, we suggest, is always to our advantage.

7

Conclusion

Throughout this book, we use a theoretical model for examining contemporary discourses that attends to their complexity and sophistication. It consists of paying attention to who speaks, what those who speak assume to be the basis for their claims, and the perspective of the audience to whom they speak. We distinguish between civic discourse aimed at all people (but in so many instances, actually at citizens or at some other specific class of people) and vernacular discourse spoken at the local level of everyday life, as well as within local communities, with community issues in mind and to fellow community members. This distinction helps us recognize that the production and living of culture is a constant negotiation between the local spaces we inhabit and the abstract communities that link multitudes of local spaces. We also distinguish between discourses that operate within the dominant logics of powerful individuals and discourses that operate within outlaw logics in ways resistant to or indifferent to dominant discourses. This distinction emphasizes the complexity of social meaning by highlighting tensions among various logics articulated in discourse.

Our model addresses the contingencies of social location, political position, and situatedness within power structures. It suggests that resistance that challenges existing paradigms from within very often requires "thinking otherwise"—that is, honoring and promoting existing outlaw discourses. Our critical model also recognizes the need for social change and attempts to locate discourses that have the potential for substantive transformations. While working within institutions, such as courts—indeed, within various areas of legislation—has the potential for a certain kind of change, whatever change takes place there occurs within the language, logics, and contexts of those institutions. Alternatively, outlaw discourses and logics, by definition, operate in unobvious and potentially transformative ways; we encourage other students of culture like ourselves to attend to such discourses.

As critical rhetoricians, we see our own work as part of the larger cultural negotiation of what Antonio Gramsci (1971) calls "wars of position." While we do not want to overemphasize the potential social significance of critical analysis, we do want to suggest that academic work should not be seen as "outside of culture" but instead as a part of it. We see academic discourse, itself, as cultural and productive. Understanding the many ways in which academic labor interfaces with, for example, activist labor and other work toward social change is central to our project. In thinking about academics and activism, we encourage self-reflectiveness with regard to rhetorical acts made in the name of social change. Books, articles, conference papers, newspaper op-eds, television spots, and lectures make up a particular aspect of the cumulative number of rhetorical acts that take place within society; taken seriously, this work has the potential to effect a broader level of change. It is ultimately the effects of our discourses that concern us in this project.

Our examination of dominant civic discourses—those of popular television news programs and articles and magazines available in a national index, as well as the statewide discourses of the *Los Angeles Times*—reveals that these discourses both favor and oppose Proposition 187. Nevertheless, they share many logics, such as belief in bootstrapping; distinctions between good and bad immigrants and between us (citizens) and them (immigrants); constructions of immigrants as criminals (by definition as "illegals") or potential criminals (e.g., if the paternalistic state cannot provide an education); representation of immigrants as economic commodities; anxiety over a health and, ultimately, cultural contagion; commitment to the United States as a fixed nation with clear borders, fair laws, and an ideally protective Constitution; concern with nativist California issues, sometimes in opposition to an inattentive nation-state; and a racialization of contemporary immigrants that depends on racist stereotypes. Arguments against Proposition 187 often rely on rhetorical strategies that belittle—appeals to personal testimony, morality, and religion—and construct an infantile, innocent, and therefore passive immigrant subject. Although these strategies are meant to *oppose* Proposition 187, they end up reifying many of the most troubling and racist aspects of anti-immigrant rhetoric. By examining pro and anti arguments separately in chapters 3 and 4, while still pointing to their shared logics, we hope to bring a complexity to our understandings of how dominant discourses function in a civic context.

In our examination of vernacular discourse on an e-mail distribution list set up to challenge Proposition 187 we find that dominant logics still predominate, even in this activist context. Specifically, constructions of immigrants as economic units, anxiety about contagion, and faith in a trustworthy and equitable state and national court system, with the U.S. Constitution as the capstone, circulate widely in these posts. Furthermore, a general diffusion of purpose on the e-mail list away from Proposition 187 to immigration and then to social activism generally articulates a politics of disagreement rather than a more specific challenge to particular institutions. Nevertheless, textual poaching of civic discourses in the vernacular context of the list does offer a significant challenge to Proposition 187 by recontextualizing dominant logics from a critical perspective that questions truth claims, calls for activism, and reverses the dominance of English and Spanish in U.S. culture. Furthermore, as we discuss in Chapter 6, outlaw logics do emerge—although in fragmented ways—in this vernacular space. While some of these outlaw logics trouble us (e.g., those that are ahistorical, dissociated from everyday experience and therefore impractical), others offer significant challenges to both Proposition 187 and the dominant discourses that support its logic, even when they argue against it. Specifically, discussions of guerrilla theater that challenge a governmental call for display of identity, particularly in relation to racialized assumptions, problematize fixed binaries between citizen/immigrant and between legal/illegal immigrant. Additionally, noncompliance resolutions of K–12 school boards as well as University of California campuses and faculty refuse to accept the legitimacy of the government to enact or rule on Proposition 187. Finally, complex discussions of immigration across generations or beyond the boundaries of an individual and her body radically challenge the possibility of distinguishing between citizen and immigrant by drawing attention to how we are all embedded in historical and contemporary relations articulated by migration processes.

Throughout our study, we found a general tendency of discourse in both civic and vernacular contexts to operate within dominant and governmental logics as opposed to resistant logics. While acknowledging this through explicitly politically invested analysis is part of the critical rhetoric project we theorize here, we also argue for the importance of finding outlaw logics and bringing them into civic contexts through the act of criticism. Thus, Chapter 6 exemplifies some ways outlaw discourses function: that is, with cultural assumptions not of the dominant legal institutions but of those based, for example, on a global perspective, on one's religious background, or on one's role as a teacher. We are not simply encouraging people to resist the courts and legislatures of their communities but to recognize that the logics operating in those places as well as "commonsense" logics of everyday life should be taken seriously and analyzed. Additionally, we encourage readers to recognize that dominant discourses and logics need not be the only ones used to address social problems and to see the benefits that emerge and the fruitful tensions that occur when epistemologies within cultures that contradict mainstream worldviews or demand alternative ways of thinking, and often alternative solutions, are seriously considered and possibly accepted.

While one goal of this book is to theorize and enact a critical rhetoric project that is useful for students of culture in many different contexts, a second goal is to use this model to engage a specific case study. We study the rhetoric of Proposition 187 because of the tremendous effects we saw the measure having on our communities at the time it was proposed and passed. It is thus an appropriate issue for examination from a critical rhetorical perspective. Like other oppressive acts, measures, and policies (e.g., the 1882 Chinese Exclusion Act, the 1924 Immigration Act, and the incarceration of Japanese Americans during World War II), Proposition 187 pitted people against one another along lines of cultural and racial difference. Studying discourses of immigration, nation, and citizenship surrounding the Proposition 187 melee, we thought, might lead to more complex and useful public conversations about immigration, race, and contemporary culture generally. Thus, this project uses critical rhetoric to help shift understandings of borders, citizens, and the nation by suggesting the ways such terms are socially constructed through discourse, are historically contextualized, are not fixed in any indelible way, and are culturally variant.

We illustrate ways in which the border has shifted as well as ways rhetoric functionally creates the conditions for such a shift. That is, borders are provisional and are circumscribed by the discourses that attempt to fix them. Despite the fact that much discourse conceives of borders as "boundaries" and people on either side in terms of their "boundedness," borders are constantly being discussed by myriad groups with very different notions of what a border should be and, thus, cannot be said to have any particular, determinate meaning. Citizenship, too, is discussed and used in particular ways. In U.S. society, citizenship often refers to those who receive benefits, not to those who do the hard labor of society, or even those who should receive benefits. The debates over citizenship in the Proposition 187 discourse illustrate the power of the term to create insider/outsider, us/them binaries. Finally, we also examine how discourse circumscribes nation as a concept. The nation is often constructed as the entity that citizens' action should support. The national "body," that of the idealized citizen whose actions best approximate those that nationalist discourses praise, comes to be defined within discourse about immigration and Proposition 187, delineating good citizens from bad, good immigrants from bad, and good people of color from bad.

By studying and writing about Proposition 187, we hope to provide some context for future struggles, such as the fights for affirmative action, gender, race, and sexual justice, as well as for multilingual culture. While our goal has not been to provide a manual for political action, especially since there is not just one manual to be written, we do think a key part of critical rhetoric projects is to understand political events after the fact, with an eye toward shaping future political events. Such an understanding may be useful each time problematic policies arise and each time careful reflection about critical activist practice becomes necessary. This book may provide a tool kit of sorts for thinking through the many aspects of social change in contemporary postmodern spaces. For example, we discuss how to address both local and mainstream communities, what rhetorical strategies to use to make the most effective and ultimately productive change, and what kinds of boundary crossing within communities is necessary to address the multiplicity of experiences operating within complex, heterogeneous communities.

We conclude by mentioning briefly some general issues that emerge from this particular study but that nevertheless impinge upon future conversations about rhetoric, cultural studies, and political activism generally.

We begin with a brief discussion about what we might say is a preoccupation with the bodies of Mexicanas, Mexicanos, Chicanas, and

Chicanos in dominant discourses about Proposition 187 and the inti-
mately related inattention paid to undocumented Asian Pacific Americans. It is difficult to put precise figures on how many undocumented
Asian Pacific Americans live permanently or temporarily in the state of
California. Peter Kwong (1997), whose work focuses primarily on
undocumented Chinese immigrants in New York, says that a conservative estimate of the number of undocumented immigrants in the United
States would be five million, approximately 60 percent of whom are
from Mexico and Central America (235). Kwong cites Paul Smith of the
Pacific Forum, who estimates that "between 1991 and 1994, there were
25,000 Fuzhounese illegals entering the United States yearly" (97), and
that is just from one region of China. Kwong further notes that former
CIA director James Wollsey Jr. told Congress in 1994 that "some
100,000 Chinese are being smuggled into America each year" (75).
While Kwong's statistics do not estimate how many undocumented
Asian Pacific migrant people live in the state of California, certainly the
number is significant. And, given that undocumented migration affects
Asian Pacific people and Asian Pacific Americans, in addition to many
other people, we must ask: Why was the focus in Proposition 187 discourse on people from south of the U.S. border, almost exclusively?[1]

One factor that could help account for this phenomenon is that the
dominant media construction of Asian Pacific people in the United
States is as a "model minority."[2] The promotion of media images of
racial exceptionalism as applied to Asian Americans may explain why
Mexicanas, Mexicanos, Chicanas, and Chicanos were targeted as scapegoats surrounding Proposition 187 as, for women, "breeders," and, for
men, "invaders." The history of media providing images of racial exceptionalism for Asian Pacific Americans, in contrast to images of African
American and Chicana and Chicano undeservedness, dates at least to
the early 1960s civil rights era (Osajima 1988), if not to the post-"Emancipation" era, when Chinese laborers were recruited, in part, to take
low-paying jobs. The issue is not whether there is a significant number
of Asian Pacific undocumented migrant people but that by not focusing attention on undocumented Asian Pacific migrant workers and by
demonizing undocumented Mexicana, Mexicano, Chicana, and Chicano undocumented laborers, discourse functionally created racializa-
tions typical of contemporary U.S. culture. The discourse pitted those
nominated as exceptional Asian Pacific Americans against those constructed as troubled Mexicanas, Mexicanos, Chicanas, and Chicanos,

rather than recognizing common and interrelated levels of experience and traditions of oppression.

More to the point of activism, such a construction of Asian Pacific American model minorities at the expense of Mexicanas, Mexicanos, Chicanas, and Chicanos should give us pause. What is to be feared about a coalition across these lines? What possible threat exists within an alliance of migrant peoples in these groups? And, what lines of communication between groups may be affected by Proposition 187 discourse? What comparative racial dimensions exist, both internal and external to the colonial metropoles engendered by racialized immigration discourses? Perhaps the tenuous lines of communication across racially marginalized people—the different languages, traditions, and cultures, as well as the different racial positioning and the discursive production of both groups in the mainstream—are to some degree vulnerable. Nevertheless, a coalition politics that coalesces around immigration policy might have tremendous political potential to cut across various lines of difference.

The role of people of color in mainstream media, especially in print, continues to be of significance in U.S. society and continues to have an impact on racial identities. As Mercedes Lynn De Uriarte (1994, 165) points out in her review of a study conducted by Teun Van Dijk: "In television news . . . minorities are overwhelmingly portrayed as deviants, criminals, illegal aliens or failures. In entertainment, they are assimilated to white middle-class lifestyles in harmonious environments, and issues of injustice are reduced to matters of individual conflict." While, as we suggest in Chapter 2, the construction of people of color in media generally does oscillate ambivalently along a continuum of loathing and desire in the press, representations of people of color as dysfunctional, assimilated, or simply inexplicably angry predominate. Furthermore, images of one racialized group very often have dramatic effects on images of other racialized groups. Because media makers are rarely people of color, there is clearly a disproportionate number of images from one particular racial, gendered, classed, and national set of perspectives. As De Uriarte writes: "Nowhere is the struggle over history and image more critical than in the press, where minority participation is severely limited. Today, fewer than 7 percent of all newspaper journalists are African American, about 2.5 percent are Latino, 1 percent are Asian American and .03 percent are Native American" (167–68).

We hope our study helps alter the responses one can make to such limiting media constructions, not only by bringing a critical lens to what media produce but also by using strategically constructed and organized rhetorical responses to do surgery on the body of the culture in which we live. Through these responses, we can demonstrate how it is possible to threaten the dominant constructions of race, immigration, gender, and class as well as other marginal positions by examining outlaw rhetorical positions. Further, calling attention to the way bodies function, and can function, outside of dominant media constructions may encourage the social boundary crossing, the many border crossings needed, to effect substantive social change in our communities.

In the contemporary era of transnational global capital and migration, in the era of the North American Free Trade Agreement (NAFTA), the General Agreement on Trade and Tariffs (GATT), and the Asia Pacific Economic Cooperation (APEC), when governments nervously try to refurbish national boundaries even while corporations and their global, tentacular reaches significantly determine the contours of capital flow as well as laws regulating capital exchange, land use, and acquisition, careful attention to the construction of race and immigration in contemporary society is sorely needed. Whereas the study of U.S. racial politics has traditionally meant a focus on internal colonies, in the era of transnational global capitalism, the study of race must be conceived as functioning within often contradictory internal and external neocolonial processes. Thus, one needs to recognize the role, say, of corporations from Newly Industrialized Countries (NICS), such as Taiwan, Singapore, and Hong Kong, in multiracial locations.

Another example of this need for a more global outlook on immigration discourses and practices would be sweatshop labor in Saipan. It is important to recognize that immigration policies in the United States that make it more difficult for documented and undocumented migrant peoples to survive do not end the corporate exploitation of laborers. Transnational corporations and U.S.–subsidized enterprises continue to rely heavily on cheap labor wherever such labor is available. Harsher immigration laws and policies in the United States may, in the transnational marketplace, simply be a sign of a trend toward increased labor exploitation abroad. Indeed, ironically, such policies may imply a shift away from exploitation of migrant laborers to exploitation by migrating corporations elsewhere, where there may be fewer laws regulating the use of human capital. As George Lipsitz (1998, 55) says, "Low wages, low taxes, weak unions, high unemployment, and nonenforce-ment of environmental protection laws make maquiladora plants the locus of terrible exploitation and disruption in Mexico." That is, while policies in the United States such as Proposition 187 may at least sug-gest that exploitable labor is no longer acceptable, in the transnational, global world in which we live, such policies, in fact, may encourage greater exploitation of workers migrating from the same parts of the world to locations other than the United States. So, for example, a news article headlined "Saipan Sweatshop Claims Settled by Retailers" (1999) reports that Nordstrom, J. Crew, and other U.S.–based retailers allegedly were selling "clothing tagged 'Made in the USA'" that was in fact being made in Saipan factories "mostly owned by Chinese, Japa-nese and Korean subcontractors." The article says the companies had allegedly not been paying duties, tariffs, and quotas and had not been operating in compliance with U.S. labor laws and international human rights treaties. All of this is to say that the scope of discussions of migra-tion, nation, and citizenship will need to be increasingly global in order to address the complexity of gender, race, and nation contemporarily— indeed to address the issue of global human capital practices in general.

By conducting research from this perspective, we realize the inter-disciplinary nature of our approach. Rhetorical studies, such as our own, that draw on rhetorical research historically, but also contend seriously with issues of social and cultural significance, say something about the way knowledges have been segmented and conceived as disciplinary practices and continue to be conceived so by many in the present. Our research attempts to broaden the approach one takes to research and tries not to remain insularly within traditional academic disciplinary modes of address that very often lead to theoretical obfuscation. We see such an approach as part of an attempt to address the social divisions between the academy and other everyday social contexts. In this approach, we see the potential to take academic analysis to the day-to-day level at which issues of cultural and social significance are addressed, and in reverse to broach issues of everyday living in order to alter aca-demic practices.

Proposition 187 and the federal welfare and immigration legislation it helped spawn continue to resonate in and on the bodies of people in California and beyond. It is, for many in California, a resonant feature of daily living. In mentioning our project to people in California from various walks of life over these past five years of research, we have received responses ranging from apparent shock to immediate interest. Whatever the response, the very bodies of people to whom we mentioned our project immediately reacted. Thus, mention of the issue itself often manifests itself physically, even today, years after voters approved the proposition. Proposition 187 discourse registers powerfully in peoples' lives. For some, it presages a return to a scapegoating racializing discourse reminiscent of World War II. For others, it necessitates a vigilant rhetorical project able to respond to the contemporary circumstances of everyday life. And, yet for others it symbolizes the taking back of what is rightfully "ours."

Whether about ethnic Albanians, Kurds, Brazilians, Nigerians, or other groups, rhetorics of immigration fundamentally script the boundaries of future performances. Our goal in this project has been to attend to the popular frameworks—both civic and vernacular—that circumscribe such boundaries. Like Rey Chow (1990–91, 132), we have asked: If popular cultural "forms provide alternative practical consciousnesses to the dominant ideology, are the modes of subversion and resistance in them not infinitely reabsorbed by the dominant culture?" While our discussion in chapters 4 and 5 suggests the answer is yes, we are not willing to let our analysis end there. Instead, we additionally suggest that there are outlaw discourses and that they can be used to alter dominant logics and institutions as they come to replace and cover over the dominant logics and institutions they ultimately subvert.

This attention to outlaw discourses is not a call for a "human rights" paradigm based on the law of the United Nations. We neither believe the United Nations speaks for subaltern people nor believe in advocating worldwide policies that universally prescribe right behaviors. Nevertheless, we respect efforts of people such as Mallika Dutt (1998) who seek to make political conversations global conversations. And we respect her for taking on the challenging task of working through many problematic conceptions of "human rights" as well as the complex negotiation of at times contrasting interests such as race and gender. However, and we think she would agree with us on this point, any paradigms unable to see the pragmatic necessity of other and multiple grounded worldviews, multiple positions of subordination, and multiple ways of conceptualizing social change are bound to failure, even if such paradigms have within them self-critical, analytical resources with which to question their approach. Leti Volpp (1996), for example, critically examines First World Western feminist projects that make general calls for the liberation of Third World women from what are conceived of as dysfunctional cultural contexts. As Volpp suggests, such a vision does not recognize the grounded worldviews of other positions of subordination (e.g., feminist migrant women in the West and colonized people in the Third World) and thus centers a white middle-class, Western feminism as the frame through which to understand global issues. Thus, projects toward liberation are in no way immune from potential colonizing effects, even when they are conducted with the best intentions in mind.

This is to say that at different times, different strategies, appeals, and modes of employment will be effective. Whether it is the Nonaligned movement (Gupta 1992) or the efforts of Global Women's Rights (Dutt 1998), no one movement can have all the answers. Furthermore, centering "human rights," which have, for most of the period during which Europeans have been in the Americas, been conceived in terms of "free white [heterosexual] men,"[3] may be yet another form of colonization without proper attention to the legacy of Western humanism and its tendency toward destructiveness. It is in our view the critic's role to seek out that logic, that subordinated resistance, those excluded positions that have the potential to challenge whatever happens to be the structuring ideological and material principles and realities of the largest number of people at any given time. Such an approach may help address large-scale and long-standing economic, political, cultural, and historical imbalances of power.

When working on projects with social change in mind, one is always faced with questions about the interface of cultures and, therefore, must always guard against conspicuous colonizing logics in order to seek the register of knowing and living that helps explain oppression within the contexts Chow refers to when asking us to listen "otherwise." Our journey requires that we address issues and questions such as those surrounding immigration in ways that require us not to resort to, as a friend of ours is fond of saying, a logic of having "everything all worked out ahead of time." The challenge today is to listen to and to hear what is being spoken but not being heard that should be, and to encourage others to do the same.

Appendix

Excerpts from the Proposition 187 Ballot

 **Illegal Aliens. Ineligibility for Public Services.
Verification and Reporting. Initiative Statute.**

Official Title and Summary Prepared by the Attorney General

**ILLEGAL ALIENS. INELIGIBILITY FOR PUBLIC SERVICES.
VERIFICATION AND REPORTING. INITIATIVE STATUTE.**

- Makes illegal aliens ineligible for public social services, public health care services (unless emergency under federal law), and public school education at elementary, secondary, and post-secondary levels.
- Requires various state and local agencies to report persons who are suspected illegal aliens to the California Attorney General and the United States Immigration and Naturalization Service. Mandates California Attorney General to transmit reports to Immigration and Naturalization Service and maintain records of such reports.
- Makes it a felony to manufacture, distribute, sell or use false citizenship or residence documents.

**Summary of Legislative Analyst's
Estimate of Net State and Local Government Fiscal Impact:**

- Annual savings of roughly $200 million to the state and local governments (primarily counties), due to reduced costs for public social services, health care and higher education.
- Annual administrative costs of tens of millions of dollars (potentially more than $100 million in the first year) to the state and local governments (primarily counties and public schools) to verify citizenship or legal status of students and parents and persons seeking health care and/or social services.
- Places at possible risk billions of dollars annually in federal funding for state and local education, health and welfare programs due to conflicts between the measure's provisions and federal requirements.

Analysis by the Legislative Analyst

Background

According to the 1990 census, more than one in five Californians were born in another country. The number of California residents who are foreign-born now totals about 7 million. Currently, about 300,000 new residents enter the state each year from foreign countries. Federal law governs immigration, and the U.S. Immigration and Naturalization Service (INS) administers and enforces those laws.

Illegal Immigrants

The INS estimates that California's foreign-born population as of April 1994 included roughly 1.6 million unauthorized immigrants and that this number has been increasing by about 125,000 each year. Other terms applied to unauthorized immigrants include "illegal immigrants" and "illegal aliens."

Most illegal immigrants who come to California enter the country without any authorization. However, at least a third of illegal immigrants in California originally entered the country legally, but on a temporary basis—as a tourist or student, for example—and then remained after their departure date. An illegal immigrant may later become "legal" by receiving permission from the INS to remain in the country temporarily or as a permanent resident. The amnesty granted by the federal 1986 Immigration Reform and Control Act legalized about 1.6 million former illegal immigrants in California. Illegal immigrants also may become legalized through regular immigration processes or by claiming asylum from persecution in their home country.

Health and Welfare Benefits.   Illegal immigrants generally are not eligible for welfare grants. However, illegal immigrants do qualify for some social services and health care programs that are available to all Californians. For instance:
- Any child in need may receive child welfare services or foster care.
- Illegal immigrants may receive some of the health care services available to other poor people.

Public Education.   Any child who lives in California may attend public schools through high school. The U.S. Supreme Court has determined (in the case of *Plyler versus Doe*) that excluding children who are illegal immigrants from public schools violates the federal constitution. This decision, however, does not apply to publicly funded higher education. Currently, illegal immigrants may attend public colleges and universities in California. However, the University of California (UC) and the California Community Colleges (CCC) generally require students who are identified as illegal immigrants to pay the higher tuition charged to nonresident students. The California State University (CSU) currently does not charge higher fees based on the legal status of the student.

Citizen Children.   Under the U.S. Constitution, children born in this country to illegal immigrant parents are U.S. citizens—just like any other child born here. Many illegal immigrant families in California have citizen children, who have the same rights and are entitled to the same benefits as any other citizen.

Verifying a Person's Legal Status

The United States has no universal national identity card, so documenting citizenship or legal immigration status can be complex, even for native-born citizens.

Generally, several documents are needed—for example, a U.S. birth certificate to establish the basis for citizenship and a driver's license with a photo to establish identity. However, many people (especially children) do not have a driver's license or other official photo identification. Documenting citizenship for these people may involve additional steps, such as verifying the identity of a child's parents.

Most legal immigrants have an identification from the INS to verify their status, such as a "green card" issued to immigrants granted permanent residence in the U.S. The INS has developed a computer system that government agencies and employers can use to check the validity of most types of immigration documents. No similar nationwide automated system exists to check the validity of birth certificates, which are issued by thousands of local agencies throughout the country.

Federal Program Requirements

State and local agencies must comply with a variety of federal laws in order to receive federal funds for many education, health and welfare programs. These laws often set out who is eligible for a program, procedures for granting or denying benefits or services, and requirements for keeping records confidential. For example, the Family Educational Rights and Privacy Act (FERPA) generally prohibits schools that receive federal funds from disclosing information in student records without parental consent.

Proposal

Generally, this initiative prohibits state and local government agencies from providing publicly funded education, health care, welfare benefits, or social services to any person that they do not verify as either a U.S. citizen or a person legally admitted to the U.S. The measure also requires state and local agencies to report suspected illegal immigrants to the INS and certain state officials. These changes are described below.

Verification Requirements

The measure does not set out any specific requirements as to how verification of citizenship or legal presence in the United States would be done. As a result, individual public agencies and institutions could choose a variety of verification methods. They might require only a birth certificate or INS document, or they also might require a driver's license or other official photo identification. A more thorough verification process would attempt to check the validity of immigration documents and possibly also birth certificates with the issuing agency.

Exclusion of Suspected Illegal Immigrants from Public Schools

Starting on January 1, 1995, the initiative requires every school district to verify the legal status of every child enrolling in the district for the very first time. By January 1, 1996, each school district must also verify the legal status of children already enrolled in the district and of the parents or guardians of all students. The measure requires school districts to take the following steps if they "reasonably suspect" that a student, parent, or guardian is not legally in the U.S.:

- Within 45 days, report the person to the INS, the State Superintendent of Public Instruction, the California Attorney General, and to the affected parent or guardian.

- Provide 90 days of additional instruction to a suspected illegal immigrant student in order to accomplish an orderly transition to a school in the student's country of origin. After this 90-day period the student no longer could attend public school in California.

The exclusion of suspected illegal immigrant children from public schools would be in direct conflict with the U.S. Supreme Court's ruling in *Plyler versus Doe* that guarantees access to public education for all children in the United States. Consequently, this provision of the initiative would not be effective. Under the *Plyler* decision the measure still might require school districts to verify citizenship and legal status and to report suspected illegal immigrants, even though districts could not exclude any students from schools. Alternatively, the courts might decide that the verification and reporting requirements have an unacceptable "chilling effect" on school attendance and therefore invalidate these requirements.

Exclusion of Suspected Illegal Immigrants from Public Colleges and Universities

The initiative prohibits public colleges and universities from allowing students to attend who are not legally authorized to be in the United States. The affected institutions include the UC, the CSU, and the CCC. The measure requires public colleges and universities to verify the citizenship or legal status of each student at the beginning of every term or semester after January 1, 1995. If the college or university reasonably suspects that a student or applicant for admission is an illegal immigrant, then it must report its findings within 45 days to the INS, the State Superintendent of Public Instruction, the California Attorney General, and to the affected student or applicant.

Restrictions on Health Care and Social Services for Suspected Illegal Immigrants

The measure requires public agencies and publicly funded health care facilities to verify that a person is a U.S. citizen or is legally authorized to be in the United States before providing that person with social services (including welfare benefits) or health care services, except for emergency health care required by federal law. If an agency or health care facility reasonably suspects that an applicant for benefits or services is an illegal immigrant, then it must report its findings to the INS, the California Attorney General, the State Department of Social Services, or the Department of Health Services, as appropriate, and to the affected person. The reporting agency or facility also must provide any additional information that the other agencies request.

Reporting Arrests Involving Suspected Illegal Immigrants

The measure requires every state and local law enforcement agency to attempt to verify the legal status of every arrestee who is suspected of being in the United States illegally. The agencies would have to report anyone they arrest who they suspect is an illegal immigrant to the INS and to the State Attorney General. The initiative also requires the Attorney General to maintain records of these reports.

New Crimes for Making or Using False Documents

The initiative creates two new state felonies for manufacture or use of false documents to conceal true immigration or citizenship status. The penalties for these

crimes would be prison terms of five years or fines of up to $75,000 (for manufac-
turing) or up to $25,000 (for use). The manufacture or use of false immigration or
citizenship documents currently are federal crimes. Forgery of state documents, such
as driver's licenses, or obtaining them by fraud is currently a state crime.

Fiscal Effect

The most significant fiscal effects of this initiative fall into the following three
categories:

- *Program Savings.*   The state and local governments (primarily counties)
  would realize savings from denying certain benefits and services to persons
  who cannot document their citizenship or legal immigration status. These
  savings could be in the range of $200 million annually, based on the current
  estimated use of these benefits and services by illegal immigrants.
- *Verification Costs.*   The state, local governments, and schools would incur
  significant costs to verify citizenship or immigration status of students, parents, persons seeking health care or social services, and persons who are
  arrested. Ongoing annual costs could be in the tens of millions of dollars, with
  first-year costs considerably higher (potentially in excess of $100 million).
- *Potential Losses of Federal Funds.*   The measure places at risk up to $15
  billion annually in federal funding for education, health and welfare programs due to conflicts with federal requirements.

All of these fiscal effects are subject to a great deal of uncertainty. The use of
services by illegal immigrants can only be roughly estimated. In addition, the measure's fiscal effects could depend on legal interpretations of the measure.

Below, we discuss the significant fiscal impacts of the measure.

Health Care Savings

Federal law requires health facilities to provide necessary emergency care to any
person in need regardless of income or legal status. This measure would not restrict
this care. The measure, however, would place restrictions on nonemergency care
provided with public funds.

Medi-Cal.   The Medi-Cal program provides a full range of medical services to
poor families with children, as well as to poor elderly and disabled people. The program is funded jointly by the state and the federal government. Generally, illegal
immigrants are eligible only for emergency Medi-Cal services. However, California chooses to provide (using only state funds) prenatal care to pregnant women
and nursing home care to elderly or disabled persons who are illegal immigrants.
The measure would eliminate these services, which would result in an annual state
savings of about $100 million.

County Indigent Health Care.   Counties provide basic medical services to poor
residents who have no insurance and are not covered by another program (such as
Medi-Cal). This measure would prohibit counties from providing nonemergency
medical care to anyone whose citizenship or legal presence in the United States
could not be verified. Denying these services to illegal immigrants would result in
savings to counties and the state. However, reductions in special federal payments
to hospitals would offset a significant portion of the county savings—possibly half.
Hospitals receive these federal payments for serving large numbers of poor people

without compensation. The net annual savings, after taking into account the reduced federal payments, would be in the tens of millions of dollars to counties and several million dollars to the state.

Denying Some Services May Increase Future Costs. Denying some medical services to illegal immigrants could result in future increased state and local health care costs. For example, eliminating prenatal services to illegal immigrant women could result in higher Medi-Cal costs for their infants, who would be citizens. In addition, failure to treat and control serious contagious diseases, such as tuberculosis, among illegal immigrants could increase future costs to treat the disease in the general population.

Social Services

Currently, any child in need may receive child welfare services or foster care benefits under Aid to Families with Dependent Children (AFDC). These programs are supported by federal, state, and county funds. Initially, counties provide foster care for illegal immigrant children at their own expense. After the INS indicates that a child in foster care will not be deported, the state and the federal government share in the cost.

This measure would prohibit counties and the state from providing these services and benefits to children whose citizenship or legal status has not been verified. Withholding these services would result in annual savings of roughly $50 million to the counties and the state.

Public Schools

Based on the INS estimate of the total illegal immigrant population in California, we estimate that roughly 300,000 students in California public schools, out of a total of 5.3 million, are illegal immigrants. Excluding all of these students from public schools could save the state up to $1.2 billion annually. However, the U.S. Supreme Court decision in *Plyler versus Doe* held that illegal immigrants could not be denied a public education, so these savings would not be realized.

Public Colleges and Universities

The UC charges identified illegal immigrant students nonresident tuition. The CCC charges these students nonresident tuition if they are taking courses for credit. This tuition generally covers the state's cost of educating these students. Consequently, there would not be any net savings from excluding these already-identified students from those institutions. However, there would be savings from this measure if more students who are currently paying resident tuition are identified as illegal immigrants and excluded as a result of more frequent and/or thorough verification.

The CSU and the CCC (for noncredit courses) do not charge students nonresident tuition on the basis of the student's legal status. The CSU's annual cost per student is about $3,000 higher than the amount of resident fees. The CCC's annual net cost per noncredit student is $1,500. Consequently, excluding illegal immigrant students from the CSU and from noncredit courses at the CCC would result in savings.

Overall, this measure would result in savings to public colleges and universities that could be up to tens of millions of dollars annually.

Potential Risk of Losing Federal Funds

The measure requires school districts to report students who are suspected illegal immigrants to the INS and the state Attorney General. Making these reports without parental consent appears to violate the FERPA. Compliance with FERPA is a condition of receiving federal education funds, which total about $2.3 billion annually to school districts in California. The Secretary of the U.S. Department of Education has indicated that the reporting requirement in this measure could jeopardize the ability of California school districts to receive these funds.

Public colleges and universities in California receive at least $1.1 billion in federal funds subject to FERPA requirements. For these institutions, FERPA prohibits release of student information without the student's consent. The measure's reporting requirements also would put these funds in jeopardy.

Federal matching funds for the AFDC program and the Medi-Cal program also would be put at risk by the measure's reporting requirements. Existing federal and state law require verification of legal status in order for persons to qualify for most benefits and services provided by these programs. However, federal regulations require the state and counties to keep confidential the information provided by applicants in order to continue receiving federal matching funds. The total amount of federal funds at stake is about $3 billion in the AFDC program, and more than $9 billion in the Medi-Cal program.

Other provisions in the measure may conflict with federal laws that (1) establish procedures agencies must follow before they can deny health or welfare benefits to anyone and (2) make some immigrants who do not have formal legal status eligible for benefits.

In total, the measure places at risk about $15 billion of federal funds. Given the magnitude of this potential loss, the state and federal governments would likely seek ways to avoid, or at least minimize, the loss. A solution, however, would likely require changes in state and/or federal laws.

Verification and Reporting Costs

This measure would impose significant administrative costs on the state and local governments to meet its verification provisions. These costs could vary considerably, depending on the verification methods used.

Public Schools.   School districts could incur large costs in 1995 in order to meet the measure's deadline of January 1, 1996 to verify all students and their parents. These one-time costs could range anywhere from tens of millions of dollars to in excess of $100 million. Ongoing costs for verification would be less, potentially in the tens of millions of dollars annually statewide.

Public Colleges and Universities.   These institutions currently review the legal status of many students, primarily to determine whether they qualify for resident tuition. The measure, however, requires these institutions to verify the legal status of all of their students (1.9 million statewide) at the beginning of each semester or term. This requirement probably would cost public colleges and universities a total of at least several million dollars annually.

Social Service Agencies.   County welfare offices currently must verify the legal status of persons applying for welfare benefits in the AFDC or county general assistance programs. There would be some additional costs, possibly several million dollars annually statewide, to verify legal status in a variety of smaller programs, such as child welfare services.

Publicly Funded Health Care Facilities. The legal status of Medi-Cal recipients must be verified under current law (generally by the county welfare office or the Social Security Administration). This measure also requires verification of persons seeking other publicly funded health services, such as county indigent health care and various public health services. The cost of this verification process to counties and UC hospitals could be up to several million dollars annually.

Law Enforcement

The costs to local law enforcement agencies to report suspected illegal immigrants to the Attorney General could be up to $5 million annually. The state costs to process the information from local law enforcement and other reporting agencies (such as school districts) would be at least several millions of dollars annually.

New Crimes

By creating new state crimes for making or using false documents to conceal legal status, this measure could increase state and local costs to arrest, prosecute, and incarcerate violators. However, these activities already constitute federal crimes and also may be covered under existing state laws. The state and local governments would incur additional costs only to the extent that more persons are apprehended for these crimes and prosecuted under state law. However, the state cost would be about $2 million annually for every hundred persons incarcerated. These costs could be offset in part by revenue from fines.

---

187 | Illegal Aliens. Ineligibility for Public Services. Verification and Reporting. Initiative Statute.

Argument in Favor of Proposition 187

California can strike a blow for the taxpayer that will be heard across America; in Arizona, in Texas and in Florida in the same way Proposition 13 was heard across the land.

Proposition 187 will go down in history as the voice of the people against an arrogant bureaucracy.

WE CAN STOP ILLEGAL ALIENS.

If the citizens and the taxpayers of our state wait for the politicians in Washington and Sacramento to stop the incredible flow of ILLEGAL ALIENS, California will be in economic and social bankruptcy.

We have to act and ACT NOW! On our ballot, Proposition 187 will be the first giant stride in ultimately ending the ILLEGAL ALIEN invasion.

It has been estimated that ILLEGAL ALIENS are costing taxpayers in excess of 5 billion dollars a year.

While our own citizens and legal residents go wanting, those who choose to enter our country ILLEGALLY get royal treatment at the expense of the California taxpayer.

IT IS TIME THIS STOPS!

Welfare, medical and educational benefits are the magnets that draw these ILLEGAL ALIENS across our borders.

Senator Robert Byrd (D-West Virginia), who voted against federal reimbursement for state funds spent on ILLEGAL ALIENS, said "states must do what they can for themselves".

PROPOSITION 187 IS CALIFORNIA'S WAY.

Should those ILLEGALLY here receive taxpayer subsidized education including college?

Should our children's classrooms be over-crowded by those who are ILLEGALLY in our country?

Should our Senior Citizens be denied full service under Medi-Cal to subsidize the cost of ILLEGAL ALIENS?

Should those ILLEGALLY here be able to buy and sell forged documents without penalty?

Should tax paid bureaucrats be able to give sanctuary to those ILLEGALLY in our country?

If your answer to these questions is NO, then you should support Proposition 187.

The federal government and the state government have been derelict in their duty to control our borders. It is the role of our government to end the benefits that draw people from around the world who ILLEGALLY enter our country. Our government actually entices them.

Passage of Proposition 187 will send a strong message that California will no longer tolerate the dereliction of the duty by our politicians.

Vote YES on Proposition 187.

The Save Our State Coalition is comprised of Democrats, Republicans and Independents. It includes all races, colors and creeds with the same common denominator. We are American, by birth or naturalization; we are Americans!

We were outraged when our State Legislature voted on July 5th to remove dental care as a medical option and force the increase of the cost of prescription drugs for Senior Citizens. Then, as a final slap in the face, they voted to continue free pre-natal care for ILLEGAL ALIENS!

Vote YES ON PROPOSITION 187. ENOUGH IS ENOUGH!

ASSEMBLYMAN DICK MOUNTJOY
Author of Proposition 187
RONALD PRINCE
Chairman of the "Save Our State" Committee
MAYOR BARBARA KILEY
Co-Chair of the "Save Our State" Committee

Rebuttal to Argument in Favor of Proposition 187

Proposition 187 promoters claim their initiative would go down in history. We agree.

- PROPOSITION 187 IS ONE OF THE MOST POORLY DRAFTED INITIATIVES IN CALIFORNIA'S HISTORY.

"The initiative is filled with provisions that collide with state and federal laws, state and U.S. constitutional protections and with state and federal court rulings."

—California Senate Office of Research

- PROPOSITION 187 ALSO MAY SET A RECORD FOR COSTING TAXPAYERS $10 BILLION!

"Because the requirements of the S.O.S. initiative (187) violate federal Medicaid law, the state's entire Medi-Cal program would be in jeopardy of losing all regular Medicaid funding . . ."

"To make up for the upwards of $7 billion in lost federal funds, state spending on Medi-Cal would have to double."

—National Health Law Program

". . . school districts will most likely be required to disclose information from education records in violation of FERPA (Family Educational Rights and Privacy Act) in order to comply with the proposed State law (Proposition 187)."

As a result, *"schools would no longer be able to receive Federal education funds."*

—U.S. Secretary of Education Richard Riley

California's Senate Office of Research estimates the loss to our public schools and colleges could exceed $3 billion.

Proposition 187 would go down in history, all right. If approved, 187 would be long remembered as the initiative that TOOK A BAD SITUATION AND MADE IT MUCH WORSE—$10 BILLION WORSE!

Meanwhile, PROPOSITION 187 DOES ABSOLUTELY NOTHING TO BEEF UP ENFORCEMENT AT THE BORDER or CRACK DOWN on EMPLOYERS WHO HIRE UNDOCUMENTED WORKERS.

VOTE NO on PROPOSITION 187!

PAT DINGSDALE
President, California State PTA
MICHAEL B. HILL, M.D.
President, American College of Emergency Physicians, California Chapter
HOWARD L. OWENS
Legislative Director, Congress of California Seniors

Arguments printed on this page are the opinions of the authors and have not been checked for accuracy by any official agency.

Illegal Aliens. Ineligibility for Public Services. Verification and Reporting. Initiative Statute. | 187

Argument Against Proposition 187

Something must be done to stop the flow of illegal immigrants coming across the border.

Unfortunately, PROPOSITION 187 DOESN'T DO A THING TO BEEF UP ENFORCEMENT AT THE BORDER. It doesn't even crack down on employers who hire illegal immigrants.

Illegal immigration is a REAL problem, but Proposition 187 is NOT A REAL SOLUTION. It's not even a start in the right direction.

Proposition 187 would only COMPOUND EXISTING PROBLEMS and cause a host of new ones—EXPENSIVE ones!

PROPOSITION 187 COULD END UP COSTING TAXPAYERS $10 BILLION.

Education, health care and legal analysts all come to the same conclusion. Because Proposition 187 is POORLY DRAFTED, it directly conflicts with several important federal laws. As a result, CALIFORNIA COULD LOSE BILLIONS in FEDERAL FUNDING.

Even the U.S. Secretary of Education has concluded Proposition 187 could cause California schools to lose federal funds. Our schools could lose more than $3 BILLION.

Health care experts have further determined Proposition 187 could cost California $7 BILLION in lost federal funding for Medi-Cal for seniors and other legal residents.

PROPOSITION 187 WOULD TURN OUR SCHOOLS INTO IMMIGRATION OFFICES.

It requires public school officials to thoroughly verify the citizenship of EVERY child and EVERY parent—more than 10 MILLION people.

The costs and time involved in undertaking this PAPERWORK NIGHTMARE is impossible to calculate. Schools already are hurting from budget cuts. Proposition 187 would divert even more funds away from classrooms.

PROPOSITION 187 WOULD KICK 400,000 KIDS OUT OF SCHOOL AND ONTO THE STREETS.

An estimated 400,000 KIDS would be kicked out of school, but Proposition 187 WON'T result in their deportation. Just what we need—400,000 kids hanging out on street corners. We all know what happens to kids who don't finish school.

Is this supposed to reduce CRIME and GRAFFITI?

PROPOSITION 187 CREATES A POLICE STATE MENTALITY.

It forces public officials to deny vital services to anyone they SUSPECT might not be a legal resident. But Proposition 187 doesn't define the basis for such suspicion. Is it the way you speak? The sound of your last name? The shade of your skin?

PROPOSITION 187 THREATENS THE HEALTH OF ALL CALIFORNIANS.

It would forbid doctors and nurses from giving immunizations or basic medical care to anyone SUSPECTED of being an illegal immigrant.

Every day, hundreds of thousands of undocumented workers HANDLE OUR FOOD SUPPLY in the fields and restaurants. Denying them basic health care would only SPREAD COMMUNICABLE DISEASES THROUGHOUT OUR COMMUNITIES and place us ALL at risk.

PROPOSITION 187 COULD COST TAXPAYERS $10 BILLION, BUT IT WON'T STOP THE FLOW OF ILLEGAL IMMIGRANTS OVER THE BORDER.

Illegal immigration is ILLEGAL. Isn't it time we enforce the law?

Proposition 187 doesn't beef up enforcement at the border or crack down on the employers who continue to hire illegal immigrants.

Send the politicians a message. Tell them to start enforcing the law. VOTE NO on PROPOSITION 187.

SHERMAN BLOCK
Sheriff, Los Angeles County
D. A. ("DEL") WEBER
President, California Teachers Association
RALPH R. OCAMPO, M.D.
President, California Medical Association

Rebuttal to Argument Against Proposition 187

The argument against Proposition 187 is emotional, thoughtless and pure mindless babble.

The real opponents of Proposition 187, the special interests who have pledged millions of dollars to defeat our initiative, have a deep financial interest in continuing the present policy. Remember. Illegal aliens are a big business for public unions and well connected medical clinics. You pay the bills, they reap the benefits.

These monied interests have the unmitigated gall to tell the California voter that by ending illegal immigration the cost to the taxpayer will skyrocket! Are they out of their minds?

Their argument states that passage of Proposition 187:

"doesn't crack down on employers."

FEDERAL LAW ALREADY PROHIBITS HIRING ILLEGALS.

"187 could end up costing taxpayers $10 billion."

NONSENSE. HOW CAN GETTING RID OF THE PRESENT COSTS END UP COSTING MORE?

they say, "187 is badly written." NONSENSE.

THE SPECIAL INTERESTS ATTACKING PROPOSITION 187 INCLUDE THE CALIFORNIA TEACHERS ASSOCIATION AND THE CALIFORNIA MEDICAL ASSOCIATION. BOTH CONSTITUTE THE STATE'S BIGGEST LOBBYING GROUPS WHO OPPOSE US. THEY PROTECT THEIR OWN INTERESTS—NOT YOURS.

Don't be deceived by greedy, special interests that benefit from the failures in our immigration policies.

Why should we give more comfort and consideration to illegal aliens than to *our* needy American citizens? Many aged and mentally impaired Americans go without government largesse. Isn't it time to consider our citizens?

The groups spending millions to maintain the failures of the status quo only do so for their own selfishness. VOTE YES ON PROPOSITION 187.

ASSEMBLYMAN DICK MOUNTJOY
Author, Proposition 187/S.O.S.
CONGRESSMAN JAY KIM
Advisor, Proposition 187/S.O.S.
JESSE LAGUNA
Chairman, Border Solution Task Force

Arguments printed on this page are the opinions of the authors and have not been checked for accuracy by any official agency.

Proposition 187: Text of Proposed Law

This initiative measure is submitted to the people in accordance with the provisions of Article II, Section 8 of the Constitution.

This initiative measure adds sections to various codes; therefore, new provisions proposed to be added are printed in *italic type* to indicate that they are new.

PROPOSED LAW

SECTION 1.   Findings and Declaration.

The People of California find and declare as follows:

That they have suffered and are suffering economic hardship caused by the presence of illegal aliens in this state.

That they have suffered and are suffering personal injury and damage caused by the criminal conduct of illegal aliens in this state.

That they have a right to the protection of their government from any person or persons entering this country unlawfully.

Therefore, the People of California declare their intention to provide for cooperation between their agencies of state and local government with the federal government, and to establish a system of required notification by and between such agencies to prevent illegal aliens in the United States from receiving benefits or public services in the State of California.

SECTION 2.   Manufacture, Distribution or Sale of False Citizenship or Resident Alien Documents: Crime and Punishment.

Section 113 is added to the Penal Code, to read:

113.   Any person who manufactures, distributes or sells false documents to conceal the true citizenship or resident alien status of another person is guilty of a felony, and shall be punished by imprisonment in the state prison for five years or by a fine of seventy-five thousand dollars ($75,000).

SECTION 3.   Use of False Citizenship or Resident Alien Documents: Crime and Punishment.

Section 114 is added to the Penal Code, to read:

114.   Any person who uses false documents to conceal his or her true citizenship or resident alien status is guilty of a felony, and shall be punished by imprisonment in the state prison for five years or by a fine of twenty-five thousand dollars ($25,000).

SECTION 4.   Law Enforcement Cooperation with INS.

Section 834b is added to the Penal Code, to read:

834b.   (a) Every law enforcement agency in California shall fully cooperate with the United States Immigration and Naturalization Service regarding any person who is arrested if he or she is suspected of being present in the United States in violation of federal immigration laws.

(b)   With respect to any such person who is arrested, and suspected of being present in the United States in violation of federal immigration laws, every law enforcement agency shall do the following:

(1)   Attempt to verify the legal status of such person as a citizen of the United States, an alien lawfully admitted as a permanent resident, an alien lawfully admitted for a temporary period of time or as an alien who is present in the United States in violation of immigration laws. The verification process may include, but shall not be limited to, questioning the person regarding his or her date and place of birth, and entry into the United States, and demanding documentation to indicate his or her legal status.

(2)   Notify the person of his or her apparent status as an alien who is present in the United States in violation of federal immigration laws and inform him or her that, apart from any criminal justice proceedings, he or she must either obtain legal status or leave the United States.

(3)   Notify the Attorney General of California and the United States Immigration and Naturalization Service of the apparent illegal status and provide any additional information that may be requested by any other public entity.

(c) Any legislative, administrative, or other action by a city, county, or other legally authorized local governmental entity with jurisdictional boundaries, or by a law enforcement agency, to prevent or limit the cooperation required by subdivision (a) is expressly prohibited.

SECTION 5.   Exclusion of Illegal Aliens from Public Social Services.

Section 10001.5 is added to the Welfare and Institutions Code, to read:

10001.5.   (a) In order to carry out the intention of the People of California that only citizens of the United States and aliens lawfully admitted to the United States may receive the benefits of public social services and to ensure that all persons employed in the providing of those services shall diligently protect public funds from misuse, the provisions of this section are adopted.

(b) A person shall not receive any public social services to which he or she may be otherwise entitled until the legal status of that person has been verified as one of the following:

(1) A citizen of the United States.

(2) An alien lawfully admitted as a permanent resident.

(3) An alien lawfully admitted for a temporary period of time.

(c) If any public entity in this state to whom a person has applied for public social services determines or reasonably suspects, based upon the information provided to it, that the person is an alien in the United States in violation of federal law, the following procedures shall be followed by the public entity:

(1) The entity shall not provide the person with benefits or services.

(2) The entity shall, in writing, notify the person of his or her apparent illegal immigration status, and that the person must either obtain legal status or leave the United States.

(3) The entity shall also notify the State Director of Social Services, the Attorney General of California, and the United States Immigration and Naturalization Service of the apparent illegal status, and shall provide any additional information that may be requested by any other public entity.

SECTION 6.   Exclusion of Illegal Aliens from Publicly Funded Health Care.

Chapter 1.3 (commencing with Section 130) is added to Part 1 of Division 1 of the Health and Safety Code, to read:

CHAPTER 1.3.   PUBLICLY-FUNDED HEALTH CARE SERVICES

130.   (a) In order to carry out the intention of the People of California that, excepting emergency medical care as required by federal law, only citizens of the United States and aliens lawfully admitted to the United States may receive the benefits of publicly-funded health care, and to ensure that all persons employed in the providing of those services shall diligently protect public funds from misuse, the provisions of this section are adopted.

(b) A person shall not receive any health care services from a publicly-funded health care facility, to which he or she is otherwise entitled until the legal status of that person has been verified as one of the following:

(1) A citizen of the United States.

(2) An alien lawfully admitted as a permanent resident.

(3) An alien lawfully admitted for a temporary period of time.

(c) If any publicly-funded health care facility in this state from whom a person seeks health care services, other than emergency medical care as required by federal law, determines or reasonably suspects, based upon the information provided to it, that the person is an alien in the United States in violation of federal law, the following procedures shall be followed by the facility:

(1) The facility shall not provide the person with services.

(2) The facility shall, in writing, notify the person of his or her apparent illegal immigration status, and that the person must either obtain legal status or leave the United States.

(3) The facility shall also notify the State Director of Health Services, the Attorney General of California, and the United States Immigration and Naturalization Service of the apparent illegal status, and shall provide any additional information that may be requested by any other public entity.

(d) For purposes of this section "publicly-funded health care facility" shall be defined as specified in Sections 1200 and 1250 of this code as of January 1, 1993.

SECTION 7.   Exclusion of Illegal Aliens from Public Elementary and Secondary Schools.

Section 48215 is added to the Education Code, to read:

48215.   (a) No public elementary or secondary school shall admit, or permit the attendance of, any child who is not a citizen of the United States, an alien lawfully admitted as a permanent resident, or a person who is otherwise authorized under federal law to be present in the United States.

(b) Commencing January 1, 1995, each school district shall verify the legal status of each child enrolling in the school district for the first time in order to ensure the enrollment or attendance only of citizens, aliens lawfully admitted as permanent residents, or persons who are otherwise authorized to be present in the United States.

(c) By January 1, 1996, each school district shall have verified the legal status of each child already enrolled and in attendance in the school district in order to ensure the enrollment or attendance only of citizens, aliens lawfully admitted as permanent residents, or persons who are otherwise authorized under federal law to be present in the United States.

(d) By January 1, 1996, each school district shall also have verified the legal status of each parent or guardian of each child referred to in subdivisions (b) and (c), to determine whether such parent or guardian is one of the following:

(1) A citizen of the United States.

(2) An alien lawfully admitted as a permanent resident.

(3) An alien admitted lawfully for a temporary period of time.

(e) Each school district shall provide information to the State Superintendent of Public Instruction, the Attorney General of California, and the United States Immigration and Naturalization Service regarding any enrollee or pupil, or parent or guardian, attending a public elementary or secondary school in the school district determined or reasonably suspected to be in violation of federal immigration laws within forty-five days after becoming aware of an apparent violation. The notice shall also be provided to the parent or legal guardian of the enrollee or pupil, and shall state that an existing pupil may not continue to attend the school after ninety calendar days from the date of the notice, unless legal status is established.

(f) For each child who cannot establish legal status in the United States, each school district shall continue to provide education for a period of ninety days from the date of the notice. Such ninety day period shall be utilized to accomplish an orderly transition to a school in the child's country of origin. Each school district shall fully cooperate in this transition effort to ensure that the educational needs of the child are best served for that period of time.

SECTION 8.   Exclusion of Illegal Aliens from Public Postsecondary Educational Institutions.

Section 66010.8 is added to the Education Code, to read:

66010.8.   (a) No public institution of postsecondary education shall admit, enroll, or permit the attendance of any person who is not a citizen of the United States, an alien lawfully admitted as a permanent resident in the United States, or a person who is otherwise authorized under federal law to be present in the United States.

(b) Commencing with the first term or semester that begins after January 1, 1995, and at the commencement of each term or semester thereafter, each public postsecondary educational institution shall verify the status of each person enrolled or in attendance at that institution in order to ensure the enrollment or attendance only of United States citizens, aliens lawfully admitted as permanent residents in the United States, and persons who are otherwise authorized under federal law to be present in the United States.

(c) No later than 45 days after the admissions officer of a public postsecondary educational institution becomes aware of the application, enrollment, or attendance of a person determined to be, or who is under reasonable suspicion of being, in the United States in violation of federal immigration laws,

that officer shall provide that information to the State Superintendent of Public Instruction, the Attorney General of California, and the United States Immigration and Naturalization Service. The information shall also be provided to the applicant, enrollee, or person admitted.

SECTION 9.   *Attorney General Cooperation with the INS.*

Section 53069.65 is added to the Government Code, to read:

53069.65.   Whenever the state or a city, or a county, or any other legally authorized local governmental entity with jurisdictional boundaries reports the presence of a person who is suspected of being present in the United States in violation of federal immigration laws to the Attorney General of California, that report shall be transmitted to the United States Immigration and Naturalization Service. The Attorney General shall be responsible for maintaining on-going and accurate records of such reports, and shall provide any additional information that may be requested by any other government entity.

SECTION 10.   *Amendment and Severability.*

The statutory provisions contained in this measure may not be amended by the Legislature except to further its purposes by statute passed in each house by rollcall vote entered in the journal, two-thirds of the membership concurring, or by a statute that becomes effective only when approved by the voters.

In the event that any portion of this act or the application thereof to any person or circumstance is held invalid, that invalidity shall not affect any other provision or application of the act, which can be given effect without the invalid provision or application, and to that end the provisions of this act are severable.

Notes

Chapter One

1. Throughout this book, we use *migration* to refer to migration generally and use "immigration" and "emigration" only to register their appearance in the discourse we examined. We prefer "migration" because "immigration" and "emigration" tend to imply the narcissistic view of the already-landed citizen. These terms make sense in a logic system that privileges the perspective of the destination to which one is coming and from which one is leaving.

2. A *Los Angeles Times* article (Bustillo 2000) suggests that as early as August 2000 the Republican Party was distancing itself from Proposition 187.

3. For background on the Chinese Exclusion Act, see Chan 1991 and Gyory 1998.

4. In the Appendix, please see the section titled "Proposition 187: Text of Proposed Law."

5. Examples of legislation that severely limited Asian immigration include the 1917 act creating an Asiatic Barred Zone, the 1924 Immigration Act virtually eliminating Japanese migration, and the 1934 act creating restrictions on Filipino migration.

6. For a discussion of the fact that undocumented immigrants were already ineligible to take advantage of most federal public assistance programs at the time of Proposition 187's passage, see Johnson 1995b, esp. 1528–31; and Cornelius 1982, esp. 21–24.

7. The criminalization of Chicano youth, the anti–affirmative action legislation Proposition 209, as well as the anti-bilingual education, English-only legislation Proposition 227 are all examples of the aftermath of Proposition 187.

8. This act denies documented and undocumented migrants the right to receive a host of state and federal benefits. For instance, it requires women receiving what used to be called Aid to Families with Dependent Children (AFDC) income to work within two years of receiving benefits. It also further regulates the use of food stamps and supplemental security income.

9. Davis's decision not to act on the appeal may have been legally prudent, because it ultimately had the indirect effect of ending Wilson's appeal of Judge

Pfaelzer's decision. The fact, however, that Davis did not take a clear stand against Wilson's appeal from the beginning, and hence symbolically oppose Wilson's over-all campaign for Proposition 187, in a sense depoliticizes the issue as if to sweep it under the rug.

10. On feminist immigration research see, e.g., Boris 1995; Grace Chang 1994; Nakano Glenn 1992; Sapiro 1984; and Weinberg 1992. For critical race theory proj-ects see, e.g., Biegel 1995; Bosniak 1996; Cervantes, Khokha, and Murray 1995; Cooper 1995; Garcia 1995; Gotanda 1991; Hing 1993a,b; Johnson 1993, 1995a,b, 1998; Reynoso 1995; Sklansky 1995; and Wagley 1995. For literary studies see, e.g., Anzaldúa 1987; Gutiérrez-Jones 1995; Lowe 1996; Michaels 1995; Michaelson and Johnson 1997; and Saldívar 1991, 1997. For anthropological studies see, e.g., Coutin and Chock 1995; and Schiller, Basch, and Blanc 1995.

11. For books specifically on media representations of immigration, see Fer-nandez and Pedroza 1981 and Simon and Alexander 1993. We found only fourteen essays that relate to immigration by searching under the terms migration, migra-tions, migrating, migrant, migrants, immigration, immigrant, immigrants, immi-grate, immigrates, immigrated, and immigrating in the CommSearch CD ROM index of communication periodicals. See Chaffee, Nass, and Yang 1990; Friedman 1977; Hofstetter and Loveman 1982; Kim 1977; Lum 1991; McCann, Hecht, and Ribeau 1986; McCue 1975; Mondello 1967; Parry-Giles 1998; Regis 1989; Ross 1994; Sunoo, Trotter, and Aames 1980; Wang and Kincaid 1982; and Yum 1982. The primary focus of many of these articles is on English-language acquisition; none focuses on media representations of immigration.

12. Whereas, in his research Michel Foucault saw discursive patterns organized around specific regimes of truth, such as discipline, sexuality, and sanity, other dis-cursive patterns can be seen to exist, as we demonstrate in this book.

13. For a discussion of this transition from literature to rhetorical studies, see Bitzer and Black 1971. Dilip Gaonkar (1990) provides one of the strongest analytic histories of rhetorical criticism and its purposes in his comments on the work of Michael Leff and Michael Calvin McGee.

14. To understand the relevance of this debate to rhetorical studies research, see Crowley 1992. The introduction to Lucaites and Condit 1999, a contemporary rhetorical theory reader, provides a history of contemporary changes in the brand of rhetorical studies that has emerged from departments of Speech Communica-tion and Communication Studies. The essays of "the early 1980s" we refer to in the text were published in the spring 1983 and winter 1984 issues of the *Central States Speech Journal.*

15. Through analysis of speeches (and other texts) by women in U.S. history, Karlyn Kohrs Campbell (1989a,b) has brought forward the voices of women denied access to public forums or denied a place in history.

16. Moreover, as we suggest elsewhere (Ono and Sloop 1995), Wander assumes in his "Third Persona" essay (1984) that all groups of people want to become part of the larger public forum. In effect, he ignores the politics of silence, the politics of being, in Peggy Phelan's words (1993), "unmarked." He does not consider the possibility that there are times when it is best to separate oneself from the civic dom-inant discourse, to remove oneself from engagement with the general polis.

17. The term "postmodern" should not be equated with "poststructural." Whereas postmodern refers to a particular contemporary cultural condition, poststructural refers to an academic, theoretical project aimed at critiquing and transforming Western logics and cultural assumptions associated with the historical ways modernism and, more recently, structuralism have been seen to operate. Indeed, a great deal of confusion in contemporary debates has occurred because of the looseness of the use of the terms "postmodern" and "poststructural" and because they are often used interchangeably.

18. See Wicheln 1925 and Bryant 1966, which includes Wicheln's "Literary Criticism of Oratory."

19. Our understanding of the condition comes, in large part, from reading Lyotard 1984 and Baudrillard 1983, as well as the summary of various theories in Connor 1997.

20. Indeed, Samuel Becker (1971), in his early contribution emerging from the Wingspread Conference on Rhetorical Criticism, makes the argument that rhetorical studies needs to expand its analysis of objects beyond that of public speeches. Given the increasing role television and other media were beginning to play in influencing audiences in the late 1960s and early 1970s, it only made sense to Becker at the time to broaden the field of analysis to include the study of mass mediated texts.

21. This is not meant to ignore the fact that McGee's work, especially 1980a,b, 1982, 1990, and 1998, was a major force in the move toward poststructural assumptions within rhetorical theory and criticism. McGee recognizes postmodernity as a reason to construct a critical rhetoric, and he has helped usher in the theory that made critical rhetoric a theoretical possibility. Although Carole Blair, Martha Cooper, and Dilip Gaonkar conducted early studies into the relationship between Foucault and rhetoric (see Blair 1987; Blair and Cooper 1987; Cooper 1988; Gaonkar 1982), and Maurice Charland (1987) drew on a nascent poststructuralism, Raymie McKerrow's article on critical rhetoric (1989) attempts to synthesize the greater poststructural movement within the academy. No one, save McKerrow, has attempted in print to theorize the larger academic field of poststructuralism in relation to rhetoric. Since McKerrow's essay was first published, numerous essays have explored aspects of the relationship between rhetoric and poststructuralism, including Biesecker 1989, 1992a,b, 1993; Blair, Jeppeson, and Pucci 1991; Goodnight 1995; McKerrow 1991, 1993; Nakagawa 1993; Nakayama and Krizek 1995; Ono and Sloop 1992, 1995; Rowland 1995; Schwichtenberg 1993; Thomas 1993; and Whitson and Poulakos 1993. Many more articles have addressed this intersection since the mid-1990s, when the focus set in and became a general approach to scholarship. Despite the growing number of articles devoted to the study of rhetoric and poststructuralism, no single essay or set of essays both develops a set of thoroughgoing theoretical assumptions and then applies those assumptions to material objects by means of a critical rhetorical practice, save our own.

22. For critiques and changes in the critical rhetoric project, see Charland 1991; Clark 1996; Hariman 1991; McKerrow 1991, 1993; Murphy 1995; Ono and Sloop 1992, 1995; Sloop and Ono 1997.

23. We do not mean to imply that we alone have posed these questions and taken these positions in the academy. Many other theorists and critics are making similar moves. The best examples that guide us are Gayatri Spivak's "strategic essentialisms" (1988, 197–221) and Foucault's "intentional fictions" (1984, 90) and "effective histories" (1980, 93).

24. Sloop and Olson (1999) argue that if cultural studies is going to be a productive "interdisciplinary" project, critics must bring to the table the insights of their own disciplinary backgrounds. Hence, we are not looking to be solely "cultural critics" but also rhetoricians who are performing cultural studies.

25. We first defined vernacular discourse in Ono and Sloop 1995. For rhetorical studies that take a similar perspective see Delgado 1998a, b; and Flores 1996.

26. Given the intricacies of target marketing, there is very little communication that could be said to be intended for "everyone." Television shows each have a particular demographic group as a driving force, presidential campaigns employ strategies based on demographics and geographics, and so forth. To some degree here, we slide into a distinction that makes the discourse of "whiteness" civic discourse (i.e., like "whiteness," the partiality of such discourses is not generally "visible") and all other discourses vernacular (e.g., *The Advocate* is a vernacular forum for gay readers). To a degree, such a distinction is unavoidable. Although all media forums have particular audiences, some are assumed to be either more objective or more "common" than others. The closer a discourse is to being seen as "objective" or "for everyone," the more we see it is a dominant civic discourse.

27. We initially developed the concept of outlaw discourse in Sloop and Ono 1997.

28. As we suggest in Sloop and Ono 1997 (62), and wish to emphasize here, outlaw discourses do not refer to individual actors or speakers but instead to overall logics, to particular phrasings of terms. That is, neither dominant nor outlaw discourses refer to individuals who are speaking but rather to the commonsense assumptions that make up the lives of those individuals who operate from a particular discourse community.

29. Here, we are referring to the current formation of governmentality, in contrast to one more to our liking that could ostensibly emerge in the future.

30. We encourage critics to look for cases of the *differend* or incommensurability "(which requires that one take into account various logics and their power relations), rather than cases of disagreement (which are seen as differences of opinion, not differences in the relative power of logics and positions), in order to provide a radical rethinking of the possibilities for any given discourse" (Ono and Sloop 1999, 528–29).

31. In this section we are playing off of Elspeth Probyn's notion of a "feminism with an attitude" (1993). Probyn is attempting to describe feminist approaches that assume no transcendent rationale but that are nevertheless pragmatic (and contingent) political projects worth carrying out.

32. In rhetorical studies, for example, see Condit 1990; Condit and Lucaites 1993; and Sloop 1996.

33. Although developing an obviously different critical tool, Gerald Hauser (1998) has also recently put forth an argument for a rhetorical study of vernacular discourse.

34. For a specific discussion of the role of critique and self-reflection about dominant discourse within Asian American studies see, in particular, Lowe 1991; Ono 1995; and Osajima 1995.

35. In a discussion of the politics of popular music fanship, Simon Frith (1996, 20) observes that "the 'difficult' appeals through the traces it carries of another world in which it would be 'easy.'" While Frith is discussing music and how we consume it, the same could be said for the way in which we "listen to" and "consume" the discourses of others.

36. See Sloop and Ono 1993, in which we make the point that one has to consider the future when doing criticism in the present, thus "futuring" traditions. Here, while we are discussing logics largely in terms of their textual construction, we readily acknowledge that consumers of discourse are also producers. Hence, we would argue that some news stories we would deem to be based in dominance are read through outlaw lenses and thus act as outlaw discourses.

37. For an example of this ideological "discipline," see Sloop's analysis (1994) of the Public Enemy controversy.

38. It is interesting to note that the same "etiquette" that disallows certain racist claims to be made is also the same "etiquette" that disallows discourses to emerge that might be seen as progressive if they ever do "catch on." "Etiquette" is, after all, an effect of the "naturalness" of ideology. As we argue in Sloop 1994, relying on Goran Therborn (1980), outlaw discourses are always limited by numerous factors, such as ideological discipline (e.g., a person speaking an outlaw discourse is seen as epistemologically suspect—ignorant, idealistic, simpleminded, closed minded, racist, etc.), physical discipline (e.g., as a result of "radical" ideas, speakers are physically and symbolically punished, kept out of sight), and economic discipline (e.g., their "radical" ideas keep them from certain types of employment in that others shun them). Hence, outlaw discourses and those who speak them are always already placed in epistemologically inferior positions. This phenomenon is similar to the "clawback" theory discussed by John Fiske and John Hartley (1978), who argue that when a radical discourse appears in mass culture, it, like a lobster attempting to escape a bucket full of other lobsters, gets "clawed back" in for the most part. Change does occur, then, but it is a very small change at any given time.

Chapter Two

1. See Susan Owen and Peter Ehrenhaus (1993), who suggest that contemporary popular cultural representations very often depict race and gender from a colonialist point of view, relying on violence against women and people of color as part of an overall encouragement of consumption practices.

2. Newsbank indexes articles of general, national interest, so while local newspapers are included in Newsbank's system, their choice is meant to help provide a national, not a local, sample.

3. Such terms or phrases are examples of what Michael McGee (1980a) calls "ideographs"—culturally resonant terms that stand in for collective understandings because they are high order, abstract concepts that can be invoked (and filled with meaning) in public arguments. Ideographs are known for the roles they have played

historically and hence cannot be completely separated from their past; the past meanings of a term act materially on how it is understood and functions in the present. For example, "democracy" played a key role in the history of the formation of the United States; hence, its present understanding is forever shaped by this historical context. Each time readers see the term or hear it invoked, they conjure up associations, possible connections between terms (e.g., between "democracy" and "liberty"), and moreover, those using the terms continually reify or reconstitute the terms and meanings associated with them. Readers imagine the many possible associations they might have with the ideograph and the particular relationships it has to their own lives. Thus, as subjects, we are embedded in culture and the discourses we speak are intrinsically cultural; to understand the struggle over ideographs is to understand struggles over culture.

4. Homi Bhabha's notion of "ambivalence" (1983)helps us understand stereotypes. Ambivalence, as Bhabha defines it, is the notion that racism depends on both attraction to and revulsion of the other; the self both desires and reviles, consumes and expels, and loves and hates the other. Dana Cloud (1992, 315) provides an apt example of the way ambivalence operates in contemporary stereotypical television representations. Drawing on Bhabha's argument, Cloud demonstrates how the popular television show *Spencer: For Hire* represents Hawk, an African American character who is Spencer's (the show's lead protagonist) sidekick. Quoting a popular review of the show, Cloud describes Hawk as " 'both ally and adversary . . . bad guy and good guy; a man to be feared but who has a code of honor identical to Spencer's.' " Thus, when the stereotype is projected onto multiple objects or others, there is in each a vacillation between desire and loathing central to the process of objectification and, often, elimination.

5. For instance, women's reproductive labor does not emerge as desirable labor necessary for national citizenship. The undocumented migrant woman giving birth is an unacceptable vision of the national body; indeed, it is figured as antithetical to national progress.

6. As Steven Perry (1983) notes in his analysis of the "infestation" metaphors in Adolph Hitler's discourse, the logical conclusion of discussions of "disease" or "invasion" is the literal erasure of those people metamorphosed as infestation agents.

7. We use the terms "Mexicana" and "Mexicano" to refer specifically to Mexican people, whether living in the United States or in Mexico. We use "Chicana" and "Chicano" to refer generally to people who describe themselves as Chicanas and Chicanos and as permanent residents of the United States, whether naturalized citizens or not. The public discourse that is aware of the difference in terms tends to differentiate between Mexicanas or Mexicanos and Chicanas or Chicanos, coding Mexicanas and Mexicanos negatively along citizenship lines. When using other terms such as Latina and Latino, we are merely referring to the choice of terms of a given article, not privileging those terms for our own discussion. For a discussion of the terms associated with Chicana and Chicano identity, such as Latina, Latino, and Hispanic, see Delgado 1994 and Gonzalez 1990.

8. It is important to say here that media gatekeepers choose what stories to tell, what evidence to use, whom to consult, and the like. Thus, words from interviewees do not appear on the pages of newspapers unedited and without what we would call

translational biases. Journalists and editors select certain arguments and counterarguments over others. So, the fact that, for instance, the media chose to highlight the economic over human arguments made by activists in Proposition 187 discourse may, at least in part, be explained by the translational biases brought to the stories and discourses of activists by the newsmakers. Nevertheless, as we suggest in Chapters 4 and 5, even when unmediated by journalist middle managers of information, oppositional discourses often maintain dominant logics.

9. Very few Asian Americans appear as sources for news stories or writers of news articles. This citation of Howard Chang is unusual, especially so because Chang is represented here as somewhat of an expert on the subject.

10. Chicanas and Chicanos were criminalized by Proposition 189 (the so-called Three Strikes You're Out Initiative) at the same time that Mexicanas and Mexicanos were criminalized by Proposition 187. That is, the initiatives affected both groups negatively but directed their messages more specifically against one group as opposed to the other. Media sometimes conflate the two groups and sometimes differentiate between them but generally portray both groups negatively.

11. It is important to note that the language used in the 1982 Supreme Court decision *Plyler v. Doe*, in which the ruling judge talked about children as innocent victims becoming juvenile delinquents, guilty and irresponsible parents, and Mexicanas, Mexicanos, Chicanas, and Chicanos as the backbone of the economy, significantly predated the current discourse in which those very same arguments are used against Proposition 187.

12. Numerous other examples emerging from sources as diverse as *Christian Century* (Gaffney 1995), *ABA Journal* (Schwartz 1995), the *Nation* (Kadetsky 1994), the *Sacramento Bee* (Rennert 1994), and NBC News (1994f) support this observation.

13. For a rhetorical study that makes similar arguments see Solomon 1985.

14. Take the example of the rhetoric of AIDS, which is very similar to the rhetoric of immigration in that it draws on other enemies in U.S. society. As Susan Sontag (1990, 140) says: "The subliminal connection made to notions about a primitive past and the many hypotheses that have been fielded about possible transmission from animals (a disease of green monkeys? African swine fever?) cannot help but activate a familiar set of stereotypes about animality, sexual license, and blacks."

The U.S. context, with its own history of fear of others, necessarily conjures up images and metaphors relating to racism. And, because of the intimate link between the constructions of race and immigration in U.S. history, relationships between the two are inevitable. Sontag alludes to the specific connection between AIDS, for instance, and immigration, linking both to an environment in which a discourse of racialized fear predominates. She writes: "Authoritarian political ideologies have a vested interest in promoting fear, a sense of the imminence of takeover by aliens—and real diseases are useful material. Epidemic diseases usually elicit a call to ban the entry of foreigners, immigrants. And xenophobic propaganda has always depicted immigrants as bearers of disease (in the late nineteenth century: cholera, yellow fever, typhoid fever, tuberculosis)" (149–50).

Like AIDS, other enemies crossed the divide between the Cold War and post–Cold War eras. Among them, and with their own historical bases, were African

Americans. During the Reagan era, Herman Gray (1995) argues, African Americans were represented as a threat to the "nation," and as such were therefore constructed, like immigrants, as "unworthy" of social benefits. When a group is constructed as the "outsider" to the nation, it is subject to exclusion, ejection, and possibly elimination but only after being configured as disease, invasion, scourge, or simply as unequivocal and unredeemable other. During the administration of Bill Clinton, "immigrants" also took up the role of the "outsider within" that African Americans more prominently played in rhetoric of 1980s' Reagan-era politics, even while African Americans continued to be the victims of contemporary media strategies of othering. In a certain way, the othering of immigrants, in this scenario, relies on the same strategies of othering used as strategies to subordinate African Americans during the 1980s; however, while immigrants in many ways have replaced African Americans as the subjects most unworthy of the benefits of citizenship, African Americans continue to be marginalized.

15. And, sometimes the new enemy is logically related to the old one. For instance, in the anticommunist agenda overall, the Soviet Union was not the only target of U.S. imperialism. El Salvador, Nicaragua, Cuba, and Guatemala were also targets of U.S. anticommunist militarism in ideological warfare. One result of creating enemies in Latin America, as in China, Vietnam, and Korea, has been an influx of prodemocracy, anticommunist immigrants and refugees.

16. Analyzing the historical relationship between racism and nationalism in western contexts, Ann Stoler (1995, 93) observes, "The discourse of race was not on parallel track with the discourse of the nation but part of it; the latter was saturated with a hierarchy of moralities, prescriptions for conduct and bourgeois civilities that kept a racial politics of exclusion at its core." Also see Berlant 1997.

17. Our argument here is that without a clearly defined external enemy, such as the Soviet Union, the potential for interior enemies within the nation-state to emerge increases.

18. Charles Ramírez Berg (1989, 8) in his discussion of Sander Gilman's work suggests that a child begins the psychological process of stereotyping at a very early age, when it is beginning to understand that the world is both different and larger than itself. He writes: "As the child realizes that the world is much more than the self, anxiety arises due to the concomitant loss of control. As a coping strategy the child divides the self and the world into good (able to be controlled and anxiety-free) and bad (unable to be controlled and anxiety-full) halves. Next, the child distances the good self from the bad, creating an 'us = good'/'them = bad' dichotomy." According to Ramírez Berg, the us/them dichotomy becomes "situational." That is, the "other" is like a chameleon and takes on different forms depending on the situation. Since there are aspects of the other that are desirable and aspects that are loathsome, the anxiety produced by being like, or becoming, the other forces the child to project anxieties about the self onto the other. Ramírez Berg quotes Gilman as saying, "'The former is that which we fear to become; the latter, that which we fear we cannot achieve'" (8). Here, we argue that the ambivalent nature of racial identification may help explain the proliferation of enemy others in the post-Cold War context; now, the enemy can be anywhere, even among those (we thought) we trusted.

19. The proliferation of media technology, including the Internet, cell phones, electronic beepers, car alarms, visual monitors for telephones, satellite television, fiber optics, and video cameras, as well as an amalgam of surveillance devices have rendered archaic linear communication models.

20. For James Holston and Arjun Appadurai (1996), transnationalism creates the potential for radical resistance; in their view, immigrants cross cultural and national boundaries, thus physically effacing the space mapped out by greater national capitalist interests. However, we would argue that one should not be wholly optimistic about the effects of transnationalism and should question the degree to which liberatory side effects that emerge in transnationalism actually challenge and resist the larger processes of commodification.

21. For example, over the past several years, discourse about the campaign finance scandal in the United States has focused heavily on China as the new Cold War enemy. William Safire (1997), a key ideologue of the Cold War era, seems not to have noticed that the Soviet Union has dissolved. In one of a series of articles on China's supposed conspiracy to "infiltrate" U.S. electoral politics, Safire observes, "Chinese intelligence operations are sophisticated, patient, disciplined, and underrated by a C.I.A.-F.B.I. counterintelligence culture still transfixed by Primakov's disciples in Moscow." For Safire, the Cold War enemy still exists: while in the new form of "China," it is for him dependent on the old form of "Soviet Union." In addition, the discourse about campaign finance reform links the Cold War villain—China—to the post–Cold War villain—Asians and Asian immigrants in the United States.

22. The ad that portrayed shadowy figures along the border was powerful rhetoric. It was also politically significant. It ran nightly on prime-time television. Pete Wilson's endorsement of Proposition 187 was the key to his reelection and defeat of Kathleen Brown. We would argue, then, that the ad made real, as if by providing evidence of Wilson's scapegoating of undocumented migrants, the problem California faced and hence enhanced his own authority in understanding and possibly being able to change the problem.

23. Mike Davis argues in his classic *City of Quartz* (1990, 151–220) that homeowners associations have been used traditionally in Los Angeles to separate middle-class property owners, assumably white, from all other peoples. The figure of the white, middle-class homeowner is not named in this discourse but instead exists as the de facto intended receiver of this rhetorical address.

24. Today, the term "breeders" is used primarily in popular cultural contexts in reference to breeding dogs for racing and show. For a nice critical popular cultural article on the use of women's bodies as reproductive incubators see Shalit 1995. Unfortunately, the article does not examine the racialized aspect of this contemporary construction of women, which focuses almost wholly on women of color, and more specifically on Mexicanas and Chicanas.

25. A particularly good contemporary example of a narrative that constructs the overall fear of the invading other for elimination is the Hollywood blockbuster science fiction film *Independence Day*. In the film, the alien poses a direct threat to the coherence of a U.S. polity, demonstrated in part by the aliens' violent and explosive demolition of the "White House," an emblem of a coherent, national family.

To save the otherwise helpless world, the president of the United States, himself, acts as a fighter pilot who goes on an apparent suicide mission to destroy the alien m/other ship. Against what appear to be unbelievable odds, the president speeds toward the alien ship and successfully jettisons a projectile through the porthole into the interior of the m/other ship out of which the audience has seen myriad tiny baby ships exit. The m/other ship then explodes from the inside out, destroying the alien civilization and thus returning people on Earth to safety. Along with the ever-changing negotiation of self/other is the rhetoric of family values, in which complex social issues are solved through an imagined return to times when comfort ostensibly resulted primarily because families remained intact. In only thinly veiled terms, the family is a metonym for the return of a coherent public sphere and national order and therefore is the edifice upon which social and psychological support is said to rest. See, for instance, Stacey 1990.

Chapter Three

1. As Mike Davis points out in *City of Quartz* (1990, 140), the *Los Angeles Times* in recent decades has found itself in a politically and commercially difficult position. The *Times*, he notes, "is now at the receiving end of a regional backlash against the cultural and political liberalism of Los Angeles's Westside." Because the *Times* attempts to maintain the readership of the fiscally dominant citizens of Los Angeles, it is losing its appeal "to the city's most rapidly growing ethnic groups.... The *Times*'s dilemma, in other words, almost precisely outlines the problem of ruling class hegemony in a postmodern city of secessionist suburbs and burgeoning barrios." Hence, Davis sees the *Times* struggling to take up positions that appeal to both dominant and nondominant groups. This tension is clearly evident in our reading of the *Times*'s coverage of the battle over Proposition 187.

2. We think the *Los Angeles Times* printed more articles about Proposition 187 than did any other mainstream daily newspaper. The *Times* had daily coverage of the story from 17 October 1994 through 23 November 1994, publishing 331 articles between 24 July 1994 and 29 September 1995 and 192 articles between 17 October 1994 and 23 November 1994. Twenty-eight different reporters covered the story between 24 July 1994 and 29 September 1995.

3. See, for instance, Billington 1938; Gordon 1964; Higham 1955; and Perea 1997.

4. The act was put in place primarily to limit the number of Europeans from southern and eastern Europe (Hing 1993b, 32).

5. We should say, because Michaels's work (1995) is controversial, that we object to his overall preoccupation with the logical fallacy of what he calls "identitarian claims" (6), invoking racial signifiers to account for the entire identity of a person. Michaels limits the meaning of claims to racial identity as statements of *real* relations. Michaels assumes those making identity claims about themselves are simply replicating the mistake made by those who used such claims against them, rather than recognizing the more complex performances people make to challenge the initial use of racial claims. Like any other claim, identitarian claims play a *functional* role. Cultural and social contexts, however, suggest that claims to identity are in some contexts simply shorthand for more complex relationships. For example, the

phrase "I am an Asian American" does not mean simply that the speaker is biologically Asian and living in the United States, which in fact may not be true at all. The phrase is a political signifier suggesting in some instances a commitment to being part of a community that recognizes that certain political and historical arrangements have been made based on racial signifiers. Hence, invocations of "Asian American" are, for many, a shorthand way to challenge political arrangements that themselves were made based on fallacious claims to biological origin. For more on Asian American racial identity see Ono 1998.

6. For instance, allowing communists to enter as immigrants decreases the number of denials based on foreign policy reasons and provides undocumented Salvadorians temporary protection (Vialet and Eig 1991, 32).

7. INS agents were little more than attendants checking citizenship papers at key crossing points along the border before the act; after the act, they were officers responsible for policing national borders, and their status was upgraded so that they now had the authority to prosecute and punish wrongdoers. *Migration World* outlines Section 503 of the Immigration Act of 1990 ("Enforcement Authority of INS Personnel") in its official summary of the act: "Bringing the authority of INS personnel in line with that of employees of many other Federal law enforcement agencies, P.L. 101-649 grants INS personnel, upon adoption of regulations, statutory authority to 1) make warrantless arrests for crimes unrelated to immigration; 2) execute and serve orders, warrants, summonses, and similar legal documents issued under Federal authority other than immigration law; and 3) carry firearms" (Vialet and Eig 1991, 36).

8. The very fact that Ezell, as a past INS director and co-author of Proposition 187, emerged as a spokesperson against "illegals" and "illegal immigration" and therefore a proponent for Proposition 187 while he stood to gain politically and economically from his policy of attracting rich entrepreneurs to the United States, is an irony that illustrates the power the INS had already begun to display in media coverage on immigration.

9. Arguably, the contradictions in U.S. immigration policies are fundamental. One question behind this ambivalence is, "Do immigrants from foreign lands alter the character of what makes the United States as a nation unique?" Thus, policies that provide for immigration from foreign lands also connote, ironically, that there are fundamental questions about whether immigration should even exist. These contradictions were also present in the Simpson-Rodino-Mazzoli Immigration Reform Act of 1986. As Charles Ramírez Berg (1989, 17) suggests, Congress had difficulty arguing for increased penalties against employers of undocumented workers while simultaneously having to ensure that agricultural growers had sufficient labor to harvest their crops.

10. By saying that marginalized communities function as scapegoats, we are not professing what Ann Laura Stoler (1995) calls a "scapegoat theory of race." Furthermore, we take issue with her discussion of the subject. She writes: "Scapegoat theories posit that under economic and social duress, particular sub-populations are cordoned off as intruders, invented to deflect anxieties, and conjured up precisely to nail blame." This cordoning off is indeed what happened to undocumented migrants with Proposition 187. However, it is important to suggest that this

particular incident is not unique, nor can it be explained by economic conditions alone, which is what we take Stoler's point to be. Indeed, contingent factors, including "the expression of an underlying discourse of permanent wars" are part of what Foucault (1977, 69) calls the technologies of "incessant purification." Yet, as Stoler argues, Foucault's explanation of an embedded technology of racial discourse set on race purity is, also, not a sufficient enough explanation for the events. Indeed, habitual responses to discourses about the economy, renewed nativist rhetoric against the in-migrant as invader, the gendered discourse against Mexicanas and Chicanas, and anxieties about threats to the national body, in addition to long-standing purifying discourses, very often in the form of body metaphors, play a role in un-fixing and re-fixing racial discourses onto the bodies of undocumented migrants, especially Mexicanas and Mexicanos, and others also represented as such: Chicanas and Chicanos.

11. One quibble we have with Aoki is that whereas he sees the incarceration of Japanese Americans as an effect of general anti–Asian American sentiment, we see it as very specifically about the international relationship between the United States and Japan at the time. Thus, Asian American ethnic groups are targeted differently at different times and for different reasons. Hence, the targeting of Chinese Americans in 2001 can be ascribed to the current relationship between the United and China. Thus, the current anti-Chinese discourse can exist simultaneously with, for example, positive discourse about unifying politics between North and South Korea.

12. For a more detailed history of institutionalized racism in California against people of color, see Almaguer 1994.

13. For instance, see the following films that came out after 1990 portraying INS agents: *The Perez Family* (1995), *Steal Big, Steal Little* (1995), and *Lone Star* (1996).

14. Doherty 1993 provides an argument similar to the one we offer here. The fact that "D-FENS," the nickname given Michael Douglas's character in the movie, is ultimately killed for his actions is not a sufficient reason to dismiss the apocalyptic xenophobia of the film and this character's role within it.

15. These very sentiments about the *mythos* of immigration to "America" were expressed repeatedly by George W. Bush during the 2000 presidential campaign season.

16. For a discussion of "internal enemies," see Stoler 1995, esp. 62, 85, 93, and 193.

17. A brief discussion of our qualitative methodology is appropriate here. We first read all of the newspaper articles attempting to locate key themes. Once we located key themes, we read the articles a second time and coded each article according to the themes from our first reading and also added new themes as they emerged. We made sure to code materials consistently in all articles and also confirmed the accuracy of the themes by comparing the findings of all coders. To provide structure for the various themes we found within the discourse we then organized all themes according to the larger themes of immigration and the nation, the law, and the individual. Finally, once we realized there were key differences between pro and con discourses, we decided to write two separate chapters, one on pro and another on con discourses.

18. While the larger themes of immigration and the nation, law, and individual remain the same in both pro and con discourse, the subthemes differ, especially with regard to immigration and the individual.

19. This sentiment recurs throughout U.S. history. Bill Hing (1993a, 32–33) points out, for example, that "the arguments advanced in support of the [Immigration Act of 1924] stressed recurring themes: the racial superiority of Anglo-Saxons, the fact that immigrants would cause the lowering of wages, and the unassimilability of foreigners, while citing the usual threats to the nation's social unity and order posed by immigration." See also Gutiérrez 1995.

20. For a discussion of the social construction of the border, see Rodríguez 1997.

21. The Treaty of Guadalupe-Hidalgo was signed on 2 February 1848, dividing Mexicans from Mexicans.

22. University of California, Davis, professor Norman Matloff (1994) characterizes undocumented migration as "flow." See also Carvajal and Martinez 1994. George Ramos (1994a) describes migration as "illegal immigrants overrunning us." For a detailed analysis of water metaphors in *Los Angeles Times* articles on Proposition 187, please see Ana, Morán, and Sánchez's cognitive linguistic study (1998). Among the water metaphors they found are larger, structuring metaphors of immigration as dangerous waters and the nation as a ship at sea. Also see their study for a discussion of conservative political sources used as experts.

23. For another example of the metaphor of invasion, see Martinez and McDonnell 1994.

24. For a discussion of the gendered bases for immigration policies see Johnson 1995b, 1549–53. The construction of the undocumented Mexican woman immigrant focuses very specifically on the role she plays in giving birth to children, therefore to the ambivalent role her body plays in the political economy as both producer of much-needed laborers and producer of feared enemy noncitizens.

25. See Hoffman 1974 and more recently García 1980. The "bracero program" as it was commonly called, which extended from 1942 to 1964, was a treaty signed by the U.S. and Mexican governments, agreeing that temporary workers from Mexico would work in the Unites States and return once their help was no longer needed. In general, this policy is understood to have presaged legal immigration of people from Mexico to the Unites States. Thus, the program prefigured the continuing historical phenomenon of Mexican workers in the United States being treated as second class noncitizens. See also Gutiérrez (1995, 117–51) for a discussion of this program. He argues that the program worked two ways for Mexican Americans and Mexicans. While it centered divisions based on citizenship, it also helped Mexicans and Mexican Americans to see a link between themselves (that was implied by dominant discourses) that ultimately encouraged the creation of categories that produced identification rather than differentiation (e.g., la raza, hispanic).

26. Of course Prince does not mention that this is precisely what the U.S. military and government have done for generations in other countries (e.g., Nicaragua). For example, the attempt by the military, the government, and the media to render Slobodan Milosevic unpopular with Yugoslavians is exactly an attempt to influence internally determined leadership processes.

27. Sometimes immigration is even described as a game rather than a means of survival. See, e.g., Skelton 1994a: "Wilson intends to do just that in a new TV ad starting today. It will say there's a right way and a wrong way to immigrate; people should play by the rules."

28. This argument follows a long-standing public argument made since the early 1970s against the "welfare state" mentality. Seeing welfare as part of a bygone era, many argue it puts an unfair damper on an otherwise capitalist-driven economy.

29. The *Los Angeles Times* devotes an entire article to this point. See Stall and Wallace 1994. See also Shogren 1994, in which Newt Gingrich is quoted as saying he would have voted for the initiative because of the federal government's irresponsibility, and Dolan 1994, which focuses on state versus federal jurisdiction over immigration.

30. Wilson responds to out-of-state critics by saying, "We don't need lectures from people outside California" (Skelton 1994b, A3). A later article quotes him saying, "We really don't need any lectures from anyone from outside of California on the vast contributions of legal immigrants" (Bornemeier 1994, A27).

31. While we have no direct evidence to support this inference, the similarity to the way nativism within California leading to the incarceration of Japanese Americans during World War II was taken to the national level, despite the federal government's initial opposition to the very idea of incarceration, is uncanny. We are not suggesting that Wilson literally studied the textbook of the history of successful nativist campaigns in California but that in both instances, the incarceration of Japanese Americans and Proposition 187, what began as an internal Californian nativist campaign to which the federal government was initially opposed later became almost an obligation by the government to support California in its efforts.

32. See United States v. Wong Kim Ark, 169 U.S. 649 (1898). Clearly, this is a very complicated issue, but with regard to Proposition 187, the *Los Angeles Times* articles throughout the ordeal failed to distinguish between a child born to an undocumented parent or parents in the United States and children brought with an undocumented parent or parents from outside of the United States to the United States.

33. It is important to point out that all of these aspects regarding children have not occurred without dispute. See Johnson 1995b, esp. 1573. Also see Schuck and Smith 1985 regarding arguments about children of those without (U.S.) legal approval being in the United States.

34. See also an article reporting Dan Lungren's late personal support of the measure (Bailey 1994). Another article discusses Wilson's pledge to uphold the voting public of California on the issue (Feldman and Connell 1994). In that same article, Lungren also encourages people to follow the law, despite court challenges.

35. Following these challenges, an article reports that four San Jose school officials decided that since others had filed suits they would withdraw theirs. The article quotes the reasoning of the superintendent of the East Side Union High School: "There is no need for us to expend any dollars or legal fees to pursue this" ("Schools Plan" 1994).

36. For a discussion of Prince and others' efforts to recall public officials, see also Shuster 1994a.

37. After the elections, discourse about constitutionality focuses on more specific details relating to Judge Marianne Pfaelzer's handling of the case and challenges to her court-ordered postponement of implementation of the measure.

38. See also Martinez and McDonnell (1994, A30) for a discussion of demonstrators arguing *for* Proposition 187: "The crowd of 100 or so who came to listen to an array of pro-187 pitches provides a window of sorts into the core support for Proposition 187. Participants were overwhelmingly white suburbanites, including many elderly. Most of them are clearly troubled by population shifts that, they said, have rapidly transformed their once-familiar communities into *strange* and *dangerous* places where English is heard less and less. Illegal immigration is to blame, they all agreed. 'We are becoming a Third World state,' said Robert Lacey, a computer executive who traveled from Riverside County to attend. Many of his neighbors have opted to leave California, he noted, adding that his home's value had plummeted and his wife had found it difficult to find work because she could not speak Spanish" (emphasis added).

39. In summarizing Proposition 187, Feldman (1994a, A3) writes, "Furthermore, they said, it is racist on the part of opponents to declare that the crime rate would increase if young illegal immigrants are expelled from school."

Chapter Four

1. In a discussion of the economic and social factors leading up to the role the *Los Angeles Times* played in the early 1970s, Jack Robert Hart (1975) describes the sometimes ruthless way this family-owned business developed. According to Hart, the newspaper survived by buying up other newspapers and putting many others out of business and by buying land, buildings, and other businesses. Originally quite conservative, the newspaper adapted to market conditions by taking a more "objective" approach to news and information in order to gain an even larger share of the market. Also see Davis 1990 (138–40) for an interesting discussion of the ideological position of the *Los Angeles Times.*

2. We are suggesting here that "racializing"—attributing characteristics of race to a person, issue, or context—is commonplace in U.S. cultural politics. It is important to note that despite attempts to "deracialize" matters—that is to say to attempt to diminish the importance of race, to pretend structures of race do not exist, or to assume racism has ended and therefore to suggest attention need not be paid to it—all of these strategies, in fact, "racialize" matters (or code them in implicitly racial ways) even while they say overtly they are attempting to do otherwise.

3. It is important to point out that taking a political position against a policy is not easy. Furthermore, we would not want to suggest that we know precisely what political position would actually have been effective against the proposition. What we are arguing here is that even a political position that appears to be against a policy may unwittingly actually create the conditions for such a policy's ultimate adoption.

4. Similarly, David G. Gutiérrez (1995, 69) notes that the history of the representation of Mexicans in the United States has always worked in such a way that both those who wanted to use Mexicans for labor and those who wanted to keep them from entering the country ultimately reified the same stereotypes. As he notes, "Although the restrictionists shared many of the ethnocentric or racist assumptions held by their opponents, spokesmen for this position turned these assumptions on their heads, arguing that the characteristics southwestern employers had long touted as reasons for the use of Mexican labor were precisely why Mexican immigrants should be *barred* from the U.S."

5. See, for instance, Bennett 1994; Feldman 1994d, A25, 1994h, A16; Lauter and Broder 1994, A23. Additionally, James Bornemeier (1994, A27) reports, "Kemp and Bennett advocate a stronger Border Patrol presence, accelerated deportation process, crackdown on counterfeit documents and reform of the Immigration and Naturalization Service to combat illegal immigration."

6. Incidentally, the call for stricter regulation of fraudulent documents and their reproduction, which was a rather minor argument in the *Los Angeles Times*, became a key issue with regard to the courts, as it was one provision of Proposition 187 not ruled unconstitutional by Judge Marianne Pfaelzer.

7. The authors are summarizing a position taken by Doris Meissner.

8. These uses of the terms "legal" and "illegal" did not always hold. As Mae M. Ngai (1999, 90) points out, "During the 1920s Congress made provisions for the enforcement of immigration laws that hardened the difference between legal and illegal immigration. It lifted the statute of limitations on deportation in 1924 and formed the Border Patrol in 1925. In 1929 Congress made unlawful entry a felony, a move that was intended to solve the problem of illegal immigration from Mexico."

9. There was a general tendency in these articles to construct undocumented migrants as criminals who regularly use "illegal" documents to avoid detection and punishment.

10. McDonnell (1994c) also suggests that Proposition 187's ban on education for children of undocumented migrants could send thousands into lives of juvenile delinquency.

11. Beth Shuster (1994b, B8) quotes Los Angeles County District Attorney Gil Garcetti as going further by saying, "The reason we work so hard at getting truants into school is we know that if they stay in school they are much, much less likely to be involved in crime and the criminal justice system."

12. Herman Gray (1989) discusses media rhetoric and public broadcasting narratives that privilege tropes of "personal interest" over those of worsening economic and social conditions for African Americans.

13. Furthermore, those opposed to Proposition 187 use the figure of uneducated criminal delinquents strategically, going so far as to suggest that white supremacists support Proposition 187, which will lead to delinquent criminality. As Feldman (1994a, A3) writes, "Opponents of Proposition 187 launched their radio advertising campaign Tuesday, airing a tough 60-second spot charging that the anti-illegal immigration ballot measure would lead to increased crime and is being backed by white supremacists."

14. See Roberts 1997 on the increased role of the state in the regulation of black bodies and families.

15. See, for instance, Decker 1994, A3; King 1994a, A3; and McDonnell and Lesher 1994, A1.

16. Summarizing William Bennett and Jack Kemp on the subject, this article suggests Bennett and Kemp teamed up to argue against Proposition 187.

17. For another article objecting to children turning in their parents, see Cornelius 1994.

18. The *Los Angeles Times* ran articles on increased activism by school boards as well. One article reads, "In a 3-2 vote after an emotional debate Tuesday night, the Santa Ana Unified School District Board asserted that the measure is unconstitutional and would turn district employees 'into inquisitors and adversaries of the students'" (Nalick and Feldman 1994).

19. Feldman (1994c) uses the phrase "police state" in a report on a news conference, saying, "Max Turchen, chairman of the Los Angeles chapter of the seniors' organization, charged that the measure fosters a police state mentality by requiring the investigation of people suspected of being illegal immigrants. 'What are the criteria? The color of your skin? The way you speak? Your last name?' he asked.'"

20. Brown first mentioned "Snoop or Snitch" right before the election. See Stall and Weintraub 1994, A10.

21. Despite his unwillingness to prosecute teachers who failed to turn in students, Lungren ended up supporting the initiative late in the campaign. When the *Times* reported Lungren's announcement that he supported Proposition 187, his Democratic opponent, Tom Umberg, charged him with "caving in to adherents on a measure that an Umberg aide said was unconstitutional and close to being racist" (Bailey 1994). During Lungren's run for governor, the media recalled his late support for the proposition.

22. An editorial published a month later ("Error" 1994) points out that such intrusion would spread to the schools, requiring "an illegal-immigration surveillance system . . . that is repulsive even to contemplate." Worse, Proposition 187 would lead people to make racial identifications based on visual clues: "School administrators would be required to peer into the faces of children and puzzle over their citizenship. How are they to separate the legal from the illegal? Are they going to question a blond, blue-eyed child who doesn't look like an 'apparent illegal alien,' to use 187's key phrase, even though she may be here illegally from Canada? Or will they question a dark-skinned, brown-eyed child who was born in this country but looks as if she might be from Latin America? This is the perniciousness, even terror, of Proposition 187."

23. See, for instance, an article that says Kathleen Brown spoke against Proposition 187 because the federal government threatened to withhold money from California schools were the measure to pass (Decker 1994, A28).

24. In September Secretary Riley pointed out that the measure would violate the federal Family Educational Rights and Privacy Act by requiring schools to disclose information from education records (Shuster 1994b). In the same article district officials and Board of Education members were quoted as saying, "The Los

Angeles Unified School District could lose more than $450 million in federal funds—almost 11% of its current budget" if Proposition 187 were to pass (B1). In July Riley had said that the federal government at the time granted about $2.3 billion in annual aid to the California public schools (Feldman 1994g). By October the Board of Education president Mark Slavkin warned that "all schools and students would be affected by the initiative" and that the system stood to lose "up to $628 million in federal funds" (Shuster 1994c, B3). The school district sent out a letter to about two thousand community leaders, addressed "Dear Friend," reiterating Slavin's warning about the potential loss of $628 million in federal funds (Pyle and Feldman 1994b).

25. An editorial ("Proposition 187 and the Law" 1994) focusing on the cost of Proposition 187 to California points to the lengthy, and therefore costly, legal battle ahead. Other articles cite the exorbitant cost of the legal battle. See, for instance, Feldman 1994j and the editorial "Proposition 187: One" 1994.

26. A later editorial ("Schools Plan" 1994), after the election, makes it clear that the *Los Angeles Times* endorses the state's challenge of the federal government on this issue, citing the newspaper's often-expressed belief that "while federal immigration law put a phenomenal burden on the affected states to cope with immigration pressures, it did not provide the states with the resources to respond to those needs." Thus, "the overwhelming passage of Proposition 187 was in part the result of that chronic neglect."

27. See, for instance, Stall and Wallace 1994, which reports that Janet Reno believes Proposition 187 is unconstitutional.

28. See, for instance, Fuentes 1994. Incidentally, a California Supreme Court decision, *Butt v. California*, ruled that children have a fundamental right to public education ("Sounds" 1994).

29. A Justice Department memorandum released by the Clinton Administration likened the California initiative to the Texas law that was declared unconstitutional in *Plyler v. Doe* (Ostrow 1994). And, according to University of Southern California law professor Erwin Chemerinsky, only the Supreme Court could overturn *Plyler v. Doe:* "If it went first to either the state or federal court system, all the lower courts would have to declare it unconstitutional because only the Supreme Court could overrule Plyler vs. Doe" (Feldman 1994j, A16).

30. Similarly, Pete Mehas, a Fresno County educator, was quoted as saying, "I say we don't deserve to be part of some grand legal experiment" (King 1994c).

31. One article quotes Los Angeles city attorney James K. Hahn, who filed a lawsuit on behalf of the city of Los Angeles against the measure. Hahn called Proposition 187 "vague" and "over-broad" and said it could "result in thousands of persons suffering violations of their constitutional right against discrimination on the basis of race or ethnicity" (Feldman and Rainey 1994a, A38). When confronted for using public money to challenge the public's vote, Hahn is reported to have replied, "We want to know whether we deny library cards, playing golf at a city golf course or being in a victim assistance program . . . if they are in the country illegally" (Connell, Shuster, and Rainey 1994, A22).

32. As we suggest in Chapter 3, the larger themes of immigration and the nation, law, and individual remain the same in both pro and con discourse. However, the subthemes differ, especially with regard to immigration and the individual.

33. Kathleen Brown is also quoted expressing concern about the scapegoating of children: "Courage would be to admit that just because our elected officials haven't been smart enough to stem the tide and the flow of illegal immigration, we shouldn't now be punishing children through Proposition 187. That's not courage. That's political chicken" (Wallace 1994, A27). Another article quotes Mexican president Carlos Salinas de Gortari also expressing concern for children: "What will happen to the children? Will they return to Mexico? Wash windshields in California? Sell newspapers on the streets or beg?" (Fineman 1994a).

34. See also Shusterman 1994, which focuses on the measure's impact on students in particular and asks, "How is it, then, that Nelson and Ezell have suddenly emerged to propose that California adopt its own immigration policy—one that targets schoolchildren rather than illegal workers or their employers?"

35. Another article reports that "a coalition of elected officials, child welfare workers and religious leaders Monday urged the defeat of Proposition 187, contending that it would hamper the county's ability to serve abused and neglected children if they or their parents are undocumented" (Feldman and Garcia 1994, A22).

36. Rivera and Feldman (1994, A22) quote David Langness, vice president of the Hospital Council of Southern California: "It means people are jeopardizing their health for fear of being turned in to the INS. We want to emphasize that we're not turning anyone in." About two weeks later Langness also said, "Very few people understand what a temporary restraining order is, and what they've heard is that the overwhelming majority of Californians voted to turn [undocumented] people in. . . . That frightens many folks and keeps them away from health care" (McDonnell 1994b, A33). Mark D. Rosenbaum, legal director of the ACLU of Southern California, expressed the same concern, contending, according to Feldman and Rainey 1994b, that "because of ambiguous statements by state officials including Gov. Pete Wilson since last week's election, many illegal immigrants have been scared to keep appointments at public health clinics for fear that they would be reported to immigration authorities." One unusual article in this vein, by Fred Alvarez (1994), requires further discussion. Alvarez describes a migrant woman from Mexico as fearful of medical and police services and then suggests that her returning home to Mexico will be a positive, viable alternative. Articles like this may imply, indirectly and unintentionally, that migrants from Mexico in fact do not need to be "here" in the United States and should (if they only knew better) stay where they belong and where they would have more comfortable lives. "For Alfaro," Alvarez points out, "the choices at this point are simple. She could continue to live in fear, worried that every contact with a doctor or a police officer would result in her deportation, and perhaps her separation from her children. Or she can return home voluntarily, her family intact and her mind at rest" (A22).

37. A *Los Angeles Times* editorial ("Why California" 1994) calls the referendum "wrong morally, because it would cast an indiscriminate shadow on people whose only real sin is to try to escape grinding poverty and make something of themselves." Mike Davis (1990) devotes an entire chapter (chapter 6) of his *City of Quartz* to the increasing conservatism of the Roman Catholic Church in Los Angeles throughout the 1980s and the Church's seemingly willful ignorance of the incoming Mexican population.

38. Jack Kemp and William Bennett, recognizing that the Republican Party hurt itself in the past with what they are quoted as calling "its hostile stand toward the last generation of immigrants from Italy, Ireland and the nations of Central Europe," which "helped to create a Democratic base in many of America's cities," warned, according to Ronald Brownstein and Patrick J. McDonnell (1994), that the Republican Party now "risks alienating entrepreneurial family-oriented immigrants who might otherwise be attracted to the party's message." The article continues, "Can anyone calculate the political cost of again turning away immigrants, this time . . . Asians, Hispanics and others?" (A26).

39. For example, the U.S. Commission on Immigration Reform opposed the elimination of benefits for undocumented migrant people, while nevertheless lobbying for increased border controls.

Chapter Five

1. We could come up with a much longer list of scholarship making such an argument, since this argument has essentially come to define an entire body of media studies literature, but for sake of brevity, we mention Cloud 1996; Dow 1990; Gray 1995; Hanke 1990; and Schwichtenberg 1984.

2. All cited posts are listed alphabetically according to subject titles in a separate list, "187-L Sources," following References. For posts that do not give a subject title, we give the first few words of the post. Although contemporary style manuals recommend citing distribution list sources by the author's name, we list no authors' names here because of the impracticality of getting permission from every person on the list whose post we cite. Furthermore, given the political nature of the list, some authors might have very good reasons for not wanting their names republished elsewhere. Thus, despite the fact that the list is open to all subscribers, it seemed prudent in this study to cite sources according to subject titles.

3. We examined posts for repeating and resonant themes. Examples given in each section are, in our estimation, representative and subsequent posts on the same subject or event, for the most part, are not cited. Our goal is to give an overall sense of the general thematic consistencies within the discourse.

4. For the title of his book on contemporary popular media fandom, *Textual Poachers*, Henry Jenkins (1992) draws on Michel de Certeau's creative coining (1984) of the term "poaching," by which he means ways nondominant groups "poach" or "steal" aspects of dominant culture, such as texts and discourses, and then re-author them within new contexts to produce non-dominant forms of cultural expression and politics. DeCerteau's and Jenkins's uses of the term "poaching" coincide in large measure with other concepts, such as "sampling," in which one takes material from one source or context and then creatively reuses it in another context with a wholly different effect. Poaching, however, necessarily adds a specific power dimension to the phenomenon; whereas, sampling may not imply specific power relations.

5. By using the term "legislation" here, we do not mean to imply that all of the arguments deal with legal issues; instead, we mean that the logic of a vast majority of the arguments works within both the legal-political structure and the general "discourse" concerning the proposition. Arguments are, in a sense, *legislativistic*. That

is, not only do the arguments often suggest structures to fight anti-immigration policies within the existing legal system but they do so by employing the metaphors
and logics concerning the costs and benefits of immigration that those in favor of
the proposition use.

6. See also "UNITE," which argues that Proposition 187 will "lead to an
increase in the spread of disease among the entire population."

7. See also another post by this group, "Florida Community."

8. Sontag (1990) points out that illness is often associated with the poor, "who
are, from the perspective of the privileged, aliens in one's midst," and this perception "reinforces the association of illness with the foreign: with an exotic, often primitive place" (51). She explains also that when "New World" explorers, having
brought disease to the Americas, returned home, their stories told the opposite
narrative: they thought they must have contracted their diseases in the "New World"
and brought them back to the "Old World," not vice versa (47–48). In the same
sense, immigrants today evoke a general fear of a disintegrating world, like the
construction of androids in *Bladerunner.* Writing about the film, Charles Ramírez
Berg (1989, 13) comments that "the teeming multicultural make-up of the people
in the streets is depicted as the dark side of the melting pot: chaos, filth, over-
crowding, disorder" (13).

9. Cohen 1987 draws on Castells 1979 to suggest that the availability of migrant
labor (and the ability to not use it at times) has become a structural necessity for
capitalist nations, because such external labor can be used to break up the class solidarity of indigenous workers and can help iron out the bust and boom nature of
economies. See also Gutiérrez 1995, 46.

10. Here, as in Chapter 3 in our discussion of Ann Stoler (1995), we are not
assuming an essentialist way of viewing these events. While economics and race
played key roles here, the discourse of the nation-state is not parallel to discourses
of economics or racism. A study such as ours that examines the operations of discourses of migration draws attention to larger forces at work than can the "scapegoat theory" Stoler criticizes.

11. One post ("[SFC] New Data"), which is simply a repost of a *San Francisco
Chronicle* article with no comment on the article by the poster, concentrates on
showing how much undocumented immigrants cost the state, mentioning at the very
end of the article that studies have been inconclusive. Thus, while the article clearly
favors the position that undocumented workers cost the state money and resources,
in the end it takes the "balanced," "equivocating" position that no conclusions have
been reached. The article does not discuss the ethics of talking about people in terms
of cost-benefit analysis.

12. The article also lists various studies of the cost and benefits of immigrants.

13. See also a post providing a "myth" and "fact" sheet ("Action Sheet"). One
of the myths the sheet debunks is that immigrants are a "drain" on the U.S. economy and do not contribute "their fair share."

14. Beginning in August 1995, news releases by the National Committee on
Immigration were posted on the list approximately every two weeks, providing
updates on immigration legislation. We chose not to list every post here. However,
one post ("First they came") explains why these posts were being forwarded and

criticizes the organizations creating and distributing them for dividing "legal" from "illegal" immigrants. For this point, see also "Federal Bill"; "H.R. 1915"; "Immigration/English"; "Immigration in Counter-Terrorism"; "Immigration Update Alert" A; "Immigration Update Alert;"B "Immmigrant [*sic*]"; "Libertarian"; "[NALEO]"; "National Committee"; "Re: FREE"; "Re: S. 269"; "State Anti-Immigrant"A; "State Anti-Immigrant"B.

15. See also Hasian and Delgado 1998 on this point.

16. See, e.g., "187 Boycott"; "AAAS"; "Conference"; "Denver"; "Interesting"; "Latino Law"; "Message"; "More boycott"; "NCSS"; "prop 187"; "RMAASC"; "Speech."

17. Another *telos* often discussed is the creation of government support programs. For instance, arguments for government to produce more social welfare programs often draw on a logic of dependency on women ultimately doing even more work in the labor force than they already do in order to maintain the smooth running of capitalism.

18. On this point, see also "CALL TO US-MEX"; "Correx"; "Fla Convention"; "FL press"; "Free SF"; "Friday 3/29"; "Go Back"; "immigrant rights"; "Immigration Issues"; "LABORNOTES"; "Lafayette Park Protests"; "NPW"; "Oregon Coalition"; "picket"; "Population"; "Sacramento"; "Sparticist"; "Stanford"; "THINGS."

19. See, e.g., "Huge"; "Chicago Forum"; "FOUR WINDS ALERT"; "MAY 1"; "MAY 1st"; "Chicago Contract."

20. Boyd 1996 offers a fascinating account of the ways in which the *Star Trek* writers, rather than the fans, in fact had to alter the Borg from its original conception as an inhuman consciousness to more of a group of individuals in order to fit "the Borg" within the *Star Trek* universe of romantic individuality. The radical difference represented by the Borg offered such an incommensurability to the *Star Trek* universe that its continued existence would have forced a change in the show's concept of individuality.

21. See also "[AP] Mexico City"; "(AP) U.S. Beefing"; "BORDER WALL"; "BORDER WAR"; "boston march"; "THE BRACERO PROGRAM"; "CALIFORNIA: ID Cards"; "California Videotaped"; "[Carlos Fuentes] 'Hey'"; "Congress's"; "[Cox] N. Nusser"; "DEADLY"; "Florida News"; "FOREIGN WORKER"; "For Most"; "FRENCH"; "GOP passes"; "Hemsptead [*sic*]"; "House Panel"; "Immigrant Basher"; "Immigrant Bashing"; "Immigrant Deaths"; "Immigrants Clash"; "IMMIGRANTS FEELING"; "Immigration Legislation"; "INS BUDGET"; "INS DIDN'T ACT"; "INS EXPECTS"; "INS to Commandeer"; "Intra-Hispanic"; "JUDGE RULES"; "LEGAL IMMIGRANTS"; "MERVYN'S"; "Mexican Consular"; "MI: Migrant Workers Make a Difference"; "Michigan's Governor"; "Migration News Sept," "More on Affirmative Action," "More Time"; "NETWAR"; "NJSP"; "[NYT] ADMINISTRATION"; "(NYT) Despite"; "[NYT] Police"; "[THE PARTISAN]"; "Pat's"; "President Backs"; "Pulling"; "Rodney King"; "SIMPSON"; "South Africa's"; "UK"; "U.S. COMMISSION"; "U.S. FOREIGN-BORN"; "U.S.-IMMIGRATION"; U.S. LOOKS"; "Violence Up"; "Visa Categoris [*sic*]"; "WHITE HOUSE PLEDGES"; "(W. Post) Trouble." (Many of the titles in the subject heading of the e-mail posts are in capital letters, perhaps alerting readers, albeit haphazardly, to the fact that the post is or will be a reprint.)

22. See also "Gingrich wants"; "INS SWOOPS"; "JUDGE APPEARS"; "JUDGE TAKING"; "OPPONENTS TRY"; "ORANGE COUNTY CON-GRESSMAN"; "Prop 187 Debate"; "Prop 187 Lessons."

23. See, e.g., "Another"; "Anti-immigration Legislative Alert"; "Chinese"; "denying"; "Fwd: S1394"; "Pressuring"; "Texas"; "Welfare."

24. See, e.g., the "Black Panther Party: Platform and Program" (1984) and the 1848 Seneca Falls "Declaration of Sentiments and Resolutions" (Campbell 1989b, 33–39) for their uses of the wording of the Declaration of Independence.

25. Doug E. Thomas (1993, 337) makes a similar argument: "The subject in language is confronted by language itself as a necessary outcome of the intersubjective creation of community and is forced to enter into a rhetoric of order that makes ideological demands on the individual as a means of preservation for the community itself."

26. See also Gupta 1992 for a discussion of the political potential in organizing transnationally and creating identities forged against/beyond national ones.

27. For a discussion of how transnational corporations have displaced nation-state governments as models and orchestrators of government, see Miyoshi 1993.

Chapter Six

1. For a complex discussion of resistant practices within Mexican migrant communities in the United States, see Rouse (n.d.). He suggests that the use and occupation of space can function in resistant ways.

2. We should also observe that, as David G. Gutiérrez (1995, 30) argues throughout his work, this creative sense of diaspora has been long-standing with Mexican Americans and Hispanics in the United States. As he points out, "In the quarter century before annexation [to the United States], many, if not most, Spanish-speaking residents of Mexico's northern provinces did not even identify themselves as Mexicans and instead probably thought of themselves first as Nuevomexicanos, Tejanos, or Californios." However, in the 1850s, he notes, Mexican Americans throughout the Southwest began to speak of themselves as members of a broad "linguistic/cultural community that was distinct from the North Americans." Indeed, the entire history of Mexicans and Hispanics in the United States is recounted by Gutiérrez as one in which they were forced to take on a collective identity in order to survive economic and ideological challenges and disciplines; once taking on that identity, they were able to make creative use of it.

3. Khacha Toloyan (1991, 3) notes in the founding Preface to *Diaspora* that the journal would be concerned "with the way in which nations, real yet imagined communities, are fabled, brought into being, made and unmade, in culture and politics, both on the land people call their own and in exile."

4. See, for example, Holston and Appadurai 1996 for a discussion of creative resistances created by diasporic groups in inner city contexts. For the authors, transnationalism allows citizens with radical potentials to cross cultural and national boundaries, and thus with their bodies they transgress social spaces and transform the physical surroundings where they live. They argue that the development of social movements as a result of the influx of migrant populations into cities whose

current forms do not accommodate those living within urban spaces leads to the
development of movements for social change at the local level. City-dwellers lead
movements that "affirm access to housing, property, sanitation, health services,
education, child care, and so forth on the basis of citizenship" (197). As a result of
these local social movements, "the urban poor create unprecedented claims on and
to the city, they expand citizenship to new social bases. In so doing, they create new
sources of citizenship rights and corresponding forms of self-rule" (198).

5. In our use of the term "thinking otherwise," we are purposefully referring to
the phrase "listening otherwise" used by Rey Chow (1990–91). While we take Chow
to be making a specific point about individual resistance to nationalist government
in China, at one particular point in the essay, if we substitute "thinking" for "listening," her claim resonates with what we argue here. She writes "[Thinking] is a
'silent' sabotage of the technology of collectivization with its own instruments"
(145). If we consider the technology of governmental thinking in general, and the
"silent" but sometimes "vocal" protests to dominant ways of thinking, this illustrates
our concept of "thinking otherwise."

6. We recognize the wide range of possible "civic articulations" that might be
implied here, from discussions in academic journals to sound bites on newscasts.
As for all rhetorical projects, each decision authors such as we make—which discourses and outlets to investigate and which terms of articulation to use—is a rhetorical one that must be made with the audience and desired effect in mind.

7. Here, we are building on both Michael Calvin McGee's (1990) celebrated turn
to a performative criticism and our own attempt to build a rhetorical "future ante-
rior"—a logic that, if enacted, would work in a world that we would like to help
promote (Sloop and Ono 1993, 1997).

8. Of course, individual critics will answer this question differently, but we
should all be diligent in thinking through the multiple types of people to be affected
by the judgments that would be made if the critics' sense of a "better logic" were
enacted. We are not being so arrogant as to expect that a "rhetorical critic's" essay
will indeed change an entire community's logic. Rather, we are arguing that the
implications of judgment and logics should be taken very seriously in all contexts,
including rhetorical criticism. In this sense, we endorse Robert Hariman's description (1996) of a "cautious postmodernism." While Hariman is discussing political
style, and we are discussing logics of judgment, we would feel comfortable swap-
ping logics for his terms in the following: "This is not to endorse uncritically a world
of autonomous individuals, social sciences, competitive markets, and bureaucratic
states, but at the least it suggests that the choice of a political style ought to include
an appraisal of the various risks involved on each side" (9).

9. For an elaboration of "minor" versus "major" logics, see Deleuze and Guattari 1986.

10. For a discussion of a case study of ideological discipline, see Sloop 1994.

11. This is why revolution must be seen as "a long revolution," in the words of
Raymond Williams (1961). Or, to borrow from McGee 1998, we must begin to see
revolution in terms of generations rather than in terms of decades. Because discourse
has a materiality of use, it is only through transitions in the actual people who have

used a particular vocabulary that change takes place. This change of people is obviously based on changes in generations.

12. Of course the definitions of "human" and generally "U.S. citizen" are themselves rhetorical.

13. McGee (1998) plays off of England's "glorious" nonviolent revolution as his idea of "good" change.

14. For a nice discussion of resistance through production of new subject positions, see Biesecker 1992b.

15. In an argument very similar to that of McGee 1998 and Spivak 1990, Judith Butler (1993, 226–27) suggests that citationality can be effective so long as it draws on prior historical enunciations and then covers them over in the process. We quote her at length here: "If a performative provisionally succeeds (and I will suggest that "success" is always and only provisional), then it is not because an intention successfully governs the action of speech, but only because that action echoes prior actions, and *accumulates the force of authority through the repetition or citation of a prior, authoritative set of practices.* What this means, then, is that a performative 'works' to the extent that *it draws on and covers over* the constitutive conventions by which it is mobilized. In this sense, no term or statement can function performatively without the accumulating and dissimulating historicity of force."

16. The University of California–Berkeley's faculty resolution, also discussed on 187-L, works in a similar fashion ("UC-Berkeley version").

Chapter Seven

1. Of course, we are in no way suggesting that Mexicanas, Mexicanos, Chicanas, and Chicanos do not make up the majority of undocumented peoples in California.

2. For a discussion of media constructions of the "model minority" stereotype as a rhetoric of division between people of color see Osajima 1988.

3. We are referring here to the Naturalization Act of 1790, in which citizenship was defined in these terms.

References

Traditional Print Sources

ABC News. 1994a. 4 Nov. 5:41:20–5:43:30.
———. 1994b. 8 Nov. 5:45:08–5:48:30.
———. 1994c. 24 Nov. 5:37:40–5:39:40.
Almaguer, Tomas. 1994. *Racial Fault Lines: The Historical Origins of White Supremacy in California.* Berkeley: University of California Press.
Alvarez, Fred. 1994. "I Walk in Fear." *Los Angeles Times,* 20 Nov., A20.
Ana, Otto Santa, Juan Morán, and Cynthia Sánchez. 1998. "Awash under a Brown Tide: Immigration Metaphors in California Public and Print Media Discourse." *AZTLAN: A Journal of Chicano Studies* 23:137–76.
Anzaldúa, Gloria. 1987. *Borderlands/La Frontera: The New Mestiza.* San Francisco: Aunt Lute Books.
Aoki, Keith. 1998. "No Right to Own? The Early Twentieth-Century 'Alien Land Laws' As a Prelude to Internment." *Boston College Law Review* 40, *Third World Law Journal* 19:37–72.
Ayres, B. Drummond. 1994. "Anti-Alien Sentiment Spreading in Wake of California's Measure." *New York Times,* 4 Dec., 1, 42.
Bailey, Eric. 1994. "Lungren Backs Prop. 187; Late Stance Assailed." *Los Angeles Times,* 8 Nov., A3.
Balderrama, Francisco E., and Raymond Rodríguez. 1995. *Decade of Betrayal: Mexican Repatriation in the 1930s.* Albuquerque: University of New Mexico Press.
Banks, Sandy. 1994. "Unflagging Controversy." *Los Angeles Times,* 10 Nov., B1.
Barrett, Michele. 1998. *Women's Oppression Today: The Marxist/Feminist Encounter.* Rev. ed. New York: Verso.
Barth, Dianne. 1994. "Vigilantes Enforce 187." *The Record,* 19 Nov., Newsbank INT82, B10.
Baudrillard, Jean. 1983. *Simulations.* Trans. Paul Foss, Paul Patton, and Philip Beitchman. New York: Semiotext(e).
Becker, Samuel. 1971. "Rhetorical Studies for the Contemporary World." In *The Prospect of Rhetoric: Report of the National Developmental Project, Sponsored by Speech Communication Association,* ed. Ed Black and Lloyd Bitzer, 21–43. Englewood Cliffs, N.J.: Prentice-Hall.

211

Benites, Joe. 1994. Letter to the Editor. *Los Angeles Times*, 4 Nov., B6.

Bennett, Brian O'Leary. 1994. "An Initiative Even Conservatives Can Hate." *Los Angeles Times*, 7 Oct., B7.

Berlant, Lauren. 1997. *The Queen of America Goes to Washington City: Essays on Sex and Citizenship.* Durham, N.C.: Duke University Press.

Bhabha, Homi. 1983. "The Other Question: The Stereotype and Colonial Discourse." *Screen* 24:18–36.

Biegel, Stuart. 1995. "The Wisdom of *Plyler v. Doe.*" *Chicano-Latino Law Review* 17:46–63.

Bierly, Janice. 1994. "Teachers as INS Cops: An Ugly Lie." *Los Angeles Times*, 4 Nov., B7.

Biesecker, Barbara A. 1989. "Rethinking the Rhetorical Situation from within the Thematic of Differance." *Philosophy and Rhetoric* 22:110–30.

———. 1992a. "Coming to Terms with Recent Attempts to Write Women into the History of Rhetoric." *Philosophy and Rhetoric* 25:140–61.

———. 1992b. "Michel Foucault and the Question of Rhetoric." *Philosophy and Rhetoric* 25:351–64.

———. 1992c. "Towards a Transactional View of Rhetorical and Feminist Theory: Rereading Helene Cixous's 'The Laugh of the Medusa.'" *Southern Communication Journal* 57:83–95.

———. 1993. "Negotiating with Our Tradition: Reflecting Again (without Apologies) on the Feminization of Rhetoric." *Philosophy and Rhetoric* 26:236–41.

Billington, Ray Allen. 1938. *The Protestant Crusade, 1800–1860: A Study of the Origins of American Nativism.* New York: Macmillan.

Bitzer, Lloyd F., and Edwin Black, eds. 1971. *The Prospect of Rhetoric: Report of the National Developmental Project, Sponsored by Speech Communication Association.* Englewood Cliffs, N.J.: Prentice-Hall.

"Black Panther Party: Platform and Program." 1984. In *The Sixties Papers: Documents of a Rebellious Decade*, ed. Judith Clavir Albert and Stewart Edward Albert, 159–64. New York: Praeger.

Blair, Carole. 1987. "The Statement: Foundation of Foucault's Historical Criticism." *Western Journal of Speech Communication* 51:364–83.

Blair, Carole, and Martha Cooper. 1987. "The Humanist Turn in Foucault's Rhetoric of Inquiry." *Quarterly Journal of Speech* 73:151–71.

Blair, Carole, Marsha S. Jeppeson, and Enrico Pucci Jr. 1991. "Public Memorializing in Postmodernity: The Vietnam Veterans Memorial as Prototype." *Quarterly Journal of Speech* 77:263–88.

Bok, Chip. 1994. Cartoon. *Los Angeles Times*, 28 Oct., B7.

Boris, Eileen. 1995. "The Racialized Gendered State: Constructions of Citizenship in the United States." *Social Politics* 2:160–80.

Bornemeier, James. 1994. "Kemp, Bennett Warn of GOP Rift on Prop. 187." *Los Angeles Times*, 22 Nov., A1.

Bosniak, Linda S. 1996. "Opposing Prop. 187: Undocumented Immigrants and the National Imagination." *Connecticut Law Review* 28:555–619.

Bourdieu, Pierre. 1994. "Structures, Habitus, Power: Basis for a Theory of Symbolic Power." In *Culture/Power/History: A Reader in Contemporary Social Theory*, ed. Nicholas B. Dirks, Geoff Eley, and Sherry B. Ortner, 155–99. Princeton: Princeton University Press.

Bové, Paul. 1990. "Discourse." In *Criticial Terms for Literary Study*, ed. Frank Lentricchia and Thomas McLaughlin, 50–65. Chicago: University of Chicago Press.

Boyd, Katrina. 1995. "Cyborgs in Utopia: The Problem of Radical Difference in *Star Trek: The Next Generation*." In *Enterprise Zones: Critical Positions on Star Trek*, ed. Taylor Harrison, Sarah Projansky, Kent A. Ono, and Elyce Rae Helford, 95–114. Boulder, Colo.: Westview Press.

"Brave Voices at a Crucial Point." 1994. Editorial. *Los Angeles Times*, 21 Oct., B6.

Brownstein, Ronald. 1994. "Wilson Proposes U.S. Version of Prop. 187." *Los Angeles Times*, 19 Nov., A1.

Brownstein, Ronald, and Patrick J. McDonnell. 1994. "Kemp, Bennett and INS Chief Decry Prop. 187." *Los Angeles Times*, 19 Oct., A1.

Bryant, Donald C., ed. 1966. *The Rhetorical Idiom: Essays in Rhetoric, Oratory, Language, and Drama, Presented to Herbert August Wichelns, with a Reprinting of His "Literary Criticism of Oratory" (1925)*. New York: Russell & Russell.

Buchanan, Patrick J. 1994. "What Will America Be in 2050?" *Los Angeles Times*, 28 Oct., B7.

Burke, Kenneth. 1969. *A Rhetoric of Motives*. Berkeley: University of California Press.

Burnett, Ron. 1995. *Cultures of Vision: Images, Media, and the Imaginary*. Bloomington: Indiana University Press.

Bustillo, Miguel. 2000. "California GOP Distancing Itself from Prop. 187." *Los Angeles Times*, 7 Aug., A3.

Butler, Judith. 1990. *Gender Trouble: Feminism and the Subversion of Identity*. New York: Routledge.

———. 1993. *Bodies That Matter: On the Discursive Limits of "Sex."* New York: Routledge.

"California Judge Limits Reach of Illegal-Immigrant Initiative." 1995. *New York Times*, 10 Feb., A20.

"California Students Leave School to Protest Alien Ballot Measure." 1994. *New York Times*, 29 Oct., 9.

Campbell, Karlyn Kohrs. 1989a. *Man Cannot Speak for Her*. Vol. 1, *A Critical Study of Early Feminist Rhetoric*. New York: Praeger.

———. 1989b. *Man Cannot Speak for Her*. Vol. 2, *Key Texts of the Early Feminists*. New York: Greenwood Press.

Carter, Paul. 1992. *Living in a New Country: History, Traveling and Language*. London: Faber.

Carvajal, Doreen, and Gebe Martinez. 1994. "Clergy Struggles to Address Volatile Issues of Prop. 187." *Los Angeles Times*, 3 Oct., A1.

Cassyd, Donna, Cindy Chung-Mi Choi, Gwenn Perez, and Paula Ward. 1994. "Prop. 187." Letter to the Editor. *Los Angeles Times*, 8 Oct., B7.

Castells, Manuel. 1979. "Immigrant Workers and Class Struggle in Advanced Capitalism." In *Peasants and Proletarians: The Struggles of Third World Workers*, ed. Robin Cohen, Peter C. W. Gutkind, and Phyllis Brazier, 353–79. New York: Monthly Review Press.

CBS News. 1994a. 13 Oct. 5:54:00–5:58:00.

———. 1994b. 16 Nov. 5:48:20–5:50:50.

Cervantes, Nancy, Sasha Khokha, and Bobbie Murray. 1995. "Hate Unleashed: Los Angeles in the Aftermath of Proposition 187." *Chicano-Latino Law Review* 17:1–23.

Chaffee, Steven, Clifford I. Nass, and Seung-Mock Yang. 1990. "The Bridging Role of Television in Immigrant Political Socialization." *Human Communication Research* 17:266–88.

Chambers, Iain. 1994. *Migrancy, Culture, Identity.* New York: Routledge.

Chan, Sucheng, ed. 1991. *Entry Denied: Exclusion and the Chinese Community in America, 1882–1943.* Philadelphia: Temple University Press.

Chang, Grace. 1994. "Undocumented Latinas: The New 'Employable Mothers.'" In *Mothering: Ideology, Experience, and Agency,* ed. Evelyn Nakano Glenn, Grace Chang, and Linda Rennie Forcey, 259–85. New York: Routledge.

Chang, Howard. 1994. "Shame on Them, Picking on Children." *Los Angeles Times,* 6 Sept., B5.

Charland, Maurice. 1987. "Constitutive Rhetoric: The Case of the *Peuple Quebecois.*" *Quarterly Journal of Speech* 73:133–50.

———. 1991. "Finding a Horizon and Telos: The Challenge to Critical Rhetoric." *Quarterly Journal of Speech* 77:71–74.

———. 1998. "Property and Propriety: Rhetoric, Justice, and Lyotard's *Differend.*" In *Judgment Calls: Rhetoric, Politics, and Indeterminacy,* ed. John M. Sloop and James McDaniel, 220–36. Boulder, Colo.: Westview Press.

Chavez, Stephanie, and Sandy Banks. 1994. "Prop. 187 Is Sore Subject for Illegal Immigrant Students." *Los Angeles Times,* 17 Sept., 1, A24.

Chow, Rey. 1990–91. "Listening Otherwise, Music Miniaturized: A Different Type of Question about Revolution." *Discourse* 13:129–48.

Clark, Norman. 1996. "The Critical Servant." *Quarterly Journal of Speech* 82:111–25.

Cloud, Dana L. 1992. "The Limits of Interpretation: Ambivalence and the Stereotype in *Spencer for Hire.*" *Critical Studies in Mass Communication* 9:311–24.

———. 1996. "Hegemony or Concordance? The Rhetoric of Tokenism in 'Oprah' Winfrey's Rags-to-Riches Biography." *Critical Studies in Mass Communication* 13:115–37.

Cohen, Robin. 1987. *The New Helots: Migrants in the International Division of Labour.* Brookfield, Vt.: Gower.

———. 1991. *Contested Domains: Debates in International Labour Studies.* Atlantic Highlands, N.J.: Zed Books.

———. 1997. *Global Diasporas: An Introduction.* London: UCL Press.

Coleman, James. 1994. "Illegal Immigrants Are, by Definition, Criminals." *Los Angeles Times,* 12 Sept., B7.

Condit, Celeste Michelle. 1987. "Crafting Virtue: The Rhetorical Construction of Public Morality." *Quarterly Journal of Speech* 73:79–97.

———. 1990. *Decoding Abortion Rhetoric: Communicating Social Change.* Urbana: University of Illinois Press.

Condit, Celeste Michelle, and John Louis Lucaites. 1993. *Crafting Equality: America's Anglo-African Word.* Chicago: University of Chicago Press.

Connell, Richard, Beth Shuster, and James Rainey. 1994. "Officials Draw Fire for Use of Tax Funds to Fight 187." *Los Angeles Times*, 11 Nov., A1.

Connor, Steven. 1997. *Postmodernist Culture: An Introduction to Theories of the Contemporary.* 2d ed. Cambridge, Mass.: Blackwell.

Cooper, Martha. 1988. "Rhetorical Criticism and Foucault's Philosphy of Discursive Events." *Central States Speech Journal* 39:1–17.

Cooper, Phillip J. 1995. "*Plyler* at the Core: Understanding the Proposition 187 Challenge." *Chicano-Latino Law Review* 17:64–87.

Cornelius, Wayne A. 1982. *America in the Era of Limits: Migrants, Nativists, and the Future of U.S.-Mexican Relations.* La Jolla, Calif.: Center for U.S-Mexican Studies, University of California, San Diego.

———. 1994. "Don't Vote for a Fix That Won't Work." *Los Angeles Times*, 28 Oct., B7.

Coutin, Susan Bibler, and Phyllis Pease Chock. 1995. "'Your Friend, the Illegal': Definition and Paradox in Newspaper Accounts of U.S. Immigration Reform." *Identities* 2:123–48.

Crowley, Sharon. 1992. "Reflections on an Argument That Won't Go Away; or, A Turn of the Ideological Screw." *Quarterly Journal of Speech* 78:450–65.

Davis, Mike. 1990. *City of Quartz.* New York: Verso.

de Certeau, Michel. 1984. *The Practice of Everyday Life.* Trans. Steven Randall. Berkeley: University of California Press.

Decker, Cathleen. 1994. "Brown Raps Wilson for His Support of Prop. 187." *Los Angeles Times*, 20 Oct., A3.

Deibert, Ronald J. 1997. *Parchment, Printing, and Hypermedia: Communication in World Order Transformation.* New York: Columbia University Press.

de la Torre, Adela. 1994. "Many a Slip 'Twixt Passage and Enforcement." *Los Angeles Times*, 16 Nov., B7.

Deleuze, Gilles, and Felix Guattari. 1986. *Kafka: Toward a Minor Literature.* Trans. Dana Polan. Minneapolis: University of Minnesota Press.

Delgado, Fernando Pedro. 1994. "The Complexity of Mexican American Identity: A Reply to Hecht, Sedano, and Ribeau and Mirandé and Tanno." *International Journal of Intercultural Relations* 18:77–84.

———. 1998a. "Chicano Ideology Revisited: Rap Music and the (Re)articulation of Chicanismo." *Western Journal of Communications* 62:95–113.

———. 1998b. "When the Silenced Speak: The Textualization and Complications of Latina/o Identity." *Western Journal of Communications* 62:420–38.

De Uriarte, Mercedes Lynn. 1994. "Exploring (and Exploding) the U.S. Media Prism." *Media Studies Journal* 8:163–75.

Dibble, Sandra. 1996. "S.D.-Tijuana Ties Called Strong Despite Prop. 187." *San Diego Union-Tribune*, 14 Jan., Newsbank INT7, A2.

Doherty, Tom. 1993. "*Falling Down.*" Review of *Falling Down* (Warner Brothers movie). *Cineaste* 20:39–41.

Dolan, Maura. 1994. "Parts of Prop. 187 May Be Blocked Two or More Years." *Los Angeles Times*, 16 Nov., A1.

Dow, Bonnie. 1990. "Hegemony, Feminist Criticism, and *The Mary Tyler Moore Show.*" *Critical Studies in Mass Communication* 7:261–74.

Dunn, Ashley. 1991. "$1-Million Visas Seeking to Lure the Wealthy to U.S." *Los Angeles Times*, 21 July, A1.

Dutt, Mallika. 1998. "Reclaiming a Human Rights Culture: Feminism of Difference and Alliance." In *Talking Visions: Multicultural Feminism in a Transnational Age*, ed. Ella Shohat, 225–46. New York: MIT Press.

Eaton, Tracey. 1994. "California Measure's Passage Angers Mexicans." *Dallas Morning News*, 10 Nov., Newsbank INT74, F3.

Ebert, Teresa L. 1996. *Ludic Feminism and After: Postmodernism, Desire, and Labor in Late Capitalism*. Ann Arbor: University of Michigan Press.

Enriquez, Sam. 1994a. "Prop. 187 Opponents Confront Ezell." *Los Angeles Times*, 13 Oct., B1.

———. 1994b. "Students Fear Their Hopes Will Be Dashed." *Los Angeles Times*, 23 Oct., B1.

———. 1994c. "Valley Business Groups Back Measure." *Los Angeles Times*, 17 Sept., B3.

"The Error of Prop. 187." 1994. Editorial. *Los Angeles Times*, 30 Oct., M6.

"Fearful Aliens in California Staying Away from Clinics." 1994. *New York Times*, 12 Nov., A9.

Feldman, Paul. 1994a. "Foes Launch Radio Ad Campaign." *Los Angeles Times*, 12 Oct. 1994, A3.

———. 1994b. "Former Mayor Bradley Opposes Prop. 187 in Rare Appearance." *Los Angeles Times*, 23 Sept., A3.

———. 1994c. "Group's Funding of Immigration Measure Assailed." *Los Angeles Times*, 10 Sept., B3.

———. 1994d. "Immigrant Measure Foes Open Drive." *Los Angeles Times*, 19 Aug., A3.

———. 1994e. "Judge Lets City Join Prop. 187 Lawsuit." *Los Angeles Times*, 13 Dec. 1994, B1.

———. 1994f. "Measure's Foes Try to Shift Focus from Walkouts to Issues." *Los Angeles Times*, 4 Nov., A3.

———. 1994g. "Opponents of Measure Vow to Sue if It Passes." *Los Angeles Times*, 11 Oct., B1.

———. 1994h. "Prop. 187 Foes' Strategy Has a Twist." *Los Angeles Times*, 26 Sept., A1.

———. 1994i. "Prop. 187 Sponsors Blame Foes for Illegal Immigrants' Fears over Seeking Health Care." *Los Angeles Times*, 26 Nov., A33.

———. 1994j. "Uncertainty, Lawsuits Would Greet Prop. 187." *Los Angeles Times*, 31 Oct., A1.

———. 1995a. "Federal Judge Schedules Full Prop. 187 Trial." *Los Angeles Times*, 14 Mar., A1.

———. 1995b. "Judge Allows Two Church Groups to Enter Prop. 187 Court Fight." *Los Angeles Times*, 10 Jan., A3.

———. 1995c. "Major Portions of Prop. 187 Thrown Out by Federal Judge." *Los Angeles Times*, 21 Nov., A1.

———. 1995d. "Uncertain Fate of Prop. 187 Tests Patience." *Los Angeles Times*, 28 Mar., A3.

Feldman, Paul, and Rich Connell. 1994. "Wilson Acts to Enforce Parts of Prop. 187: Eight Lawsuits Filed." *Los Angeles Times*, 10 Nov., A1.

Feldman, Paul, and Jon Garcia. 1994. "Emotions High at Last-Minute Protests." *Los Angeles Times*, 8 Nov., A3.

Feldman, Paul, and Carl Ingram. 1994. "Will Defend Prop. 187 in Courts, Lungren Says." *Los Angeles Times*, 1 Nov., A1.

Feldman, Paul, and Patrick J. McDonnell. 1994a. "Prop 187 Foes Urge Boycott of Nabisco, Disney." *Los Angeles Times*, 9 Dec., A3.

———. 1994b. "Prop. 187 Sponsors Swept Up in National Whirlwind." *Los Angeles Times*, 14 Nov., A1.

———. 1994c. "U.S. Judge Blocks Most Sections of Prop. 187." *Los Angeles Times*, 15 Dec., A1.

Feldman, Paul, and James Rainey. 1994a. "L.A. Joins Challenge to Prop. 187." *Los Angeles Times*, 18 Nov., A1.

———. 1994b. "Parts of Prop. 187 Blocked by Judge." *Los Angeles Times*, 17 Nov., A1.

———. 1994c. "U.S. Judge Extends Ban on Prop. 187." *Los Angeles Times*, 23 Nov., B1.

Fernandez, Celestino, and Lawrence R. Pedroza. 1981. *The Border Patrol and News Media Coverage of Undocumented Mexican Immigration During the 1970's: A Quantitative Content Analysis in the Sociology of Knowledge*. Tucson: Mexican American Studies and Research Center, University of Arizona.

Fineman, Mark. 1994a. "Mexico Assails State's Passage of Prop. 187." *Los Angeles Times*, 10 Nov., A28.

———. 1994b. "Mexico Fights Prop. 187—Delicately." *Los Angeles Times*, 29 Oct., A13.

Fiske, John, and John Hartley. 1978. *Reading Television*. New York: Methuen.

Flanigan, James. 1994. "Keep Immigration on the Side of Common Sense." *Los Angeles Times*, 30 Oct., D1.

Flores, Lisa A. 1996. "Creating Discursive Space through a Rhetoric of Difference: Chicana Feminists Craft a Homeland." *Quarterly Journal of Speech* 82:142–56.

Foucault, Michel. 1977. *Discipline and Punish*. Trans. Alan Sheridan. New York: Pantheon.

———. 1980. "Two Lectures." In *Power/Knowledge: Selected Interviews and Other Writings, 1972–1977*, ed. Colin Gordon, 78–108. New York: Pantheon.

———. 1984. "Nietzsche, Genealogy, History." In *The Foucault Reader*, ed. Paul Rabinow, 76–100. New York: Pantheon.

Friedman, Paul G. 1977. "Special Reports: Closing the Cultural Gap: Awareness Groups for Migrant Children." *Communication Studies* 28:134–39.

Frith, Simon. 1996. *Performing Rites: On the Value of Popular Music*. Cambridge, Mass.: Harvard University Press.

Fuentes, Carlos. 1994. "Why a Damn Great State Resource?" *Los Angeles Times*, 28 Sept., B7.

Gaffney, Edward McGlynn Jr. 1994. "The Territorial Imperative, California Style." *America*, 5 Nov., 3.

———. 1995. "Immigrant Bashing." *Christian Century*, 1 Mar., 228–29.

Gaonkar, Dilip Parameshwar. 1982. "Foucault on Discourse: Methods and Temptations." *Journal of American Forensic Association* 18:246–57.

———. 1990. "Object and Method in Rhetorical Criticism: From Wichelns to Leff and McGee." *Western Journal of Speech Communication* 54:290–316.

García, Juan Ramón. 1980. *Operation Wetback: The Mass Deportation of Mexican Undocumented Workers in 1954.* Westport, Conn.: Greenwood Press.

Garcia, Ruben J. 1995. "Critical Race Theory and Proposition 187: The Racial Politics of Immigration Law." *Chicano-Latino Law Review* 17:118-48.

Goldberg, David J., and John D. Rayner. 1989. *The Jewish People: Their History and Their Religion.* Harmondsworth, Middlesex, Eng.: Penguin.

Gonzalez, Alberto. 1990. "Mexican 'Otherness' in the Rhetoric of Mexican Americans." *Southern Communication Journal* 55:276–91.

Goodnight, G. Thomas. 1995. "The Firm, the Park, and the University: Fear and Trembling on the Postmodern Trail." *Quarterly Journal of Speech* 81:267–90.

Gordon, Milton M. 1964. *Assimilation in American Life: The Role of Race, Religion, and National Origins.* New York: Oxford University Press.

Gotanda, Neil. 1991. "A Critique of 'Our Constitution Is Color-Blind.'" *Stanford Law Review* 44:1–68.

Gramsci, Antonio. 1971. *Selections from the Prison Notebooks of Antonio Gramsci.* Ed. and trans. Quintin Hoare and Geoffrey Nowell Smith. London: Lawrence and Wishart.

Gray, Herman. 1989. "Television, Black Americans, and the American Dream." *Critical Studies in Mass Communication* 6:376–86.

———. 1995. *Watching Race: Television and the Struggle for "Blackness."* Minneapolis, University of Minnesota Press.

Greene, Ronald Walter. 1998. "Another Materialist Rhetoric." *Critical Studies in Mass Communication* 15:21–40.

Gupta, Akhil. 1992. "The Song of the Nonaligned World: Transnational Identities and the Reinscription of Space in Late Capitalism." *Cultural Anthropology* 7:63–79.

Gutiérrez, David G. 1995. *Walls and Mirrors: Mexican Americans, Mexican Immigrants, and the Politics of Ethnicity.* Berkeley: University of California Press.

———. 1999. "Migration, Emergent Ethnicity, and the 'Third Space': The Shifting Politics of Nationalism in Greater Mexico." *Journal of American History,* September, 86:481–517.

Gutierrez, Elena Rebeca. 1999. "The Racial Politics of Reproduction: The Social Construction of Mexican-Origin Women's Fertility." Ph.D. diss., University of Michigan.

Gutiérrez-Jones, Carl. 1995. *Rethinking the Borderlands: Between Chicano Culture and Legal Discourse.* Berkeley: University of California Press.

Gyory, Andrew. 1998. *Closing the Gate: Race, Politics, and the Chinese Exclusion Act.* Chapel Hill: University of North Carolina Press.

Hall, Stuart. 1981. "The Whites of Their Eyes: Racist Ideologies and the Media." In *Silver Linings,* ed. George Bridges and Rosalind Brunt, 28–52. London: Lawrence and Wishart.

———. 1992. "The Question of Cultural Identity." In *Modernity and Its Futures,* ed. Stuart Hall, David Held, and Tony McGrew, 273–316. Cambridge, Mass.: Polity Press.

———. 1997. *Representation and the Media*. Prod. and dir. Sut Jhally. Media Education Foundation, Northampton, Mass. Videocassette.

Hall, Stuart, Chas Critcher, Tony Jefferson, John Clarke, and Brian Roberts. 1978. *Policing the Crisis: Mugging, the State, and Law and Order*. London: Macmillan.

Hanke, Robert. 1990. "Hegemonic Masculinity in *thirtysomething*." *Critical Studies in Mass Communication* 7:231–48.

Hariman, Robert. 1991. "Critical Rhetoric and Postmodern Theory." *Quarterly Journal of Speech* 77:67–70.

———. 1996. *Political Style: The Artistry of Power*. Chicago: University of Chicago Press.

Hart, Jack Robert. 1975. "A History of the *Los Angeles Times* from the Era of Personal Journalism to the Advent of the Multi-Media Communications Corporation." Ph.d. diss., University of Wisconsin.

Hasian, Marouf Jr., and Fernando Delgado. 1998. "The Trials and Tribulations of Racialized Critical Rhetorical Theory: Understanding the Rhetorical Ambiguities of Proposition 187." *Communication Theory* 8:245–70.

Hauser, Gerard A. 1998. "Vernacular Dialogue and the Rhetoricality of Public Opinion." *Communication Monographs* 65:83–107.

Hayes-Bautista, David and Gregory Rodriguez. 1994. "A Rude Awakening for Latinos." *Los Angeles Times*, 11 Nov., B7.

Hayward, Brad. 1994. "Debate on Immigration Reform Crackles with Passion, Outrage." *Sacramento Bee*, 20 Sept., Newsbank INT59, D1.

Higham, John. 1955. *Strangers in the Land: Patterns of American Nativism, 1860–1925*. New Brunswick, N.J.: Rutgers University Press.

Hing, Bill Ong. 1993a. "Beyond the Rhetoric of Assimilation and Cultural Pluralism: Addressing the Tension of Separatism and Conflict in an Immigration-Driven Multiracial Society." *California Law Review* 81:863–925.

———. 1993b. *Making and Remaking Asian America through Immigration Policy, 1850–1990*. Stanford, Calif.: Stanford University Press.

Hoffman, Abraham. 1974. *Unwanted Mexican Americans in the Great Depression: Repatriation Pressures, 1929–1939*. Tucson: University of Arizona Press.

Hofstetter, C. Richard, and Brian Loveman. 1982. "Media Exposure and Attitude Consistency about Immigration." *Journalism Quarterly* 59:298–302.

Holston, James, and Arjun Appadurai. 1996. "Cities and Citizenship." *Public Culture* 8:187–204.

"How Many Lawsuits Are Necessary?" 1994. Editorial. *Los Angeles Times*, 12 Nov., B7.

Ibarra, Rafael. 1994. "Looking at Proposition 187 through the Eyes of an Illegal Valedictorian." *Los Angeles Times*, 6 Nov., M6.

Impoco, Jim, and Mike Tharp. 1994. "California Propositions Will Cost Plenty." *U.S. News and World Report*, 26 Dec., 60.

Jameson, Fredric. 1981. *The Political Unconscious: Narrative as a Socially Symbolic Act*. Ithaca, N.Y.: Cornell University Press.

Jenkins, Henry. 1988. "*Star Trek* Rerun, Reread, Rewritten: Fan Writing as Textual Poaching." *Critical Studies in Mass Communication* 5:85–107.

———. 1992. *Textual Poachers: Television Fans and Participatory Culture*. New York: Routledge.

Johnson, Kevin R. 1993. "*Los Olvidados:* Images of the Immigrant, Political Power of Noncitizens, and Immigration Law and Enforcement." *Brigham Young University Law Review*, 1139–256.

———. 1995a. "An Essay on Immigration Politics, Popular Democracy, and California's Proposition 187: The Political Relevance and Legal Irrelevance of Race." *Washington Law Review*, 629–73.

———. 1995b. "Public Benefits and Immigration: The Intersection of Immigration Status, Ethnicity, Gender, and Class." *UCLA Law Review*, 1509–75.

———. 1998. "Race, the Immigration Laws, and Domestic Race Relations: A 'Magic Mirror' into the Heart of Darkness." *Indiana Law Journal*, 1111–59.

Kadetsky, Elizabeth. 1994. "School's Out." *Nation*, 21 Nov., 601.

Kang, K. Connie. 1994. "Asian American Groups Organize to Fight Measure." *Los Angeles Times*, 9 Oct., B1.

Katz, Jesse. 1995. "Prop. 187 Gives Texas a Selling Point in Mexico." *Los Angeles Times*, 6 Feb., A1.

Kim, Young Yun. 1977. "Communication Patterns of Foreign Immigrants in the Process of Acculturation." *Human Communication Research* 4:66–77.

King, Peter H. 1994a. "Be Careful What You Pray For . . ." *Los Angeles Times*, 2 Oct., A3.

———. 1994b. "Let's Make a Deal." *Los Angeles Times*, 2 Nov., A3.

———. 1994c. "A Roll Call of Second Opinions." *Los Angeles Times*, 26 Oct., A3.

———. 1994d. "They Kept Coming." *Los Angeles Times*, 9 Nov., A3.

Klinge, Dan. 1994. Letter to the Editor. *Los Angeles Times*, 2 Nov., B6.

Krikorian, Greg, and Dave Lesher. 1994. "Huffington Declares Support for Prop. 187." *Los Angeles Times*, 21 Oct., A1.

Krikorian, Greg, and Amy Wallace. 1994. "Prop. 187 Rises as Key Theme in Top Two Races." *Los Angeles Times*, 25 Oct., A1.

Kwong, Peter. 1997. *Forbidden Workers: Illegal Chinese Immigrants and American Labor*. New York: The New Press.

Lacan, Jacques. 1977. *Ecrits: A Selection*. Trans. Alan Sheridan. New York: Norton.

Laguna, Jesse. 1994. "Latinos Want a Tighter Border, Too." *Los Angeles Times*, 23 Sept., B7.

Lauter, David, and John Broder. 1994. "Clinton Attacks Prop. 187 at City Hall Rally." *Los Angeles Times*, 5 Nov., A1.

Lipsitz, George. 1990. *Time Passages: Collective Memory and American Popular Culture*. Minneapolis: University of Minnesota Press.

———. 1998. "California: The Mississippi of the 1990s." Chapter 10 in *The Possessive Investment in Whiteness: How White People Profit from Identity Politics*. Philadelphia: Temple University Press.

Lorde, Audre. 1984. "The Master's Tools Will Never Dismantle the Master's House" In *Sister/Outsider: Essays and Speeches*. Freedom, Calif.: The Crossing Press.

Lowe, Lisa. 1991. "Heterogeneity, Hybridity, Multiplicity: Marking Asian American Differences." *Diaspora* 1:24–44.

————. 1996. *Immigrant Acts: On Asian American Cultural Politics*. Durham, N.C.: Duke University Press.

Lucaites, John Louis, and Celeste Michelle Condit, eds. 1999. Introduction to *Contemporary Rhetorical Theory: A Reader*. New York: Guilford.

Lum, Casey Man Kong. 1991. "Communication and Cultural Insularity: The Chinese Immigrant Experience." *Critical Studies in Mass Communication* 8: 91–101.

Lyotard, Jean-François. 1984. *The Postmodern Condition: A Report on Knowledge*. Trans. Geoff Bennington and Brian Massumi. Minneapolis: University of Minnesota Press.

————. 1985. *Just Gaming*. Trans. Wlad Godzich. Minneapolis: University of Minnesota Press.

————. 1988. *The Differend: Phrases in Dispute*. Trans. Georges Van Den Abbeele. Minneapolis: University of Minnesota Press.

Mahony, Roger. 1994. "Protect the Children from Politics." *Los Angeles Times*, 25 Oct., B7.

Martinez, Al. 1994. "Pride and Prejudice." *Los Angeles Times*, 22 Oct., B3.

Martinez, Gebe, and Patrick McDonnell. 1994. "Prop. 187 Backers Counting on Message, Not Strategy." *Los Angeles Times*, 30 Oct., A1.

Martinez, Ruben. 1994. "The Nightmare Is Coming True." *Los Angeles Times*, 28 Nov., B7.

Matloff, Norman. 1994. "American Minorities Try to Hold the Line." *Los Angeles Times*, 30 Sept., B7.

McCann, Lynn D., Michael L. Hecht, and Sidney Ribeau. 1986. "Commmunication Apprehension and Second Language Acquisition among Vietnamese and Mexican Immigrants: A Test of the Affective Filter Hypothesis." *Communication Research Reports* 3:33–38.

McCue, Andy. 1975. "Evolving Chinese Language Dailies Serve Immigrants in New York City." *Journalism Quarterly* 52:272–76.

McDonnell, Patrick J. 1994a. "Foes of Prop. 187 Toeing a Difficult Line." *Los Angeles Times*, 26 Sept., A16.

————. 1994b. "Health Clinic Report Declines after Prop. 187." *Los Angeles Times*, 26 Nov., A1.

————. 1994c. "L.A. Police Panel Joins Foes of Measure." *Los Angeles Times*, 19 Oct., B4.

————. 1994d. "Mahony to Fight Ballot Measure on Immigrants." *Los Angeles Times*, 24 July, B1.

————. 1994e. "Police Fear Prop. 187 Will Crush Hard-Earned Trust." *Los Angeles Times*, 5 Nov., A1.

————. 1994f. "Prop. 187 Turns Up Heat in U.S. Immigrant Debate." *Los Angeles Times*, 10 Aug., A1.

————. 1998. "Judge's Final Order Kills Key Points of Prop. 187; Permanent Injunction Is Levied on the '94 Measure Targeting Illegal Immigrants Use of Public Benefits." *Los Angeles Times*, 19 Mar., A3.

McDonnell, Patrick J., and Paul Feldman. 1994a. "Spreading the Word on Prop. 187 Tests Patience." *Los Angeles Times*, 16 Dec., A3.

————. 1994b. "State Counsel Questions Parts of Prop. 187." *Los Angeles Times*, 2 Nov., A1.

McDonnell, Patrick J., and Dave Lesher. 1994. "Clinton, Feinstein Declare Opposition to Prop. 187." *Los Angeles Times*, 22 Oct., A1.

McDonnell, Patrick J., and Robert J. Lopez. 1994a. "70,000 March through L.A. against Prop. 187." *Los Angeles Times*, 17 Oct., A1.

————. 1994b. "Some See New Activism in Huge March." *Los Angeles Times*, 18 Oct., B1.

McGee, Michael Calvin. 1980a. "The Ideograph: A Link between Rhetoric and Ideology." *Quarterly Journal of Speech* 66:1–16.

————. 1980b. "The Origins of 'Liberty': A Feminization of Power." *Communication Monographs* 47:23–45.

————. 1982. "A Materialist's Conception of Rhetoric." In *Explorations in Rhetoric: Studies in Honor of Douglas Ehninger*, ed. Raymie E. McKerrow, 23–48. Glenview, Ill.: Scott, Foresman.

————. 1990. "Text, Context, and the Fragmentation of Contemporary Culture." *Western Journal of Speech Communication* 54:274–89.

————. 1998. *Rhetoric in Postmodern America: Conversations with Michael Calvin McGee*. Ed. Carol Corbin. New York: Guilford.

McKerrow, Raymie E. 1989. "Critical Rhetoric: Theory and Praxis." *Communication Monographs* 56:91–111.

————. 1991. "Critical Rhetoric in a Postmodern World." *Quarterly Journal of Speech* 77:75–78.

————. 1993. "Critical Rhetoric and the Possibility of the Subject." In *The Critical Turn: Rhetoric and Philosophy in Postmodern Discourse*, ed. Ian Angus and Lenore Langsdorf, 51–67. Carbondale: Southern Illinois University Press.

McLaughlin, Ken. 1994. "'SOS' Initiative Is Not a Sure Bet." *San Jose Mercury News*, 13 Sept., Newsbank INT67, F7.

McLaughlin, Ken, and Mary Anne Ostrom. 1994. "Proposition 187 Drew from Wide Spectrum in Lopsided Victory." *San Jose Mercury News*, 13 Nov., Newsbank INT74, A9.

Merl, Jean, and Paul Feldman. 1994. "Business Leaders Attack Immigration Measure." *Los Angeles Times*, 21 Oct., A3.

Michaels, Walter Benn. 1995. *Our America: Nativism, Modernism, and Pluralism*. Durham, N.C.: Duke University Press.

Michaelson, Scott, and David E. Johnson, eds. 1997. *Border Theory: The Limits of Cultural Politics*. Minneapolis: University of Minnesota Press.

Miller, Martin. 1994. "Fund-Raiser by Supporters Draws 100 in Orange County." *Los Angeles Times*, 29 Oct., A24.

"The Missing $3 Billion." 1994. *Economist*, 19 Nov., 30–31.

Mitchell, Alison. 1996. "U.S. Launches a Second Strike against Iraq after Clinton Vows to Extract 'A Price.'" *New York Times*, 4 Sept., A1.

Miyoshi, Masao. 1993. "A Borderless World? From Colonialism to Transnationalism and the Decline of the Nation-State." *Critical Inquiry* 19:726–51.

Mondello, Salvatore. 1967. "The Magazine Charities and the Italian Immigrants, 1903–14." *Journalism Quarterly* 44:91–98.

Mouffe, Chantal. 1993. *The Return of the Political*. New York: Verso.

Murphy, John M. 1995. "Critical Rhetoric as Political Discourse." *Argumentation and Advocacy* 32:1–15.

Nakagawa, Gordon. 1993. "Deformed Subjects, Docile Bodies: Disciplinary Practices and Subject-Constitution in Stories of Japanese-American Internment." In *Narrative and Social Control: Critical Perspectives*, ed. Dennis K. Mumby, 143–63. Newbury Park, Calif.: Sage.

Nakano Glenn, Evelyn. 1992. "From Servitude to Service Work: Historical Continuities in the Racial Division of Paid Reproductive Labor." *Signs* 18:1–43.

Nakayama, Thomas K., and Robert L. Krizek. 1995. "Whiteness: A Strategic Rhetoric." *Quarterly Journal of Speech* 81:291–309.

Nalick, John, and Paul Feldman. 1994. "Santa Ana Schools Condemn Immigrant Measure." *Los Angeles Times*, 29 Sept., A21.

Navarrette, Ruben Jr. 1994. "At the Birth of a New—and Younger—Latino Activism." *Los Angeles Times*, 13 Nov., M1.

———. "Is This What Prop. 187 Sought? More Latino Citizens?" 1995. *Los Angeles Times*, 30 Apr., M6.

NBC News. 1994a. 17 Oct. 5:51:30–5:53:40.

———. 1994b. 4 Nov. 5:38:40–5:40:40.

———. 1994c. 8 Nov. 5:45:00–5:48:30.

———. 1994d. 10 Nov. 5:30:20–5:32:50.

———. 1994e. 14 Nov. 5:48:50–5:52:30.

———. 1994f. 17 Nov. 5:30:20–5:33:00.

———. 1994g. 21 Nov. 5:40:00–5:42:10.

Ngai, Mae M. 1999. "The Architecture of Race in American Immigration Law: A Reexamination of the Immigration Act of 1924." *Journal of American History* 86:67–92.

Noble, Kenneth B. 1994. "Initiative on Aliens Suffers Its Biggest Setback Yet." *New York Times*, 15 Dec., A18.

Ono, Kent A. 1995. "Re/signing 'Asian American': Rhetorical Problematics of Nation." *Amerasia Journal* 21:67–78.

———. 1998. "Communicating Prejudice in the Media: Upending Racial Categories in Doubles." In *Communicating Prejudice*, ed. Michael L. Hecht, 206–20. Thousand Oaks, Calif.: Sage Publications.

Ono, Kent A., and John M. Sloop. 1992. "Commitment to Telos: A Sustained Critical Rhetoric." *Communication Monographs* 59:48–60.

———. 1995. "The Critique of Vernacular Discourse." *Communication Monographs* 62:19–46.

———. 1999. "Critical Rhetorics of Controversy." *Western Journal of Communication* 63:526–38.

Osajima, Keith. 1988. "Asian Americans as the Model Minority: An Analysis of the Popular Press Image in the 1960s and 1980s." In *Reflections on Shattered Windows*, ed. Gary Okihiro, Shirley Hune, Arthur Hansen, and John Liu, 165–74. Pullman: Washington State University Press.

———. 1995. "Postmodern Possibilities: Theoretical and Political Directions for Asian American Studies." *Amerasia Journal* 21:79–87.

Ostrow, Ronald. 1994. "U.S. Justice Official's Memo Assails Prop. 187." *Los Angeles Times*, 28 Oct., A1.

Owen, Susan, and Peter Ehrenhaus. 1993. "Animating a Critical Rhetoric: On the Feeding Habits of American Empire." *Western Journal of Communication* 57:169–77.

Parry-Giles, Trevor. 1998. "Stemming the Red Tide: Free Speech and Immigration Policy in the Case of Margaret Randall." *Western Journal of Speech Communication* 52:167–83.

Perea, Juan F., ed. 1997. *Immigrants Out! The New Nativism and the Anti-Immigrant Impulse in the United States.* New York: New York University Press.

Perry, Steven. 1983. "Rhetorical Functions of the Infestation Metaphor in Hitler's Rhetoric." *Central States Speech Journal* 34:229–35.

Perry, Tony. 1994. "Anti-187 Protester Honored for Halting Burning of Flag." *Los Angeles Times*, 5 Nov., A24.

Phelan, Peggy. 1993. *Unmarked: The Politics of Performance.* New York: Routledge.

Prince, Ronald. 1994a. "Americans Want Illegal Immigrants Out." *Los Angeles Times*, 6 Sept., B5.

———. 1994b. Letter to the Editor. *Los Angeles Times*, 25 Aug., B6.

Probyn, Elspeth. 1993. *Sexing the Self: Gendered Positions in Cultural Studies.* New York: Routledge.

"Proposition: Text of Proposed Law." 1994. In *Illegal Aliens. Ineligibility for Public Services. Verification and Reporting. Initiative Statute,* 91–92. Sacramento: State of California.

"Proposition 187: One Is More than Enough." 1994. *Los Angeles Times*, 22 Nov., B6.

"Proposition 187 and the Law of Unintended Consequences." 1994. Editorial. *Los Angeles Times*, 2 Oct., M4.

Purdum, Todd S. 1999. "Governor Seeks Compromise on Aid to Illegal Immigrants: Davis Tries Not to Anger Hispanic Backers." *New York Times*, 16 Apr., A14.

Pyle, Amy. 1994a. "L.A. Teachers Sign Pledges to Ignore Measure." *Los Angeles Times*, 2 Nov., B1.

———. 1994b. "Some Question Wisdom of Nov. 2 Student Walkout." *Los Angeles Times*, 26 Oct., B3.

———. 1994c. "Suit Cites Impaired Children Aided by Services." *Los Angeles Times*, 11 Nov., A22.

Pyle, Amy, and Paul Feldman. 1994a. "Investigation of Walkouts Urged." *Los Angeles Times*, 5 Nov., A24.

———. 1994b. "School Letter on Prop. 187 Draws Fire." *Los Angeles Times*, 1 Nov., B1.

Pyle, Amy, and Beth Shuster. 1994. "10,000 Students Protest Prop. 187." *Los Angeles Times*, 3 Nov., A1.

Quintanilla, Michael. 1995. "Rage and Raves." *Los Angeles Times*, 11 Jan., E4.

Ramírez Berg, Charles. 1989. "Immigrants, Aliens, and Extraterrestrials: Science Fiction's Alien 'Other' as (among *Other* Things) New Hispanic Imagery." *CineAction!* 18:3–17.

Ramos, George. 1994a. "Prop. 187 Debate: No Tolerance but Abundant Anger." *Los Angeles Times*, 10 Oct., B3.

———. 1994b. "Prop. 187 Foes Get a Boost from an Unlikely Ally." *Los Angeles Times*, 19 Sept., B3.

Regis, Humphrey A. 1989. "A Theoretical Framework for the Investigation of the Role and Significance of Communication in the Development of the Sense of Community among English-Speaking Caribbean Immigrants." *Howard Journal of Communications* 2:57–80.

Rennert, Leo. 1994. "Clinton Calls State's Prop. 187 Unconstitutional, Harmful." *Sacramento Bee*, 22 Oct., Newsbank INT67, E11.

Reynoso, Cruz. 1995. "Introduction." *Chicano-Latino Law Review* 17:ix–xi.

Richardson, Lisa. 1994. "A System in Jeopardy." *Los Angeles Times*, 5 Nov., B1.

Rivera, Carla, and Paul Feldman. 1994. "L.A. Supervisors Decline to Join Prop. 187 Challenges." *Los Angeles Times*, 11 Nov., A1.

Roberts, Dorothy E. 1997. *Killing the Black Body: Race, Reproduction, and the Meaning of Liberty*. New York: Pantheon Books.

Rodriguez, Antonio H., and Carlos A. Chavez. 1994. "Latinos Unite in Self-Defense on Prop. 187." *Los Angeles Times*, 21 Oct., B7.

Rodríguez, Néstor P. 1997. "The Social Construction of the U.S.-Mexico Border." In *Immigrants Out! The New Nativism and the Anti-Immigrant Impulse in the United States*, ed. Juan F. Perea, 223–43. New York: New York University Press.

Romero, Simon. 1994. "1,500 Students Leave Class to Protest against Prop. 187." *Los Angeles Times*, 15 Oct., B3.

Romney, Lee. 1994. "Boy in Prop. 187 Controversy Mourned."*Los Angeles Times*, 29 Nov., A22.

Rosello, Mireille. 1998. "Representing Illegal Immigrants in France: From Clandestins to L'affaire-de-sans-papiers-de-Saint-Bernard." *Journal of European Studies* 28:137–51.

Rosin, Hanna. 1994. "Raisin Hell." *New Republic*, 14 Nov., 15–16.

Ross, Felecia G. Jones. 1994. "Preserving the Community: Cleveland Black Papers' Response to the Great Migration." *Journalism and Mass Communication Quarterly* 71:531–39.

Rouse, Roger. N.d. "Men in Space: Power and the Appropriation of Urban Form among Mexican Migrants in the U.S." Manuscript.

Rowland, Robert C. 1995. "In Defense of Rational Argument: A Pragmatic Justification of Argumentation Theory and Response to the Postmodern Critique." *Philosophy and Rhetoric* 28:350–64.

Safire, William. 1997. "I Remember Larry." *New York Times*, 2 Jan., A15.

Said, Edward. 1989. "Representing the Colonized, Anthropology's Interlocutors." *Critical Inquiry* 15:205–25.

"Saipan Sweatshop Claims Settled by Retailers." 1999. *Davis Enterprise*, 9 Aug., A7.

Saldívar, José. 1991. *The Dialectics of Our America: Genealogy, Cultural Critique, and Literary History*. Durham, N.C.: Duke University Press.

———. 1997. *Border Matters: Remapping American Cultural Studies*. Berkeley: University of California Press.

Sanchez, Edgar. 1994. "Immigrants Flocking to Citizenship Classes." *Sacramento Bee*, 22 Nov., Newsbank INT82, B8.

Sandbrook, Richard. 1982. *The Politics of Basic Needs: Urban Aspects of Assaulting Poverty in Africa*. London: Heinemann Educational Books.

Sapiro, Virginia. 1984. "Women, Citizenship, and Nationality: Immigration and Naturalization Policies in the United States." *Politics and Society* 13:1–26.

Scheer, Robert. 1994a. "The Dirty Secret behind Proposition 187." *Los Angeles Times*, 29 Sept., B7.

———. 1994b. "Prop. 187: Stick It to the Kids." *Los Angeles Times*, 13 Oct., B7.

———. 1994c. "Prop 187 Is a Search for Scapegoats." *Los Angeles Times*, 27 Oct., B7.

Schiller, Nina Glick, Linda Basch, and Cristina Szanton Blanc. 1995. "From Immigration to Transmigrant: Theorizing Transnational Migration." *Anthropological Quarterly* 68:48–63.

"Schools Plan to Drop Their Prop. 187 Suit." 1994. *Los Angeles Times*, 16 Nov., A24.

Schuck, Peter H., and Rogers M. Smith. 1985. *Citizenship without Consent: Illegal Aliens in the American Polity*. New Haven: Yale University Press.

Schwartz, Herman. 1994. "The Constitutional Issue behind Proposition 187." *Los Angeles Times*, 9 Oct., M1.

———. 1995. "No: The Law Is Clear, Only the Court has Changed." *ABA Journal*, Feb., 43.

Schwichtenberg, Cathy. 1984. "*The Love Boat:* The Packaging and Selling of Love, Heterosexual Romance, and Family." *Media, Culture, and Society* 6:301–11.

———. 1993. "Madonna's Postmodern Feminism: Bringing the Margins to the Center." Chapter 6 in *The Madonna Connection: Representational Politics, Subcultural Identities, and Cultural Theory*. Boulder: Westview Press.

Seo, Diane. 1994. "CSU Case May Become Legal Test for Prop. 187." *Los Angeles Times*, 21 Nov., A3.

Shalit, Ruth. 1995. "Breeders." *New Republic*, 14 Aug., 42.

Shogren, Elizabeth. 1994. "Gingrich Says He Opposes U.S. Version of Prop. 187." *Los Angeles Times*, 5 Dec., A1.

Shohat, Ella, and Robert Stam. 1994. *Unthinking Eurocentrism: Multiculturalism and the Media*. London: Routledge.

Shuit, Douglas. 1994. "Initiative Would Hasten Spread of TB, Study Says." *Los Angeles Times*, 19 Oct., A1.

Shuster, Beth. 1994a. "Prop. 187 Backers Plan Recall Campaign." *Los Angeles Times*, 15 Nov., B3.

———. 1994b. "Prop. 187 Cost to L.A. Schools Put at $450 Million." *Los Angeles Times*, 21 Sept., B1.

———. 1994c. "Prop. 187 Would Cut 10,000 Teaching Jobs, Officials Say." *Los Angeles Times*, 22 Oct., B3.

Shuster, Beth, and Chip Johnson. 1994. "Hundreds of Students Stage Walkouts to Protest Prop. 187." *Los Angeles Times*, 21 Oct., B3.

Shusterman, Carl 1994. "Make It 'SOS' for Snake-Oil Salesmen." *Los Angeles Times*, 15 Sept., B7.

Simon, Laura. 1999. Telephone interview with Kent A. Ono. 29 Mar.

Simon, Rita James, and Susan H. Alexander. 1993. *The Ambivalent Welcome: Print Media, Public Opinion, and Immigration.* Westport, Conn.: Praeger.

Skelton, George. 1994a. "Politicians Lay Out Cards in Prop. 187 Game." *Los Angeles Times,* 24 Oct., A3.

———. 1994b. "Wilson's Key Task: Handling Prop. 187." *Los Angeles Times,* 10 Nov., A3.

Sklansky, David A. 1995. "Proposition 187 and the Ghost of James Bradley Thayer." *Chicano-Latino Law Review* 17:24–45.

Sloop, John M. 1994. "'Apology Made to Whoever Pleases': Cultural Discipline and the Grounds of Interpretation." *Communication Quarterly* 42:345–62.

———. 1996. *The Cultural Prison: Discourse, Prisoners, and Punishment.* Tuscaloosa: University of Alabama Press.

Sloop, John M., and Mark Olson. 1999. "*Cultural Struggle:* A Politics of Meaning in Rhetorical Studies." In *At the Intersection: Cultural Studies and Rhetorical Studies,* ed. Thomas Rosteck, 248–65. New York: Guilford Press.

Sloop, John M., and Kent A. Ono. 1993. "Futuring Traditions: Making Postmodern Judgments." In *Argument and the Postmodern Challenge: Proceedings of the Eighth SCA/AFA Conference on Argumentation,* ed. Raymie McKerrow, 143–48. Annandale, Va.: Speech Communication Association.

———. 1997. "Out-law Discourse: The Critical Politics of Material Judgment." *Philosophy and Rhetoric* 30:50–69.

Solomon, Martha. 1985. "The Rhetoric of Dehumanization: An Analysis of Medical Reports of the Tuskegee Syphilis Project." *Western Journal of Speech Communication* 49:233–47.

Sontag, Susan. 1990. *Illness as Metaphor* [1977]; *and, AIDS and Its Metaphors* [1988]. New York: Doubleday, Anchor Books.

"Sounds as if He's Doing His Job." 1994. *Los Angeles Times,* 18 Nov., B6.

Spivak, Gayatri Chakravorty. 1988. *In Other Worlds: Essays in Politics.* New York: Routledge.

———. 1990. "Reading *The Satanic Verses.*" *Third Text* 11:41–60.

Stacey, Judith. 1990. *Brave New Families: Stories of Domestic Upheaval in Late Twentieth Century America.* New York: Basic Books.

Stall, Bill, and Cathleen Decker. 1994. "Wilson and Prop. 187 Win." *Los Angeles Times,* 9 Nov., A1.

Stall, Bill, and Dave Lesher. 1994. "Stressing GOP Unity, Wilson Backs Prop. 187." *Los Angeles Times,* 18 Sept., A3.

Stall, Bill, and Amy Wallace. 1994. "Prop. 187 Key to Getting U.S. Aid, Wilson Argues." *Los Angeles Times,* 29 Oct. 1994, A1.

Stall, Bill, and Dan Weintraub. 1994. "Brown, Wilson Swap Attacks on Prop. 187, Crime." *Los Angeles Times,* 2 Nov., A3.

"Stiffer Punishment for Hiring of Aliens." 1996. *New York Times,* 14 Feb., A16.

Stoler, Ann Laura 1995. *Race and the Education of Desire: Foucault's History of Sexuality and the Colonial Order of Things.* Durham, N.C.: Duke University Press.

Sullivan, Deborah. 1995. "Students Avoiding College over Fear of Prop. 187, Educator Says." *Los Angeles Times,* 14 Jan., B8.

Sunoo, Don H., Edgar P. Trotter, and Ronald L. Aames. 1980. "Media Use and Learning of English by Immigrants." *Journalism Quarterly* 57:330–33.

Takaki, Ronald. 1989. *Strangers from a Different Shore: A History of Asian Americans.* New York: Penguin.

Therborn, Goran. 1980. *What Does the Ruling Class Do When It Rules?* London: Verso.

Thomas, Douglas E. 1993. "Burke, Nietzsche, Lacan: Three Perspectives on the Rhetoric of Order." *Quarterly Journal of Speech* 79:336–55.

———. 1997. "Deconstruction and Rationality: A Response to Rowland, or Postmodernism 101." *Philosophy and Rhetoric* 30:70–81.

Toloyan, Khacha. 1991. "Preface." *Diaspora* 1:3–7.

Torres, Art. 1994. "It Can Still Be a Golden State." *Los Angeles Times*, 21 Nov., B7.

Unz, Ron. 1994. "Scaling the Heights of Irrationality." *Los Angeles Times*, 3 Oct., B7.

Vasquez, Daniel. 1994. "Rally Blasts Immigrant Backlash." *Oakland Tribune*, 13 Oct., INT 67: F3.

Verhovek, Sam Howe. 1999. "Illegal Immigrant Workers Being Fired in I.N.S. Tactic." *The New York Times*, 2 Apr., A1.

Vialet, Joyce C., and Larry M. Eig. 1991. "Immigration Act of 1990." *Migration World* 19:32–42.

Volpp, Leti. 1996. "Talking Culture: Gender, Race, Nation, and the Politics of Multiculturalism." *Columbia Law Review*, 1573–617.

Wagley, Anne Paxton. 1995. "Newly Ratified International Human Rights Treaties and the Fight against Proposition 187." *Chicano-Latino Law Review* 17:88–117.

Wallace, Amy. 1994. "Brown Attacks Wilson on Illegal Immigration." *Los Angeles Times*, 26 Oct., A3.

Wander, Philip. 1983. "The Ideological Turn in Modern Criticism." *Central States Speech Journal* 34:1–18.

———. 1984. "The Third Persona: The Ideological Turn in Rhetorical Theory." *Central States Speech Journal* 35:197–216.

Wander, Philip, and Steven Jenkins. 1972. "Rhetoric, Society, and the Critical Response." *Quarterly Journal of Speech* 58:441–50.

Wang, Georgette, and D. Lawrence Kincaid. 1982. "News Interest of Immigrants in Hawaii." *Journalism Quarterly* 59:573–80.

Weinberg, Sydney Stahl. 1992. "The Treatment of Women in Immigration History: A Call for Change." *Journal of American Ethnic History* 11:25–67.

Weintraub, Daniel W. 1994. "Voter Group Favors Brown, Feinstein; Opposes Prop. 187." *Los Angeles Times*, 4 Nov., A3.

Weintraub, Daniel, and Bill Stall 1994. "Wilson Would Expel Illegal Immigrants from Schools." *Los Angeles Times*, 16 Sept., A1.

Whitson, Steve, and John Poulakos. 1993. "Nietzsche and the Aesthetics of Rhetoric." *Quarterly Journal of Speech* 79:131–45.

"Why California Should Vote 'No' on Proposition 187." 1994. *Los Angeles Times*, 2 Nov., B6.

"Why Proposition 187 Won't Work." 1994. *New York Times*, 20 Nov., S4.

Wichelns, Herbert A. 1925. "The Literary Criticism of Oratory." In *Studies in Rhetoric and Public Speaking in Honor of James A. Winans.* New York: Century.

Will, George 1994. "1982 Court's Hubris Comes Home to Roost." *Los Angeles Times*, 30 Oct., M7.
Williams, Raymond. 1961. *The Long Revolution*. New York: Penguin.
Wood, Robin. 1985. "An Introduction to the American Horror Film." In *Movies and Methods*, vol. 2, ed. Bill Nichols. Berkeley: University of California Press.
Yum, June Ock. 1982. "Communication Diversity and Information Acquisition among Korean Immigrants in Hawaii." *Human Communication Research* 8: 154–69.
Zuckerman, Mortimer B. 1994. "Beyond Proposition 187." *U.S. News and World Report*, 12 Dec., 124.

187-L E-Mail Postings

All citations are online postings at 187-L-Resisting and Organizing Against Prop 187. 187-L@CMSA.BERKELEY.EDU.

"1-800 number to Congress is FREE (for a while)—see last paragraph." 26 Apr. 1995.
"1-800 to Congress: Paid for by Exxon." 4 Aug. 1995.
"6 DAY MARCH TO THE BORDER. . . ." 9 Apr. 1996.
"8-27: Rally against National Immigration Bill." 11 Aug. 1995.
"9th Circuit Ruling on English as State Language." 9 Dec. 1994.
"25th Chicano Moratorium Commemoration Marcha." 2 Aug. 1995.
"[51] REPORT: MORE BORDER PATROLS WON'T FIX IMMIGRATION WOES." 10 Mar. 1995.
"70 IMMIGRANTS FOUND IN RAID ON SWEATSHOP." 26 Sept. 1995.
"187." 23 Feb. 1995.
"187 boycott against California—Nat. Ass. Of Hispanic Journalists." 23 Nov. 1994.
"187's status: constitutional v. statutory." 31 Jan. 1995.
"1995-05-03 Fact Sheet Immigration Enforcement Improvements Act." 4 May 1995.
"1995-06-23 Statement by President on New Guestworker Program." 27 June 1995.
"AAAS RESPONSE TO 187 << The Board Statement." 29 Nov. 1994.
"AAW v. Board of Trustees—Ca." 2 Feb. 1995.
"ABC DAY ONE." 11 Jan. 1995.
"Action Sheet: Anti-Immigrant Racism." 5 Mar. 1996.
"ACT NOW!—Ban on Funded Student Groups." 21 July 1995.
"AFFAM-L: List on Affirmative Action info & organizing." 21 July 1995.
"Affirmative Action Poll." 24 Mar. 1995.
"AFL-CIO 800-Number to Congress." 8 July 1995.
"Aftermath of Prop 187: Licensing Human Rights Abuses Against Racial. . . ." 22 Aug. 1995.
"ALERT: Leahy petition has 20K, needs more this week." 9 June 1995.
"Another Welfare Reform Updatem, Pt. 2." 3 Apr. 1995.
"Anti-enslavement legislation (AB 81 and 83)." 6 Mar. 1995.

"Anti-immigrant legislation synopsis...." 26 July 1995.

"Anti-immigration Legislative Alert." 18 Mar. 1995.

"Anti-immigration movement builds in Florida." 6 Feb. 1995.

"[AP] Larry Gerber, 'Law Enforcement Crowd Cheers Gates.'" 17 Apr. 1996.

"[AP] Mexico City: Protest at U.S. Embassy for Beatings." 13 Apr. 1996.

"(AP) U.S. Beefing Up Border Forces." 14 Jan. 1996.

"API-FIRE: Educational Forum on Welfare Reform." 31 May 1995.

"Apr 9: to be sent out NOW." 5 Apr. 1995.

"Are We Immigrants?" 26 Apr. 1995.

"Asian Hate Crime—PLEASE FORWARD!" 18 Apr. 1996.

"Asian Law Caucus Statement on Immigrant Beatings." 4 Apr. 1996.

"Aug 5: YOUTH IN STRUGGLE '95 Planning Meeting." 29 July 1995.

"Bilingual Ed." 12 Sept. 1995.

"BOOK: Immigration and Ethnic Communities/A Focus on Latinos." 28 Mar. 1996.

"BORDER CRISIS WORSENS." 11 Feb. 1996.

"[BORDERLINES] Belated Thoughts about Prop187." 7 Mar. 1995.

"BORDER WALL A WORLD AWAY FROM THE TWO LAREDOS." 13 Mar. 1996.

"BORDER WAR TURNS CHURCH SHELTER INTO WAYSTATION." 30 Jan. 1996.

"boston march." 26 Mar. 1995.

"Boycott of American Economic Association California meeting." 14 Sept. 1995.

"THE BRACERO PROGRAM IS BACK!!!" 12 Mar. 1996.

"Buchanan's Bigoted Statements." 27 Feb. 1996.

"CALIFORNIA: ID Cards Proposed for Immigrants." 16 Jan. 1996.

"Californias [sic] Still Pro-187." 13 Mar. 1995.

"California Summer: 1995." 3 July 1995.

"California Videotaped Beating of Two Mexicans." 4 Apr. 1996.

"A CALL FOR JUSTICE!" 3 Apr. 1996.

"CALL TO ACTION." 29 Apr. 1995.

"CALL TO US-MEX BORDER FORUM." 17 Feb. 1996.

"CANET: e-mail lists for campus activists." 27 July 1995.

"[Carlos Fuentes] 'Hey, Mike Royko, Pick a Few Strawberries!'" 15 Apr. 1996.

"Chicago Contract Demonstration." 21 Apr. 1995.

"Chicago Forum on Prop. 187." 10 Apr. 1995.

"Chinese Immigrants Organize Against PRA." 5 June 1995.

"Columbia U takeover for Ethnic Studies." 6 Feb. 1996.

"Conference Boycott." 15 Nov. 1994.

"Congress's Anti-Immigrant Effort." 28 Mar. 1996.

"COORDINADORA 96: CALIFORNIA REGIONAL MEETING." 16 Jan. 1996.

"Coordinadora 96: Regarding California ID Card Initiative." 23 Jan. 1996.

"Correx to Immigration Report." 28 Mar. 1996.

"[Cox] N. Nusser, 'California Beating Provokes Mexican Outcry.'" 15 Apr. 1996.

"[CSPM] Houston Declaration (Spanish) (June 1995)." 8 June 1995.

"DEADLY CAMPAIGN AGAINST IMMIGRANTS IN AUSTRIA EVOKES NAZI PAST." 23 Aug. 1995.
"Denver 187-Vigil." 23 Dec. 1994.
"denying prenatal care." 23 Feb. 1995.
"DV96 and DOS Visa Bulletin." 20 Aug. 1995.
"east coast student coordination resolutions." 25 Jan. 1995.
"ENDORSERS FOR MARCH 29 LOCAL ACTION." 5 Mar. 1995.
"English First/U.S. English resignation. . . ." 17 July 1995.
"English-only Update." 13 Apr. 1996.
"Environmental Justice and the University." 13 Sept. 1995.
"'ethnic humor' on LA radio show." 13 July 1995.
"Fall 1995: Western Youth Activist Conference." 5 May 1995.
"Federal Bill to Deny Benefits." 2 Mar. 1995.
"Feinstein Action Alert." 10 Jan. 1995.
"FIRST ANNUAL FOUR WINDS YOUTH SUMMIT." 28 Jan. 1996.
"First they came for. . . ." 17 Sept. 1995.
"Fla. Bishops Statement on Immigration." 20 Jan. 1996.
"Fla Convention for Immigrant Rights." 1 Aug. 1995.
"Fla. Prop 187 summaries." 13 Aug. 1995.
"FL convention statements." 12 Aug. 1995.
"Florida 187 Convention Statements." 9 Aug. 1995.
"Florida Community Health Assn. statement on 187." 19 Jan. 1996.
"Florida Immigrant Rights." 9 July 1995.
"Florida News Item." 8 Sept. 1995.
"FL press conference on federal legislation." 8 Mar. 1996.
"FOREIGN WORKER HIRING FEE PROPOSED BY IMMIGRATION PANEL." 13 Sept. 1995.
"For Most Immigrants, 'Immersion' Failed." 2 Aug. 1995.
"FOUR WINDS ALERT!!!!!!!!!!!!" 14 Apr. 1995.
"FOUR WINDS STUDENT MOVEMENT: DEMANDS AND ACTION PLAN." 25 Jan. 1995.
"FREEDOM SUMMER." 4 Apr. 1996.
"Free SF Legal Clinic." 7 Mar. 1996.
"FRENCH HR Abuse Targets Ethnics." 13 Aug. 1995.
"Friday 3/29 Immigrant Rights Hunger Strikers Picket of Feinstein's Office." 28 Mar. 1996.
"Frontline Anti-Affirmative Action Legislation." 11 Mar. 1995.
"Fwd: S1394 is SPLIT!!!" 20 Mar. 1996.
"Germany to Deport 40,000 Vietnamese." 3 July 1995.
"Gingrich wants U.S.-Mexco border sealed." 6 Feb. 1995.
"Go Back to where you came from. . . ." 19 Apr. 1996.
"Good Luck: Get on TV while you're at it." 17 Feb. 1995.
"GOP passes 'moderate' attack on Noncitizens." 15 Mar. 1995.
"Greetings from Nicaragua." 22 Aug. 1995.
"H.R. 1915 Leaflet Draft." 27 July 1995.
"Hate Groups Suspected in Bombing." 26 Apr. 1995.

"Help Texas Farm Workers!" 17 May 1995.
"Hemsptead [sic], LI, NY-Salvadorean Beaten." 26 Feb. 1996.
"HERE/SEIU Job Openings to Organize the Unorganized." 17 July 1995.
"House Panel Urges Drastic Steps on Immigration." 29 June 1995.
"Huge March April 9 (corrected post)." 5 Mar. 1995.
"Immigrant Basher Turns to Politics." 13 Apr. 1996.
"Immigrant Bashing Politicians." 28 Feb. 1996.
"Immigrant Deaths During Border Pursuit." 13 Apr. 1996.
"Immigrant Rights and the PRA." 20 Apr. 1995.
"Immmigrant [sic] Rights Hunger Strike—correction." 15 Mar. 1996.
"immigrant rights in fla." 14 July 1995.
"Immigrants Clash with Police in NJ Detention Center." 20 June 1995.
"IMMIGRANTS FEELING GOP HEAT/THREAT OF LOSING WELFARE
    PROMPTS RUSH TOWARD CITIZENSHIP." 23 Mar. 1995.
"Immigrants' Right." 5 July 1995.
"Immigration/English Only Alert." 13 Apr. 1996.
"Immigration in Counter-Terrorism Bill." 13 Mar. 1996.
"Immigration Issues Resource List." 21 Mar. 1996.
"Immigration Legislation." 16 Apr. 1996.
"Immigration Update Alert" A. 16 Mar. 1996.
"Immigration Update Alert" B. 19 Mar. 1996.
"[xH-LABOR] Impact of Immigrants." 15 Mar. 1996.
"INS BUDGET FOR NATURALIZATION CRITICIZED." 23 Aug. 1995.
"INS DIDN'T ACT ON SWEATSHOP TIP—FEDS RECEIVED INFORMA-
    TION 3 YEARS AGO." 8 Aug. 1995.
"INS EXPECTS FLOOD OF 1 MILLION FARMWORKERS FOR CITI-
    ZENSHIP." 13 Sept. 1995.
"INS SWOOPS DOWN ON DAY LABORERS IN BAY AREA." 9 May 1995.
"INS to Commandeer Cops?" 10 Feb. 1996.
"InterAction." 27 July 1995.
"Interesting protest . . . I LIKE IT!! 'Flu Day' in CA." 10 Dec. 1994.
"Internet Censorship Alert." 6 June 1995.
"Intra-Hispanic Tensions Tied to Anti-Immigrant Mood." 17 Aug. 1995.
"Istook Amendment: 'Non-Profit Gag Rule.'" 10 Sept. 1995.
"Jobs at Student Activism Clearinghouse." 1 Aug. 1995.
"[LA JORNADA] ARTICLES; AGRESSION [sic] AGAINST UNDOCU-
    MENTED [SPANISH]." 13 Apr. 1996.
"JUDGE APPEARS SKEPTICAL OF STATE'S PROP 187 REASONING." 28
    July 1995.
"JUDGE RULES AGAINST RAIDING FOR ILLEGALS." 22 Apr. 1995.
"JUDGE TAKING STATEMENTS IN PROP !*& [sic] TRIAL." 25 July 1995.
"June 22 Sacramento Immigration Meeting w/Assemblyperson." 1 June 1995.
"June 24: Protest AA Decision at Berkeley." 21 July 1995.
"LABNEWS: E-mail List for Labor News." 7 Aug. 1995.
"LABORNOTES: Lafayette Park organizing in Shadow of Prop 187." 5 Sept.
    1995.

"Lafayette Park: Fax/Phone Corporate Clients of Hotel." 6 June 1995.
"Lafayette Park Protests Stir up Establishment in Contra Costa County." 31 July 1995.
"LA Justice for Janitors & SEIU Democracy struggle." 31 July 1995.
"LA Office: Californians for Justice/AA Mobilization." 18 Sept. 1995.
"LA TIMES: An Ocean Away, Prop. 187 Protested." 20 Feb. 1995.
"Latino Law Students @ Rutgers." 6 Mar. 1995.
"Latino Leaders in Arizona Plan California Boycott." 17 Dec. 1994.
"LEGAL IMMIGRANTS IN LINE OF FIR [sic] ON WELFARE." 27 Mar. 1995.
"Legal Notice from UCSD re: Proposition 187." 29 Mar. 1995.
"Legal Representation for People." 6 June 1995.
"Libertarian Mag on National ID." 12 Sept. 1995.
"Los Angeles: Thousands March/Justice for Janitors!" 10 Feb. 1995.
"MAASU Spring Conference." 7 Feb. 1996.
"March 29 Action Summary." 12 Apr. 1995.
"MARCHA: Needs Your Support." 12 Apr. 1996.
"MAY 1 MOBILIZATION: FOUR WINDS." 18 Apr. 1995.
"MAY 1st MOBILIZATION." 27 Apr. 1995.
"May 2: Forum on Resisting unjust laws." 26 Apr. 1995.
"MERVYN'S MIRED IN LABOR PROBE—SWEATSHOP RAID FINDS PRISON-LIKE CONDITIONS." 9 Aug. 1995.
"Message from AAS UC Berkeley, about the AAAS Conference." 1 Dec. 1994.
"Mexican Consular Offices in the USA." 28 Jan. 1996.
"Mexican Hero Seeks U.S. Presidency (fwd)." 22 Mar. 1996.
"MI: Migrant Workers Make a Difference." 20 Aug. 1995.
"Michigan's Governor Makes Immigration Gaffe." 9 June 1995.
"Migrants against HIV/AIDS: IMPORTANT INFO." 5 Jan. 1996.
"Migration News Sept Issue." 6 Sept. 1995.
"Moratorium's Position on Lincoln Heights Murder." 15 Aug. 1995.
"More boycott discussion//From the Board//No decision as yet." 21 Nov. 1994.
"More News on Skinhead Attack in Phoenix." 3 July 1995.
"More on Affirmative Action." 23 Mar. 1995.
"More Time for Asylum Claims: Central American Refugees Benefit." 4 Aug. 1995.
"More U.S. Population Stats. . . ." 6 Mar. 1995.
"Nader on Immigration." 2 Mar. 1996.
"[NALEO] INS Green Card Replacement Program Info." 3 Apr. 1995.
"National Committee on Immigration News Release No 10." 24 Aug. 1995.
"NCSS refuses to boycott California." 1 Jan. 1995.
"NETWAR COULD MAKE MEXICO UNGOVERNABLE." 21 Mar. 1995.
"Network for Withdrawing INS Troops from Border."
"New FBI Charter to Investigate Political Groups." 2 Mar. 1995.
"News Releases." 12 Nov. 1994.
"NJSP-DWNSI Acquittal." 11 Feb. 1996.
"NPC: Resist "English Only." 27 Feb. 1995.
"NPW: Hotel Workers Update." 9 Aug. 1995.

"NY Community Wide Forum on anti-immigrant legislation." 18 July 1995.

"[NYT] ADMINISTRATION VOWS VETO/SENATE CONSIDERS IMMI-GRATION." 17 Apr. 1996.

"(NYT) Despite Increased Patrols, the Border Remains Porous." 13 Feb. 1996.

"[NYT] Police Gave Orders—In English—Before They Beat Mexicans." 13 Apr. 1996.

"Oakland: Anti-187 Educational Event, Mar 25." 8 Mar. 1995.

"Oakland School Board votes for non-compliance w. Prop 187." 11 May 1995.

"Oakland School Board votes on 187 on Wednesday, May 3." 21 Apr. 1995.

"Oakland School Board votes on non-compliance May 10." 26 Apr. 1995.

"OCT. 12 CIVIL DISOBEDIANCE [sic]: FOUR WINDS." 27 July 1995.

"[LA OPINION] CALIFORNIA: ACTIONS CONTINUE (Spanish)." 13 Apr. 1996.

"OPPONENTS TRY TO AVOID TRIAL ON PROP. 187." 2 May 1995.

"Orange County." 16 Apr. 1996.

"ORANGE COUNTY CONGRESSMAN EMPLOYED ILLEGAL IMMI-GRANT." 10 May 1995.

"OREGON: ANTI-IMMIGRANT INITIATIVES (51, 52, 53, 54) [VOTE "NO]." 23 Feb. 1996.

"Oregon Coalition." 24 Mar. 1996.

"Oregon march (4/29)." 18 Apr. 1995.

"Organizing Training & Rally against McClintock." 26 June 1995.

"[THE PARTISAN] Beyond November?" 28 Feb. 1995.

"Pat's Great Wall of the United States." 4 Mar. 1996.

"Perm Residents & Financial Aid???" 9 Mar. 1995.

"Petition for Affirmative Action (1)." 14 July 1995.

"PHONE ALERT: Defend anti-187 Youth Organizer." 12 June 1995.

"picket feinstein's office friday march 29." 29 Mar. 1996.

"Population and World Migration." 4 Mar. 1995.

"Prensa mexicana en Internet/Mexican press on Internet." 13 June 1995.

"President Backs Plan to Cut Legal Immigration." 8 June 1995.

"Pressuring Feinstein (Calif.)." 12 Mar. 1996.

"Pro-EZLN, Anti-Racism Demo in Italy Feb.25." 8 Mar. 1995.

"PROGRESSIVE STUDENT CONFERENCE." 12 July 1995.

"prop 187." 22 Nov. 1994.

"Prop 187 Debate Goes on in Court." 28 July 1995.

"PROP187 ELECT INFO." 7 Dec. 1994.

"Prop 187 Lessons for AA Fight." 29 Mar. 1995.

"Pulling Back on Extended Families in Immigration." 2 Aug. 1995.

"R&R's call for RESIST 96." 28 Mar. 1996.

"Racist Remarks by L.A. Radio Host." 13 Apr. 1996.

"Re: anti-immigrant show: HELP." 30 May 1995.

"Re: Contract with America." 3 Jan. 1995.

"Re: FREE ISSUE OF U.S. IMMIGRANT MAGAZINE." 30 May 1995.

"Re: Madison Prop 187 Action." 21 Feb. 1995.

"Re: May 1 and May 6 Actions." 17 Apr. 1995.

"Re: 'migra' checkpoints and campus action." #1. 22 Feb. 1995.
"Re: 'migra' checkpoints and campus action." #2. 22 Feb. 1995.
"Re: 'migra' checkpoints and campus action." #3. 22 Feb. 1995.
"Re: Nader on Immigration." 2 Mar. 1996.
"Re: National English-Only Bill-Erasing A Culture (new bill)." 24 Feb. 1995.
"Re: need info on NY." 9 June 1995.
"Re: S. 269 National Call-in." 10 May 1995.
"Re[2]: Cultural contributions of immigrants?—informational." 26 Apr. 1995.
"REASON: Economic Refugees." 20 Aug. 1995.
"REPORT: Prop 13 Meets the Internet—Local Govt Roadkill on the Information
    Superhighway." 16 Aug. 1995.
"Reviving 187resist." 1 June 1995.
"Rightwingers Bomb Children in anti-government Extremism." 22 Apr. 1995.
"RMAASC Position II, BOYCOTT, 12/7/94." 7 Dec. 1994.
"Rodney King Revisited? Telvised [sic] Beating." 3 Apr. 1996.
"Sacramento demonstration 4/3." 4 Apr. 1996.
"San Francisco Immigrant Voting Rights Initiative." 17 Apr. 1996.
"Save Hightower Radio in Bay Area." 27 Aug. 1995.
"Seattle Protests Pete Wilson (corrected version)." 21 Aug. 1995.
"[SFC] Arizona: New Favorite Site Cross-Border Immigration." 12 June 1995.
"[SFC] New Data on Costs of Undocuemnted [sic]: CA." 7 Apr. 1995.
"SFSU: Cesar Chavez Institute Teach-in." 23 Mar. 1995.
"SIMPSON PROMISES FAIR IMMIGRATION BILL." 15 Mar. 1995.
"Slim GOP victory '94." 24 July 1995.
"Sonoma Co STOP i87 [sic] Strategy." 26 Sept. 1995.
"[NPW] Sonoma March." 24 May 1995.
"South Africa's Immigrant Dilemma." 28 July 1995.
"Sparticist Article on Immigration." 20 Feb. 1996.
"Speech Boycott Attempt Failed." 29 Nov. 1994.
"Stanford Park Hotel rally." 7 Mar. 1996.
"State Anti-Immigrant Measures" A. 2 Mar. 1995.
"State Anti-Immigrant Measures" B. 8 Mar. 1995.
"Stop Racist Indiana Politician." 28 Feb. 1995.
"Student leader protests 187." 2 Mar. 1995.
"Students & Community Rally for Affirmative Action." 21 July 1995.
"Texas: Anti-Immigration Bills (Urgent Action Requested)." 26 Apr. 1995.
"THINGS PEOPLE SAY ABOUT IMMIGRATION." 8 Sept. 1995.
"TIME MAGAZINE—LATINO RACISM." 19 Mar. 1995.
"Two Immigrant Hotel Workers fired for Union Organizing." 26 Feb. 1995.
"UC-Berkeley Campus 187 update." 16 Mar. 1995.
"UC-Berkeley version of a noncompliance pledge." 7 Mar. 1995.
"UC Faculty Statement Against Regents' AA Decision." 9 Aug. 1995.
"UCP: Fall Internships Available." 1 Aug. 1995.
"UC-Riverside Statement on 187." 10 May 1995.
"UC Santa Cruz Academic Senate Resolution re Prop 187." 6 June 1995.
"UFW summer internships." 31 Jan. 1996.

"UK to introduce possible National ID card." 6 June 1995.

"Undocumented Immigrants: From TQSRC/TQS Research Center." 23 Feb. 1995.

"Unfunded Mandates." 29 Jan. 1995.

"UNITE at US Civil Rights Commission Testimony." 16 Sept. 1995.

"UNITY 95—August 12 in SF." 30 July 1995.

"Unity Time for Univ. Of Mass—in Daily Collegian." 25 Feb. 1995.

"U.S. COMMISSION ON CIVIL RIGHTS INVESTIGATES ANTI-IMMI-GRANT." 7 Sept. 1995.

"U.S. FOREIGN-BORN POPULATION AT HIGHEST LEVEL IN 55 YEARS." 30 Aug. 1995.

"U.S.-IMMIGRATION: Clinton administration touts record deportation." 4 Jan. 1996.

"Using the System." 1 Dec. 1994.

"U.S. LOOKS AT HIGH TECH DEVISES TO PROTECT BORDERS." 21 Mar. 1995.

"Violence Up Sharply Against U.S. Asians." 2 Aug. 1995.

"Visa Categoris [sic] in Jeopardy." 2 Aug. 1995.

"Welfare Reform ALERT and UPDATE—Part 1." 3 Apr. 1995.

"Western Youth Activists Conference: Fall 1995." 8 May 1995.

"WHITE HOUSE PLEDGES MORE DEPORTATIONS." 25 Mar. 1995.

"White House says wait for budget on immigrants." 23 Jan. 1995.

"World Bank's World Development Report 1995: Labour." 25 July 1995.

"(W. Post) Trouble backs up in Nogales as U.S. plugs border." 8 Feb. 1996.

Index

health threat to, 76
national identity, 53, 76, 143, 195n. 9
vs. universal rights, 125
nationalism, 25, 28, 46, 144
    Mexican, 52, 76
    and racism, 192n. 16
    trans-, 5, 6, 136, 143, 152, 154, 164,
        193n. 20, 207n. 27, 207–8n. 4
    social movements, 155–56, 207–8n. 4
    Xicano "Aztlan," 156
nationality, conflated with race, 149
national sovereignty, 75
nation-state, 8, 35, 61, 143, 145
    identification, 24
    legitimacy of, 156
Native Americans
    attempts to eliminate, 98
    in California, 47, 71
    and cultural logic, 15–17, 141–42
    journalists, 163
    as noncitizens, 106
    as nonimmigrants, 153
nativism, 3, 5, 28, 42–43, 46–48, 61, 64,
        70–71, 89, 158, 196n. 10, 198n. 31
    Californian vs. national, 43, 59, 70–71
naturalization, 135
    vs. denaturalization of meanings, 25
    of meanings, 19
neglect of children, 203
negotiation, 145
Nelson, Alan, 56–57, 69, 109, 203
neocolonialism, 46, 164
newspaper industry, 199n. 1
newspapers, 2, 6, 24, 25, 47, 127–31, 133,
        199n. 1
    as "civic" discourse, 13
    Japanese American, 21
Ngai, Mae, 44, 200n. 8
noncompliance, 118, 148, 149–51, 156, 159
North American Free Trade Agreement,
        55, 60, 164
nurses as immigration officials, 85

Oakland School Board, 118, 149–51
objectification, 41, 55
objectivity, 5, 10, 13, 73, 109
Olson, Mark, 188n. 24
Ono, Kent, 15, 20, 21, 113, 139, 140,
        186n. 16, 188nn. 25, 28, 189n. 36
Operation Gatekeeper, 51

Operation Hold the Line, 51
Osajima, Keith, 162
other, 27, 36
    vs. self, 36, 37
outlaw/civic intersection disappears 18, 22
outlaw discourses. See discourse
outlaw judgments, 22
outlaw logics, 17, 21–22, 25, 140–41, 156,
        157, 159
Owen, Susan, 189n. 1
ownership, private, 16–17

"pagan style," 140
panopticon, 78
parents
    migrant, 81–82, 191n. 11
    state as substitute, 82
past, discourse of the, 23
paternalism, 51, 58, 81, 92, 106, 158
pathos, 95
    appeals to, 68, 96
    vs. appeals to logos, 68
    empathy, 65
    sympathy, 65
    testimonial, 82
the "people," 26, 146
people of color, 27, 47, 68, 73, 144, 151,
        161, 163, 196n. 12
    "depravity" of, 81
performativity, 9, 10, 209n. 15
Perry, Steven, 118, 190n. 6
persuasion, strategies of, 68
Pfaelzer, Marianne, 4, 5, 39, 91, 186n. 9,
        199n. 37, 200n. 6
phrase regimes, 133
Plyler v. Doe, 63, 64, 87, 88, 94, 191n. 11,
        202n. 29
poaching, textual, 115, 117, 127–31, 159,
        204n. 4
    defined, 127, 204n. 4
    relation to dominant discourses, 127
    reposting, 128–31
police state, 80, 83–86, 99, 201n. 19
polis, 186n. 16
political protest, 16
political style, 208n. 8
politics
    of disagreement, 126
    disaffection, 8
    dispersed, 126